IN THE
GLASS
CASE
Essays on New Zealand Literature

BY THE SAME AUTHOR

poetry　　Whether the Will is Free
Crossing the Bar
Quesada
Walking Westward

fiction　　Smith's Dream
Five for the Symbol

criticism　　The New Poetic: Yeats to Eliot

edited　New Zealand Short Stories (Second Series)
Measure for Measure: A Casebook
Letters and Journals of Katherine Mansfield
Collected Stories of Maurice Duggan

IN THE GLASS CASE

Essays on New Zealand Literature

C.K. Stead

AUCKLAND UNIVERSITY PRESS
OXFORD UNIVERSITY PRESS

*Published with the help of a grant from
the New Zealand Literary Fund*

Typographical design by Neysa Moss

ACKNOWLEDGEMENTS

These essays and reviews have variously appeared under the imprints of Blackwood and Janet Paul, Oxford University Press, Penguin Books, Allen Lane, and Auckland University Press, and in the periodicals *Landfall, Comment, Islands, Pilgrims, The New Review* (London), *The Melbourne Age,* and *The London Review of Books.* Specific acknowledgement is made at the foot of the first page of each piece.

I am grateful to all my colleagues in the English Department and to those of my colleagues in the Faculty of Arts who in 1979 supported my nomination for the University of Auckland's Senior Research Fellowship in Arts—and in particular to John Asher, Sebastian Black, Keith Sorrenson, John Irwin, Bill Pearson, Keith Sinclair, Forrest Scott, Michael Joseph, Sydney Musgrove, and Donal Smith.

C.K.S.

CONTENTS

Part III: A Poet's View 243

INTRODUCTION

Making this selection from reviews, review articles, and lectures published over a period of more than twenty years has made me conscious of something I also know simply from the day-to-day practice of teaching. There are few critical absolutes. However worthy of serious attention a literary work may be, there is always a variety of ways, positive and negative, of coming at it, and a good deal of the skill of the critic lies in the recognition, and then the communication, of the point of view which is the justification for the judgement he feels himself impelled to make. I say 'feels' because there is no criticism without personal response. To be a good critic you must be practised at self-analysis. What did I feel? Why did I feel it? Is there something personal and local in that response, or would it be reasonable to assume that many literate persons would share it? Questions of that kind are the first movements towards criticism. Too many critics fail because they allow their own truest, innermost responses, which may initially be faint, to be contradicted by some doctrinaire requirement, or by the knowledge of what others have said.

Because I change, the valuation I put on various works is likely to change too. That is not to say the earlier view was wrong. Both may be justified. Many different 'readings' of a literary work may be right (though some will be quite wrong); and many different valuations may be supported. The improvement one feels in one's own criticism is not in making better, or more sensitive judgements, but rather in getting better at seeing and making clear the grounds for judgement. In my article on John Mulgan I go to some trouble to spell out the relation between my own development as a writer and Mulgan's work because I recognize quite well that Mulgan is more important to me than he will be to (say) an English or an American reader. This is not the application of a 'double standard'—an unfortunate phrase recently resurrected by Dr Cherry Hankin. For me there has never been a double standard in the sense Dr Hankin implies, of making special allowance for local work. On the contrary, I think I am in some ways more demanding of local work because I am more concerned about it. But no work of literature exists in a vacuum. There is an added dimension to the literature of any region which only those who are of that region will fully recognize. As I put it in the second of my articles on Baxter

No poetry moved me in quite the same way, at so profound a level, as our own, not just because the sensuous world it recreated was the one I knew from day to day, but because the Eden we are all cast out from is that of the world fresh to our awakening senses. For me one of the most important functions of poetry was to take us back there, and Baxter was one of the magicians who knew the way.

We must assume that there is something in Yeats which Irish readers see and feel and which we do not, however much we may revere him. That is not a 'double standard' but the recognition that there is in most literature a regional element. Where I think a double standard may sometimes apply is *against* local writers. New Zealanders still (and I suppose always will) lack confidence in their own products. It is fortunate that Katherine Mansfield is as good a writer as she is because if she were worse and had the same reputation overseas, she would still be respected in her own country above all other writers we have produced. I remember in 1963 when I wrote about some of Allen Curnow's poems in sentences which casually yoked them with poems by Keats and by Yeats I met disbelief, embarrassment, or laughter. I think there might now be more people in New Zealand capable of recognizing that there was nothing critically absurd or naive in what I wrote. I could see no qualitative difference between the lines I was discussing and similar lines by Keats and by Yeats, and I was right not to be cowed by the universal Kiwi demand for muted statement and hedged bets.

When I consider the body of work discussed in this book, and all the work not discussed that might have been, I have to conclude that this country has produced good literature far in excess of statistical probability. Does this acknowledgement prove that I am, after all, partial? To rebut any such statistical argument I simply put together in my mind an imaginary anthology containing (for example) a selection of Mansfield letters and journals (which I rate higher than her stories), Sargeson's *That Summer* and *En Route* (early and late), some Curnow including the late sequence 'Moro Assassinato', some part of Duggan's 'Riley's Handbook', half a dozen Smithyman poems, some pages from Sylvia Ashton-Warner's 'Life in a Maori School', Chapter 9 of Janet Frame's *Daughter Buffalo,* Baxter's late sonnets, and a selection of poems by Ian Wedde, and ask where else you could find a unifying principle (the principle here being the islands of New Zealand) to bind together such an extraordinary and powerful collection of work by a group of twentieth-century authors. I am not sure why this should be, except perhaps that the lonely practice of arts and crafts is in part a substitute for what our society does not offer. We develop more inwardly, as individuals, less as social beings; but having done so we must launch the works which express that individuality out upon the grey tide of a society which does not really welcome it. Explaining his support for a book of Kevin Ireland's which won a recent New Zealand Book Award for poetry Dr Michael Neill wrote 'There's a congenially self-deprecating irony which I find particularly attractive amid so much of the inflamed egoism which seems to be our chief legacy from the Romantics'. Is this a proper plea for the infusion of a long-overdue civility? Or is it merely that the old familiar suburban repression now puts on academic airs?

One of the problems of writing criticism in New Zealand is the smallness of the literary and intellectual community. To some extent we may exaggerate this. From the inside the London literary scene can also seem small. But there is no doubt that here writers are thrown together in a way which can be inhibiting to critical frankness. Also I think New Zealanders shy away from confrontations and verbal warfare, preferring to sulk and smoulder inwardly. Of course it is right not to want to inflict pain on a fellow-writer, and there is no simple formula that will cover all cases. My 1964 review of Glover was left unfinished because I found it taking a negative turn—but that was because I was leaving for a visit overseas and I felt I needed more time to reflect and to analyse. My uncertainties about Brasch's poetry were muted in *Landfall* in 1957. But re-reading my reviews and articles it seems to me I have said pretty exactly and honestly what I have thought. Sometimes I have written a piece which was more promotional than critical—the Morrieson article is an example. Clearly one could write more analytically and searchingly of Morrieson. Yet I don't feel inclined to withdraw a word of that article, or to agree with Vincent O'Sullivan who argued in a lecture in Christchurch in 1978 that Morrieson had been overrated. Morrieson is uneven, imperfectly controlled, and in his weaker moments monstrous and absurd, but he was a breath of fresh air we needed, and he practised fiction as an art because at every point his comedy (often black) is not simply a matter of plot and situation, it is linguistic as well.

Sometimes of course one has been involved in literary/critical warfare— most notably in the 1950s when a group of poets, most of them about ten years older than I, were attacking Curnow, ten years older again, partly I think because they felt under-represented in his anthologies. They had some justice on their side; and I can no longer get excited by the subtleties of the argument about what it means to say that 'reality must be local and special at the point where we pick up the traces'. What I felt at the time was that Curnow was a poet whose work I could take hold of, admire, and use. For that I was grateful, and in return I took his side against poets who seemed to me less talented both in their practice and in the skills of literary debate. Some of the smoke of those old battles still hovers between the lines of my 1961 lecture, 'For the Hulk of the World's Between'; and my review article on Curnow in 1963 was an attempt to make up for the fact that he had been seriously undervalued and slighted as a poet during the previous decade, especially by writers whose work was in every way inferior to his own.

An opposite case is that of Fairburn. I had known Fairburn, he had admired some of my earliest poems, and as a student I had read his work with great pleasure. I don't think that pleasure can have been totally unfounded. There was—and is—a freshness in Fairburn, ease, vigour, a lucid apprehension of physical things, and especially of the Auckland isthmus, to which I could never be indifferent. But there was also provincial insecurity, uncertainty of tone, and sometimes sheer silliness, mixed in with the good qualities; and the time I reviewed his *Collected Poems* was the height of the post-mortem Fairburn adulation. It seemed to me (to put it sweepingly as I would have felt it then) characteristically Kiwi that someone comfortable, half-baked, and dead should be celebrated, while the awkward, brilliant, and very much alive Curnow should be slighted.

These are examples where the context—what I have called earlier the point of view—helps to explain the direction the criticism took. Criticism is always a dialogue; and it needs to be understood that what the critic writes follows upon other things being said or written at the time.

Counting up I find that of the seventeen writers to whom separate attention is given (nine of them now dead) the only two I never met are Mansfield and Mulgan.* Some have been close friends. Personal relations with some have gone through varying phases. But I don't believe friendship or enmity have affected my critical attitudes. When it comes to the point one must say honestly what one thinks or give up the effort to say anything at all.

Because context is so important in understanding criticism I have not altered these pieces except very slightly in a very few instances which are indicated in footnotes. I began writing when the convention was to refer to living writers as Mr Curnow or Miss Adcock and to dead ones as Mulgan or Katherine Mansfield. That convention now seems out of date, but I have not altered what I originally wrote. Nor have I done anything to alter the style of pieces written for public delivery.

One thing I have not discussed in this introduction but which should be taken for granted is that for me the act of literary criticism has never been unconnected with my own practice as a writer. If I find myself with fresh perceptions about the nature of fiction or poetry they almost always come in part from the experience of writing in these genres. In this sense I write

* A note on the dates of authors discussed will be found at the back of the book.

what T.S. Eliot calls 'workshop criticism'. But Eliot is wrong (or insincere) when he seems to imply there is something peculiar or partial about such criticism. In fact from Sidney and Dryden through Johnson, Coleridge, and Arnold to Eliot himself, the critics in English have always been practitioners.

PART I:
FICTION

PRELIMINARY:
WHAT IS FICTION?

Like anyone else, I have had to take it on trust that I have an ear for the true notes in fiction, and for the false ones. I have read passively, waiting to be gripped by something, waiting for the story to make the first move. No formal theory has governed this procedure—only the feeling that to look conscientiously for 'significance' would be to look for one, or at best a limited number of significances, and never for the unpredictable one that makes the work of fiction distinct. What I have sought might be described simply as pleasure, if that did not seem to put too commonplace a value on the qualities which achieve it. One looks of course for formal competence; or rather, one is distracted when it is absent. But no amount of competence will alone achieve the moment, or moments, of illumination (in a short story there may be no more than one) which, on the other hand, a minimal competence may be sufficient to support.

Near the beginning of this book there is a story, 'City and Suburban', by New Zealand's most distinguished writer of fiction, Frank Sargeson; and at the end, one by Marilyn Duckworth, a young writer known chiefly for her novels. That Mr Sargeson brings a high degree of consciousness to his story, while Mrs Duckworth is still working largely by instinct, will be obvious enough. What interests me, however, is the qualities the two stories have in common. Neither seems to me perfect in form. Both present a recognizable New Zealand suburban scene, and introduce into it elements of fantasy and of horror. Both writers—but Mr Sargeson especially—are possessed by an 'idea'. The ideas differ in detail, but they fit well enough together. They concern suburban life, affluence, conformity ('Pink? But that's *wrong*') and the rebellion of something that may as well be called 'the

From the introduction to World's Classics *New Zealand Short Stories (2nd Series)* (ed. C.K. Stead), London, 1966.

spirit' against these things. Simply *as* ideas, they are not ones to which I would find myself giving easy assent. What is it then, to which the 'ear' I have spoken of, has responded?

I hope it will be plain that I have not set myself this examination in order to pass with full marks, but only to push myself towards some kind of definition. There are stories it would be easier to analyse, if 'analysis' were called for; and others which are simply good and successful, in a way which leaves little to be said. But there are only a few, I think, in which, quite apart from the question of 'success', the qualities peculiar to *fiction* are so readily distinguished:

'Oh, I feel sick,' Mrs Doubleday gulped, lying back on the tartan rug and placing a hand across her eyes. Her shopping bag bosom divided over her ribs, while her soft chins multiplied. . . .
. . . 'Find me the field glasses, Jeremy.'   (Marilyn Duckworth)

And as the handkerchief-draped horror went into the picnic bag, out came the transparent packet of chocolate biscuits. . . .
. . . I recovered my speech only to say a thing which to Pam would be irritating and silly, and which in the circumstances she was quite right to ignore.
'For God's sake, Pam,' I said, 'why ever in the name of heaven and earth did you insist they be called Happy and Glad?'   (Frank Sargeson)

Two picnics. In ten years time I may well have forgotten a good deal of Mrs Duckworth's story; but it is unlikely I will have forgotten the scene in which the suburban lady calls for her field glasses. Nor does it seem possible that I will have forgotten any detail of that perfect short story within what is perhaps an imperfect one, in which Mr Sargeson's Happy and Glad bring to their parents the severed finger they have found on the beach.

Why are such scenes memorable? Why is one compelled—by that power which belongs uniquely to fiction—to store them *as if they were real?* It is not to an 'idea' one has responded. There is, I suppose it may be said, a 'perception'—about our society, about ourselves—bodied forth in these scenes; but if so, it is a perception more comprehensive, more satisfying, and more general (its instance being more particular) than anything which may be stated in intellectual terms.

There are, of course, stories which, for all their distinctness as fiction, do resolve themselves in a statement. 'The trouble is . . .' O. E. Middleton's 'The Doss House and the Duchess' concludes, 'we forget the friends of our poverty'. It is the classic conclusion to the classic pattern of the 'mateship' tale. The simple didacticism has its charm, as it had in the early stories of Frank Sargeson. But is it only for this we have come so far? What supports the statement, surpasses it in claiming our attention, and lends to it in the end a flavour almost of irony, is a quality everywhere present in the story, but most clearly exemplified in that cool and terrifying moment when 'a ripe melon falls from the sky and splits on the pavement'.

Can we call that quality the sense of style? If we can—and that is how I believe it is best described—it must be distinguished from 'fine writing'. There are times, indeed, when writing which is *noticeably* fine can seem evidence only of a fiction writer's effort, and failure, to get through to his subject. The prose stands like a dead monument to his labour, and that is all we see. Maurice Duggan is perhaps better equipped to turn a sentence than any other New Zealand writer. Yet that is not the gift which makes 'Along Rideout Road that Summer' the remarkable story it is. It is not 'prose' that tangles the heel of the father, retreating from his discovery, in the 'bra' of the girl with whom his son has assumed the 'historic disposition of flesh'; nor is it 'prose' that sends him stumbling across the field his son has ploughed, 'scattering broadcast the white and shying gulls'.

If for my own purposes I have rejected in turn the quality of the 'ideas' and of the prose as measures of the quality of the fiction, it is not so that I may conclude with a general statement about the metaphysical, or metaphorical, 'unity' of the work of literature. Literature can look after itself, and has no need of our road-blocks and check-points along the variety of routes by which it may be approached. My concern has been, not to preserve it against infiltrators, but simply to keep as close as possible to the experience of the common reader who will come to these stories as fiction. A professional critic might well study 'Along Rideout Road that Summer' simply as prose. A second might approach it sociologically, in terms of 'race relations'—and find in it a tone refreshingly casual and wholesome. A third, coming by a different route, might see it as a bringing together of two extremes—the literary and the actual—of the New Zealand consciousness. Each of these studies would have its point and its value. Each would contribute something to our awareness of the fact that Mr Duggan has done something entirely new in this story. Yet none, strictly within its terms of reference, could quite deal, for example, with Fanny Hohepa's 'bra': that would be a detail, one of many left out of the account; and without such details, without the sense they cumulatively contrive for us of something *lived through,* none of those critical approaches—stylistic, sociological, historical—would be called for at all.

Can we go a short step further and allow that 'bra', tangled round a shocked father's retreating foot, to stand for what I have called the sense of style; and to see the sense of style in turn as the direct transmission of the writer's sense of life? It is this latter sense which generates his energy at the same time that it requires precision of him; and it is this, in the scenes I have used as touchstones, that has given to Frank Sargeson and to Marilyn Duckworth their gaiety, to O. E. Middleton and to Maurice Duggan their authority, in the midst of the horrors or the complexities or the absurdities they are conceiving.

KATHERINE MANSFIELD:
THE LETTERS AND JOURNALS

When Katherine Mansfield died on 9 January 1923 at the age of thirty-four she had published three books of short stories. Of these the first, *In a German Pension* (1911), had been an immediate success, running quickly through three impressions, but it had gone out of print with the collapse of the publishing firm of Stephen Swift, and throughout the remaining twelve years of her life Katherine Mansfield resisted all efforts to persuade her to allow it to be republished. Her second book, *Bliss*, appeared in 1920 and her third, *The Garden Party*, in 1922. Both were favourably received. In 1923 Katherine Mansfield's husband, John Middleton Murry, issued the collection of stories she had been at work on before her death, *The Dove's Nest*. There followed one further book made up of uncollected and unfinished stories, *Something Childish* (1924), and a reissue of *In a German Pension*, making five books, a total of eighty-eight stories. In the fifty years since her death not one of these stories has ever been out of print* and the best of them seem to have a secure place in the history of the short story and in the development of modern British fiction.

In addition to her fiction Katherine Mansfield left a variety of writing of other kinds. She was a prolific correspondent, an irregular keeper of diaries and notebooks, a busy reviewer and an occasional versifier. In a will dated 14 August 1922 she bequeathed 'all manuscripts notebooks papers letters'

From the Introduction to *Letters and Journals of Katherine Mansfield*, selected with an introduction by C. K. Stead, Allen Lane and Penguin Books, London, 1977 (written 1973).

* U.K. publishers' figures for sales during the two decades from 1952 to 1972 show Constable's *Collected Stories* having sold 46,000 copies, Oxford's World's Classics' *Selected Stories* 67,000 copies, and Collins Classics' *Selected Stories* 24,000 copies (since 1957), while Penguin Books have kept sometimes two, sometimes three, of her titles in print, selling around 10,000 a year of each title. In a period when short stories have been described as virtually unsaleable these figures indicate a firmly established reputation.

to her husband but she added 'I should like him to publish as little as possible and tear up and burn as much as possible he will understand that I desire to leave as few traces of my camping ground as possible.' A letter written a week earlier and left to be opened in the event of her death is less sweeping but still clear enough in its intention: 'All my manuscripts I leave entirely to you to do what you like with. Go through them one day, dear love, and destroy all you do not use. Please destroy all letters you do not wish to keep and all papers. You know my love of tidiness. Have a clean sweep . . . and leave all fair—will you?'

There is no evidence that Murry destroyed anything at all. On the contrary over a period of years he transcribed and published almost everything, however apparently insignificant or fragmentary, first using the pieces in his new periodical, *The Adelphi*, to which his late wife was for some years the most regular contributor, and then editing them and publishing them as books. In 1923 Katherine Mansfield's *Poems* appeared, in 1927 her *Journal*, in 1928 a two-volume selection of her letters, in 1930 *Novels and Novelists* (reprinting her reviews of fiction written for *The Athenaeum*) and in 1939 *The Scrapbook of Katherine Mansfield*. In 1951 the almost complete texts of her letters to Murry, a 700-page volume, replaced the 1928 selection of letters; and in 1954 there was a much enlarged 'definitive' edition of the *Journal*. A rough count suggests that in addition to her short stories Murry published something like 700,000 words of those papers he was instructed to tidy and leave fair. The 'camping ground' she hoped to conceal is now open to the public.

Murry's promotion of his wife's literary remains brought him royalties and opprobrium, and increased her fame. The good and the bad seem inextricably mixed in his work on her behalf. He transcribed, edited, and wrote commentaries tirelessly but in a way which encouraged a sentimental, and sometimes a falsely mystical, interest in her talent. He could not keep himself out of the picture either, seeing the development of her art always in relation to the development of her feeling for him. He was accused of making capital out of her death. He antagonized many people previously well-disposed towards her writing and perhaps ensured something of a reaction against it at the same time that he was making it more widely known. Finally, by publishing more and more of his wife's private papers revealing tensions in the marriage, Murry cast himself publicly in the role of the husband who had failed her.

Worse might have been said of him had it been known that he was ignoring her instruction to 'tear up and burn as much as possible', and Murry must have been uneasy about it. He was fond of quoting (and misquoting) the last sentence of the letter posthumously received, in which she said 'I feel no other lovers have ever walked the earth together more joyfully—in spite of all.' But he never printed it all, and that can only have been because to do so would have revealed her wish that her 'camping ground' should not be exposed.

It must be admitted, however, that Murry's position was a difficult one. There was certainly bad taste in his manner of presenting his wife's work but it could not have been otherwise, he being the man he was, and there was no one else to do the job. He did his best; and if the financial rewards he earned were considerable* so too were the brickbats. Perhaps he published too much, and too soon; but at least, if he need not have published, it is difficult to see how he could have taken upon himself the decision of what to keep and what to destroy. In asking that, Katherine Mansfield was asking too much—and her manner of asking it (in the letter if not in the will) was ambiguous: 'destroy *all you do not use*' and 'destroy . . . *all you do not wish to keep*'. In these ambiguities he might have found a sort of justification for his own procedure.

That procedure was simply, over a period years, to publish almost everything and let the public choose what it liked. The poems were reprinted once but interest in them was slight (as were most of the poems) and they were allowed to lapse. Her letters, on the other hand, were widely read and admired. And of the *Journal* Murry was able to say by 1939 that European opinion had received it as a 'minor classic'. Whether this would have pleased Katherine Mansfield or not we can only guess, but we can be certain it would have surprised her. She had more than once announced in letters to Murry that she was starting a journal with the idea of publishing it, but the resolve had always petered out shortly afterwards. On 15 September 1920, for example, she writes 'I've begun my journal book. I want to offer it to Methuen—to be ready this Xmas. Do you think that's too long to wait? It ought to be rather special. *Dead* true. . . .' Three weeks later she is writing 'The Journal—I have absolutely given up. I dare not keep a journal. I should always be trying to tell the truth'.

How was it, then, that versions of a '*Journal*' were published in 1927 and 1954, and a '*Scrapbook*' in 1939? From what manuscript sources were these derived? Even more puzzling, how did material from the *Scrapbook* come to be incorporated into the 1954 'definitive edition' of the *Journal*?

The answers to these questions might have been arrived at by anyone who pondered carefully on the publication facts, on the nature and variety of the writing in each volume, and on the description of manuscript

* Murry's official biographer describes how in 1923 Murry, about to be remarried, 'espied the house of his dreams', bid for it £925 he did not have, and by a 'crowning stroke of luck' received almost immediately £1000 in royalties on Katherine Mansfield's books. 'I felt that Katherine's blessing was on our marriage', he wrote in an unpublished manuscript. In 1942 he was drawing about £500 a year on her royalties. Buying the farm where he and his fourth wife were to live he wrote in his journal 'It is Katherine who has bought this farm for us' (F. A. Lea, *John Middleton Murry*, London, 1959, pp. 124 and 300).

material given by Murry in his Introduction to the *Scrapbook* and his Preface to the 1954 *Journal*.* But those answers were not arrived at, probably because no one thought to ask the questions. It seems to have been generally assumed that Katherine Mansfield had kept two manuscript books, a *'Journal'* and a *'Scrapbook',* and that her husband had published most of the contents of both.

In 1957, on the death of Murry, the Alexander Turnbull Library in Wellington acquired from his estate all his Mansfield notebooks, manuscripts, and papers. The first to look closely at these was Professor Ian A. Gordon, and his findings were first published in the quarterly *Landfall* in March 1959. Gordon found that there was only one collection of manuscripts from which all of the *Scrapbook* and the two versions of the *Journal* had been derived. This collection consisted of four ordinary and rather empty diaries for the years 1914, 1915, 1920, and 1922; about thirty notebooks containing fragments of stories, scenes, snatches of conversation, ideas, notes from reading, quotations, calculations of household finances, unposted letters; and, finally about one hundred loose sheets of equally heterogeneous material. Out of this confusing pile of writing, much of it only barely legible, Murry had compiled the three separate editions of *Journal* material.

Professor Gordon seems to have been divided between admiration of Murry's 'brilliant . . . editorial patchwork' which had shaped a minor classic out of such diverse and difficult material, and uncertainty about whether it was not also a brilliant piece of editorial deception. He reported that all the material in the published *Journal* and *Scrapbook* was authentic—Murry had invented nothing. He showed that Murry's transcription, dating, and chronological ordering, though not without errors, were on the whole commendably accurate. But he was troubled by the fact that Murry seemed to have taken the rough edges off the material so that the published versions do not accurately represent the notebooks they derive from, which are 'scrappier, less tidy'.

This discrepancy between the apparent scrappiness of the manuscript material and the coherence of the published *Journal* led Gordon to make one statement which his own account of the state of the papers does not seem to support. 'It is hardly too much to claim', he wrote 'that it [the *Journal*] is as much Murry's work as Katherine Mansfield's.' It seems a

---

* '. . . notebooks—ordinary French school *cahiers,* mostly—in which finished and unfinished stories, quotations, odd observations, intimate confessions, unposted letters, and stray sentences are crammed up like some rich thievery . . .' (Introduction to the *Scrapbook,* 1939). '. . . comments, confessions, and unposted letters, which she had the habit of writing in the same exercise books as those in which she wrote her stories; fragmentary diaries . . .; brief and often difficult notes for stories; marginal comments in the books she had read. . . .' (Preface to the *Journal,* 1954).

great deal too much to claim; yet one can see a sort of metaphysical puzzle here: How can Katherine Mansfield be 'author' of a book of which, as such, she was quite unaware? She is author of the fragments of which it is composed; but if the fragments hang together as beautifully as they do, this must surely be because of Murry's 'brilliant . . . editorial patchwork'.

Such a conclusion, it seems to me, is understandable but false. Another disposition of the same material would, I feel sure, have hung together quite as well, and this is because of the essential unity of all Katherine Mansfield's writing in letters and notebooks. This writing is of considerable variety, yet it is all of a piece. Into the briefest notes and jottings just as into long letters something of the author's life is infused. She has the rare talent of being able to address herself intimately to anyone, or even to no one—to a blank page. ('She has the terrible gift of nearness,' Frieda Lawrence once wrote. 'She can come so close.') The particularity and vividness of the writing is an extension of the particularity and vividness of the personality, and it is everywhere present. That is why Murry had only to transcribe more or less at random to achieve a book coherent enough to become a 'minor classic'. The material has, it must be admitted, the fascination of a kitset which can be assembled in different ways to produce instant—and genuine—art.

In selecting from the great mass of correspondence and journals available I have been guided principally by the wish to represent Katherine Mansfield's writing at its best rather than to give a balanced biographical portrait. There are periods in her life when she suffers such deep anguish, or fear, or distrust that the quality of her letters seems to decline correspondingly. Where she is mistress of negative feelings and can give full-blooded expression to them (see for example her letter of 20 November 1919 on the subject of hate, or her journal entry of 15 December 1919 on the subject of death) the writing is often truly impressive. Where she seems defeated by such feelings (and the periods of defeat sometimes last for months on end) I have passed over material which is of importance biographically but is inferior as writing. What is meant by 'inferior as writing' is easy to recognize but difficult to explain. Perhaps it is sufficient to say that she is at her best when the writing is least deliberate, when it flows easily and naturally, governed by feeling and observation rather than by any apparent calculation of its effect. . . .

I must also admit to having found myself resistant, or at least cautious, in choosing from those passages for which in the past Katherine Mansfield may well have been most noted—the passages of 'sensibility'. This is not out of a distrust of emotional writing but rather out of the feeling that her emotion is often less genuine when she is being 'sensitive' than when she is being (for example) satirical, or bullying, or simply plain and factual.

Working on Katherine Mansfield's letters in 1950 Murry observed (in a letter to Violet Schiff preserved in the British Museum) 'It's indubitably true that she tended to assume a personality to please a correspondent. I suppose we all do it in some degree. But in her it was very pronounced.' This easy adoption of different masks, different voices, is one of the principal skills on which her success as a fiction writer rests, and it is not surprising to notice the way her recognition of the distinct character of each of her friends determines the persona she adopts in writing to them. She is always confidently herself, but it is a subtly different self for each friend. To Lady Ottoline Morrell and to Virginia Woolf she is witty, literary, professional, but just a little more fulsome than might have come naturally to her, and sometimes wary too. To her cousin 'Elizabeth' (the Countess Russell) she is inclined to be tremulous and lyrical. To Violet and Sydney Schiff she is intense, lady-like, even prim. To younger writers and painters (William Gerhardi and Richard Murry, for example) she is overwhelmingly kind, considerate, encouraging, and a bit more solemn than, no doubt, she felt. To her father she is practical and reassuring. To her Russian friend Koteliansky she is brilliant, enigmatic, dark, like a character out of a novel by Dostoyevsky. To her devoted companion Ida Baker ('L.M.') she is for the most part the practical, no-nonsense, slightly salty K.M. of everyday life. Perhaps she is most herself where she trusted most completely and where the relationship was free, sisterly, and undemanding—and one sees this in letters to her American painter friend, Anne Estelle Rice. Here she appears relaxed, witty, honest, direct, intelligent, practical. Finally, of course, to her husband she is all these things and more by turns—a Cleopatra, at once lover, companion, editorial assistant, little sister, big sister, supporter, dependent, and (not least) remorseless critic.

'As to the poetical Character [Keats says in a letter of 1818] . . . it is not itself—it has no self—it is every thing and nothing—It has no character. . . . A Poet is . . . continually informing and filling some other Body.' Katherine Mansfield has this chameleon quality. She is always adopting a mask, changing roles, assuming the identity of the person she speaks to or the thing she contemplates. Yet through all these changes we are able to say that some roles suit her better than others, even that some are false, and this is because we retain a clear notion of what is permanently and indelibly 'Katherine Mansfield'. Only the firmly resolved character can so give itself to each experience, dare so far to lose itself in the impression of the moment, as to persuade itself that it has no character at all—something which worried Katherine Mansfield as it worried Keats. She is in fact finely confident in her letters, and it is a confidence both of personality and of talent, each serving and augmenting the other. However much illness and fear undermined her there was a sort of reassurance to be got from taking up a pen and addressing herself to a friend or to a notebook. In letters and journals she is continually putting herself together again.

Suffering took its toll, however. Loneliness in foreign places to which she had gone in search of a cure for her tuberculosis, the pain of the disease itself, distress at the death of her brother, a feeling of having been deserted by her husband, fear of death—this suffering, which she bore on the whole with great fortitude, made her ashamed of her satirical self, afraid of inflicting pain on others. Suffering, she said, was the gift which had taught her to look on the world with love. And this in turn is said to be the foundation on which her best stories are built. Perhaps it is—but I am inclined to believe it is also the source of some of her weakest writing. That is why I say I find myself wary of her 'sensibility', the sensitive writing for which she has been widely praised. It is not quite natural to her personality or central to her talent. It is, rather, an accident of her disease augmented and fostered by the fashion of the day—and I think it is the real K.M. who tells Ida Baker brutally that 'yearning sentimental writing about a virginia creeper and the small haigh voices of tainy children is more than [she] can stick' (see the letter of 29 August 1921). Similarly in the stories—the K.M. who laughs and lightly caricatures her subjects seems to me to be writing more naturally and genuinely than the one who conscientiously trembles and pines at the sufferings of others. 'The Daughters of the Late Colonel', for example, which several reviewers called 'cruel' at the time of its publication, I find in every way superior to 'Miss Brill', which brought its author tender letters of thanks from numbers of readers.

She was susceptible, of course, to these responses, sensitive to the charge of cruelty and pleased to be told she had touched a reader's heart. But if she had retained her health she would undoubtedly have continued to follow the direction of that robust, anarchic intelligence apparent in all her best work, deeply committed to no social forms and niceties (in this she remained indelibly the colonial), seeing Nonsense everywhere (Male Nonsense especially), and enjoying her ability to represent it inflated to bursting point.

D. H. Lawrence, according to Frieda Lawrence's report, used to say that Katherine Mansfield's nearest literary relation was Dickens—the Dickens who pounces quick and sharp on funny details and by a slight (often satirical) exaggeration, and by the repetition of certain magically comic phrases, expands an insignificant scene or event until it becomes unforgettably significant. This, I think, places her correctly. Her talent was a comic talent. 'I don't think anyone has ever made me laugh more than she did in those days,' Leonard Woolf recalled in his autobiography, describing her sitting upright on the edge of a chair telling stories with 'not the shadow of a gleam of a smile on her mask of a face, and the extraordinary funniness of the story . . . increased by the flashes of her astringent wit'. This humour is nowhere more beautifully apparent than in her letters, and it appears too, occasionally, in the reviews when, with the same straight face, she renders a book absurd simply by retelling its story. The idea that she was some kind of mystic in search of Truth through Love is very largely a fiction built on her last desperate efforts to stay alive, and sustained after her death by her husband's critical commentaries. There was nothing mystical about her that antibiotics would not have cured.

To read Katherine Mansfield's letters and journals is to be struck again and again by the recognition that her talent was larger than her actual achievement at the time of her death—and to say that is not at all to imply that her achievement in fiction is not both significant and durable. She has her place in the development of the modern short story—and her place on the *scene*, among an impressive cast of characters who were making English literary history. But the immediacy of her contact with the natural world and her facility in representing it, her extraordinary visual memory, the acuteness of her ear both for speech and for indiscriminate sounds (like 'the *panting* of a saw'), her subtlety in following the threads of human feeling, the ease with which (even in her early twenties) she could create and satirically manipulate convincing dialogue—all these qualities together with an indefinable all-pervasive freshness in her writing, as if every sentence had been struck off first thing on a brilliant morning, make her natural talents in fiction superior to those of all her contemporaries except Lawrence. There is no reason why her performance, had she lived, should not have outstripped that of Forster and Woolf; and one is not in the least surprised to discover that on hearing the news of her death Virginia Woolf, who in the first-published version of her diary is only recorded throwing *Bliss* down exclaiming 'She's done for!', confided to the same diary 'I was jealous of her writing—the only writing I have ever been jealous of'.

Holding the various elements of her talent together, governing them, there is an artistic sense which is indistinguishable from a critical sense, is, in fact, simply the critical sense in action. As a reviewer of contemporary fiction Katherine Mansfield is interesting. But she worked, during the period of her reviewing, under great pressure and mainly on inferior novels; and she was unhappy about the conventions which required, for example, an editorial 'we' and encouraged picturesque rather than practical writing. There are remarks of great interest and value scattered through her reviews. But the real quality of her critical mind blazes forth most clearly in comments dashed down informally in letters and notebooks. One doesn't need to agree or disagree with her on the subject of Lawrence's *The Lost Girl*, for example (see the note attached to a letter to Murry written early in December 1920); but when she asks herself why the 'trill' Alvina feels 'in her bowels' is peculiarly offensive, and answers

'Because it is *not on this plane* that the emotions of others are conveyed to our imagination', one feels the kind of flash, or shock, that only a critical insight of the very highest order can give. At another level her crisp notes on Murry's editing of *The Athenaeum* show the application of critical intelligence to practical day-to-day work.

KATHERINE MANSFIELD:
THE ART OF THE 'FICTION'

Katherine Mansfield became famous only after her death, and it was as much for the extraordinary talent and personality revealed in her letters and journals as for the qualities of her stories. I think the fame was deserved; but it rested on style rather than substance, and for that reason it has survived better in France than in England. In England art is seldom valued for its own sake; it is a vehicle, like a coal truck; and from Dr Johnson to Dr Leavis the English critics have almost without exception seen their primary task as being to check the quantity and quality of the coal.

In Katherine Mansfield's letters and journals are displayed qualities of mind, imagination, sensibility, intelligence, wit—all finding verbal expression, coming to life on the page, running irresistibly day by day off the tip of the pen. This is not the same as saying that she is always revealed as a good person, a nice person, that she is always controlled, or fair minded, or strong, or sensible. She is afraid, defeated, hysterical, waspish as often as she is affirmative, joyful, witty, or wise. But whatever the state of her mind or soul, there is always distinction in the writing, distinction of intellect and of personality transmitted through all the rare and lovely skills of the natural writer. She has more than talent. She has genius—and only a part of that genius gets into the stories. Fiction writers usually do their best work after the age of forty. Katherine Mansfield died at thirty-four, leaving about ninety stories, some of them unfinished—a total of perhaps 250-300 thousand words. It is clear that she needed a longer life to produce the best

The major part of this was delivered as a lecture at University College London in January 1977. It was published in *The New Review*, London, September 1977.

work she was capable of. Nevertheless she has a distinct place as one who made certain discoveries about the form of fiction. It is the nature of these discoveries that still calls for critical definition; and at the same time, if they are to be usefully discussed, it becomes necessary to disengage the Mansfield image from some of the mythology that has surrounded it since her death in 1923.

To speak of Katherine Mansfield's discoveries in fiction is not to speak of something achieved in full consciousness, or critically articulated. In her conscious intentions she was often very conventional. She was always setting out to write a novel. What became 'Prelude' began as a novel with the title *The Aloe*. As she wrote 'Je ne parle pas français' she called its sections chapters, apparently expecting it to grow into a book. She planned a novel called *Maata,* and another called *Karori.* All these came either to nothing or to smaller items which, not being novels, we call stories, but which would be better described as fictions. It was not lack of stamina which brought this about. She had ample energy and fluency and determination as a writer. It was her instinct as an artist that gave her fictions their modern shape. She taught us the fiction as distinct from the narrative, and it is in that sense that she is an innovator.

It is usually agreed by critics that Katherine Mansfield's New Zealand stories are her best. But her identity as a New Zealander is revealed more interestingly in other ways, ways more indirect, than in the material of her stories. She is of largely Anglo-Saxon stock. But she comes from a physical environment in which there are empty spaces, distances, a great deal of sky (and usually water), and in which, whatever the season, there is ample light. Her visual sense is developed to a degree unusual in English writers; and this is just as apparent in her European stories as anywhere else:

Four of the clock one July afternoon she appeared at the Pension Müller. I was sitting in the arbour and watched her bustling up the path followed by the red-bearded porter with her dress-basket in his arms and a sunflower between his teeth. The widow and her five innocent daughters stood tastefully grouped upon the steps in appropriate attitudes of welcome.[1]

Secondly, and more importantly, in the European context she has the detachment of someone who comes from a great way off, and on whom in terms of established convention very little has been decisively stamped. Her social sense is superficial. She adopts roles easily, without any real conviction about which of them properly belongs to her. She can take nothing for granted. She has both freedom, and uncertainty about how it should be used. She has very little custom—only intelligence and instinct to guide her. Virginia Woolf, who was both fascinated by Katherine Mansfield and intensely jealous of her, set out to be a writer and in due course produced a first novel because that was what writers wrote. Katherine Mansfield had it for review and was surprised. She expected something more original of Virginia. She could not say what it ought to have been, only that this conventional item was a disappointment.

Her own first book had emerged very differently, under the pressure of painful experience which made its stories all of a piece. This was the collection called *In a German Pension*, published in 1911 when she was twenty-three. The received standard view of Katherine Mansfield, which is essentially that established by her husband, John Middleton Murry, invites us to excuse the book on the grounds of youth; yet what Murry calls its 'youthful bitterness and crude cynicism'[2] speak very directly to the 1970s. It is not, as it once seemed, an anti-German book so much as an anti-male book—but not quite simply anti-male either. It is full of that subtle humour, that dead-pan presentation of absurdities, which characterized Katherine Mansfield's talk and letters and made her seem to Leonard Woolf the most amusing conversationalist he had known. But the humour of *In a German Pension* skates on very thin ice. It is laughter right at the brink of hysteria, tears, revulsion and hatred. The gross, insensitive German males dominate and enslave their fraus and turn them into domestic animals, while natural appetite is seen to be drawing the young girls towards sexual involvement and the same destruction. In one story a young man putting his hands over the breasts of a girl is interrupted by a 'frightful, tearing shriek' upstairs where a baby is being born. In another a young woman, disillusioned with her lover and determined to leave him, viciously bites the hand of a man who tries to kiss her, and immediately feels compliant once again towards the lover. There is violence just below the surface of these stories; and these two qualities, the violence and the humour, are held together by a third—a delicate precision in the portrayal of scene and atmosphere, so that in the best of the stories everything happens at a slight remove, it floats somewhere in the middle distance, as if on a stage with misty lighting or behind a gauze curtain:

'Are you an American?' said the Vegetable Lady, turning to me.
'No.'
'Then you are an Englishwoman?'
'Well, hardly—'
'You must be one of the two; you cannot help it. I have seen you walking alone several times. You wear your—'
I got up and climbed on to the swing. The air was sweet and cool, rushing past my body. Above, white clouds trailed delicately through the blue sky. From the pine forest streamed a wild perfume, the branches swayed together, rhythmically, sonorously.

The chapter of biography that lies behind the writing of *In a German*

Pension has yet to be fully written.* Katherine Mansfield had come to London at the age of twenty to be a writer. She had had lovers. She had married a singing teacher, George Bowden, and had left him next day. She had possibly experimented with drugs. She had become pregnant to someone who was not her husband and gone to Bavaria to have the child, but the pregnancy miscarried. All this in 1909 or '10. As Brigid Brophy puts it: 'The life of the "free woman" which is now being imposed on us as a postwar phenomenon—post *our* war—was being lived by Katherine Mansfield, and with incomparably more style, before women were properly out of long skirts.'³ With more style, no doubt; but also without antibiotics and without the pill, and it was very nearly too much for her. She survived the crisis, however, and under the pressure of so much experience wrote her first book very rapidly, not at all in the confessional manner most young gentlewomen in like circumstances would have chosen, but converting it all into black comedy. In the story called 'The Modern Soul' there is a German professor who likes to eat cherries because he says they free saliva for his playing on the trombone. He is also very skilled at spitting the cherry stones great distances across the garden. He explains to a young woman that all cherries contain worms, but if you like cherries you must put up with that. '. . . it amounts to this,' he says; 'if one wishes to satisfy the desires of nature one must be strong enough to ignore the facts of nature.' That is really the dilemma Katherine Mansfield is wrestling with in these stories. Only a rare talent would have allowed it to emerge in such a bizarre and oblique way.

The book was a success. It went through three printings before the publisher vanished abroad, pursued by a charge of bigamy.⁴ But it left Katherine Mansfield uncertain what direction her writing should take. She experimented a great deal and did not publish another collection of stories for nine years. One brief experiment consists of three stories which are interesting because they indicate a whole line of development she denied herself by becoming a European writer. 'Millie', 'Ole Underwood', and 'The Woman at the Store', are New Zealand stories quite different from the evocations of a middle-class childhood for which she is best known. They are stories of raw colonial life, conventionally shaped towards a dénouement. They anticipate a whole genre of New Zealand fiction; and they lead Elizabeth Bowen to ask whether Katherine Mansfield might not, under different circumstances, have become a regional writer.⁵ The dénouement of 'The Woman at the Store' is a very professional exercise in surprising us with what on reflection we have to concede was apparent all along. The revelation comes when the strangely malevolent child does for

---

* New biographies by Jeffrey Meyers (1979) and Antony Alpers (1980) have to some considerable extent filled this gap.

the visitors the drawing her mother has forbidden her to do. Subtly the story has led us to expect something pornographic. Instead, the drawing reveals that the woman, who is portrayed as having been ruined by neglect, maltreatment, and the strain of outback life, has murdered her husband. Thus elements of the thriller and the social documentary are combined; and at the same time the story can be seen to contain another version of Katherine Mansfield's central preoccupation—female sexual involvement and the destruction she seems to feel goes inevitably with it.

The experiment of those three stories was not continued. Linear narrative was not going to be Katherine Mansfield's fictional mode. She could manage it very skilfully; but so could many writers of much more limited talents. What she worked for continually was texture, density, a feeling of richness, of reality; and it is one of the dilemmas of fiction that the more totally the reader is engaged in an on-rushing narrative, the less he is left afterwards with a sense of having experienced a piece of real life. We can move so fast through a landscape we experience, not the landscape, but only a sense of momentum.

There is a phenomenon I think characteristic of a great many respectable novels. It goes something like this. For the first twenty or thirty, or even fifty pages, we are absorbed and enchanted by the articulation of a scene, a situation, a set of characters. The development is not a straight line but a movement in slow circles over the same ground. Then all at once the novelist feels obliged to set his characters moving along a narrative path towards a climax and a conclusion. What felt real and life-like both to reader and writer now turns conventional. The imagination gives up and the magic vanishes. I think Katherine Mansfield's artistic instinct was too strong ever to let this happen. Again and again she disappointed herself by not being able to force herself onward by sheer acts of will. But the instinct was right and the effort misplaced. The cut-off point often leaves an unconventional but artistically complete work.

Quite a number of her shorter fictions do have something of the character of a 'story', though few rely primarily on narrative for their effect. They develop around a single image or scene or situation, and they move towards the recognition, or realization (in the French sense of making real) of something latent there. These pieces of five or ten pages are taken, and often written, at a single sitting. They are tightly unified, so that the mind holds them as a single item. With intermediate-length fictions, however, there is the problem for the writer of how to add on if the addition is not to be linear, and here I think Katherine Mansfield developed two methods: one might be called 'accretion', the second 'circumlocution'. Accretion is the method of 'Prelude' and 'At the Bay'; 'circumlocution' is the method of 'Je ne parle pas français' and 'The Daughters of the Late Colonel'.

'Prelude' and 'Je ne parle pas français' are crucial because each represents something of a technical breakthrough; and this means a breakthrough not merely for Katherine Mansfield but in the history of fiction. Frank O'Connor, by no means her kindest or fairest critic (he calls her 'the brassy little shopgirl of literature who made herself into a great writer'[6]), says of 'Prelude' and 'At the Bay': 'These extraordinary stories are Katherine Mansfield's masterpieces and in their own way comparable with Proust's breakthrough into the subconscious world.'[7] And Elizabeth Bowen, another practitioner: 'Had [Katherine Mansfield] not written . . . as she did, one form of art might still be in infancy. . . . We owe to her the prosperity of the "free" story: she untrammelled it from conventions . . . How much ground [she] broke for her successors may not be realized. . . . she was to alter for good and all our idea of what goes to make a story.'[8]

Can we characterize this breakthrough? If we are to try we must first disengage these stories from a certain amount of Mansfield mythology, emanating from John Middleton Murry's commentaries on his late wife's work, and abetted in certain particulars by what might be called New Zealand critical nationalism. Murry's account of his wife's fiction shows little comprehension of technical matters. He comprehends only the substance of the stories; and he divides them accordingly into two simple categories—positive and negative. At the centre of his interpretation he places a passage from a letter she wrote him on 3 February 1918. He quotes the passage in both of the full-length articles he published on her work;[9] and he refers to it again and again in introductions to, and commentaries on, her letters, journals, and stories. The passage, he insists, 'is vital to any true understanding of Katherine Mansfield'.[10] It was written while she was engaged on 'Je ne parle pas français', and it goes as follows:

I've two 'kick-offs' in the writing game. *One* is joy—real joy—the thing that made me write when we lived at Pauline, and that sort of writing I could only do in just that state of being in some perfectly blissful way *at peace*. Then something delicate and lovely seems to open before my eyes, like a flower without thought of a frost or a cold breath—knowing that all about it is warm and tender and 'ready'. And *that* I try, ever so humbly, to express.

The other 'kick-off' is my old original one, and (had I not known love) it would have been my all. Not hate or destruction (both are beneath contempt as real motives) but an *extremely* deep sense of hopelessness, of everything doomed to disaster, almost wilfully, stupidly . . . There! as I took out a cigarette paper I got it exactly—*a cry against corruption*—that is *absolutely* the nail on the head. Not a protest—a *cry*.[11]

'Into those two categories,' Murry comments, 'all Katherine Mansfield's best writing falls with remarkable precision';[12] and he proceeds to write the history of her development in these terms. *In a German Pension* represents her negative 'kick-off'—the 'cry against corruption'. 'Prelude' represents the first flowering of her positive mode—'a new range of utterance, a new comprehension of experience, new complex harmonies'—and this occurs under the influence of 'two distinct and definite strands of experience . . . woven together. . . . Her overwhelming grief at the death of her young and only brother, killed in France; and the almost simultaneous unfolding of a new love for her husband'.[13]

The 'husband' referred to here is of course Murry himself. He thus writes himself into her artistic development, and in all his commentaries he is assiduous in keeping himself there. 'Prelude' represents the happiness she found with him in Bandol in the early months of 1916. 'Je ne parle pas français' represents a return to her negative vein while she was far from him, in Bandol again, ill and disillusioned in February 1918. 'A Married Man's Story' is a continuation of that negative phase. 'At the Bay', like 'Prelude', springs from love—another period when the Murrys lived and worked at peace together, this time at the Chalet des Sapins in Switzerland in 1921.

Thus the swing from positive to negative in the material of her fiction is made to correspond with the ups and downs of her marriage; and while the downs—'Je ne parle pas français' and 'A Married Man's Story'—are interesting failures or partial successes, it is the ups, 'Prelude' and 'At the Bay', which represent the true fulfilment of the Mansfield talent.

Added on to this is the idea that with the death of her brother she returned to the material of her childhood—the New Zealand memories she and her brother had evoked together during his last leave before he went to the war in France. Under the double influence of love and grief any bitterness towards her own country and family was purged, and the New Zealand material became available to her for use in fiction. In support of this part of the mythology there are those passages in her journal in which she resolves to write for her dead brother and of New Zealand:

Now—now I want to write recollections of my own country. Yes, I want to write about my own country till I simply exhaust my store. Not only because it is 'a sacred debt' . . . because my brother and I were born there, but also because in my thoughts I range with him over all the remembered places. I am never far away from them. I long to renew them in writing. . . . Oh, I want for one moment to make our undiscovered country leap into the eyes of the Old World.[14]

This then is Murry's picture of his wife's development. A new phase opens with the death of her brother and the full discovery of her love for her husband. The advance is not technical but spiritual, and it is marked by the writing of the first draft of 'Prelude' (under the title *The Aloe*) in the period of happiness husband and wife shared in Bandol in the early months of 1916. No doubt in retrospect Murry believed this simple account, which now pervades almost every critical and biographical commentary. But a look at the evidence of letters and journals shows it to be false. Here, briefly, is the real story.

In February 1915 Katherine Mansfield left Murry and went, on what she later called 'an indiscreet journey', all the way to the war zone in France to be with the French writer Francis Carco whom she had met in Paris and with whom she had been corresponding. After a brief affair with Carco she returned to England—'disillusioned', Murry says, but there is no evidence of that.[15] In March she left Murry again and went to live alone in Carco's flat in Paris. On 24 March her journal entry reads 'kick-off'. Next day she is saying in a letter that she has written 'a huge chunk' of her 'first novel'.[16] Murry's footnote tells us that this 'almost certainly' refers, not to *The Aloe*, which became 'Prelude', but to something called 'Brave Love'. Murry is quite certainly wrong about 'Brave Love', a story mentioned in her journal as having been completed on 12 January 1915;[17] and I think the entry of 24 March must in fact record the beginning of *The Aloe*.

She returned to London during April and was back in Paris again on 5 May. On 8 May she writes in a letter to Murry 'I am writing my book. Ça marche, ça va, ça se dessine—it's good.'[18] Murry's 1951 note on this letter (a note written after his most influential commentaries on her work had had their effect) acknowledges that this refers to *The Aloe*. Hitherto, he says, he had thought the work was begun at a later date; but he has recently found a letter of his dated 11 May which refers to *The Aloe* as a matter of familiar knowledge between them.[19]

On 12 May she writes that the work continues well: 'I could write it anywhere—it goes so easily and I know it so well'—which fits the material of *The Aloe*. And on 14 May she says it is 'finished'[20]—it has only to be polished. A day later she writes to Murry 'Is your *book* worrying you? No, I can't send any of *mine* because I'm too dependent on it *as a whole* under my hand.'[21]

It is clear that even at the speed Katherine Mansfield was capable of when she was in the vein she could not have completed a draft of something she conceived of as a 'book' between 6 May and 14 May. It must have begun earlier—almost certainly on that earlier visit to Paris in March—and might have been continued in London during April. But in any case the crucial point is that the work was first conceived and largely executed in a period of separation from Murry and while her brother was still alive. Long before she wrote those passages about making her undiscovered country leap into the eyes of the Old World she was well launched on what was to become 'Prelude'.

For some months after her return to London in the latter half of May 1915 there is no reference in journals or letters to anything that might be *The Aloe*. In October 1915 her brother is killed. In November she and Murry go to Bandol in the South of France, but he returns to England after three weeks, leaving her behind. On 10 and 11 December there are references in letters to some writing—references which Murry thinks are to a second attempt at *The Aloe*.[22] I think this unlikely; but in any case whatever the letters refer to came to nothing. For the remainder of December, though she writes every day and in detail about her activities, there is no suggestion of anything being written except a sketch for a periodical called *The Signature*.

On 1 January 1916 Murry arrived back in Bandol and their three-month idyll at the Villa Pauline began. On 22 January she confides to her journal her determination to write for her brother and of New Zealand—but she is clearly not doing it.[23] On 13 February she admits she has written 'practically nothing yet. . . . There is nothing done. I am no nearer my achievement than I was two months ago'[24]—so nothing had been achieved during December and January. On 14 February she acknowledges how difficult it is, but once again promises her dead brother that she will do it. On 15 February she seems to record a start on something—'I have broken the silence'—but next day comes the crucial entry: 'I *found The Aloe* this morning.'[25] She had evidently come upon the manuscript, which had probably been laid aside entirely since the previous May—for a period, that is, of nine months. Now she can see that what she had written the previous day was a false start. It 'was not quite "right" yesterday. No. . . . *The Aloe* is right. *The Aloe* is lovely. It simply fascinates me, and I know that it is what you would wish me to write' (the 'you' being her dead brother). 'And now I know what the last chapter is. It is your birth. . . . That chapter will end the book.'

What happened at Bandol then was not the simple flowering into fiction of love and memory but quite the reverse, a complete block—a total lack of anything but the wish to write—until she rediscovered and reread a work begun and extensively written in quite different circumstances. Further, if we accept Alpers's statement that the manuscript of *The Aloe* shows it was completed on 2 March then she spent only two weeks on it in Bandol.[26]

Thus almost every statement Murry makes about the genesis of the work is misleading. It derives neither from her love for him nor from the death of her brother. It represents a technical development possibly dependent more than anything else on situations of isolation and estrangement. In such situations she learned to re-enter the characters of her childhood, to live their lives and imaginatively to reinterpret them in terms of an adult consciousness. In this way Linda and Stanley Burnell come to life, and through them she develops once again her theme of the female identity fully realizing itself only in a sexual relationship which at the same time is seen as the source of pain, fear, and ultimate destruction.

Even at Bandol the work was not completed. The 30,000-word draft apparently brought to a conclusion there was revised, cut by a third, and renamed 'Prelude' during the spring and summer of 1917—again a period when the Murrys were living apart. From start to finish it had taken two and a half years. It was published as a little book by Leonard and Virginia Woolf in 1918; and it became the principal story in her second collection, *Bliss and Other Stories,* published in 1920.

What had that prolonged exercise taught Katherine Mansfield? First I think it had taught her that fiction did not have to be shaped towards a conclusion, a climax, a dénouement; or, as I have suggested already, that a fiction is not quite the same thing as a story. A fiction survives, not by leading us anywhere, but by being at every point authentic, a recreation of life, so that we experience it and remember it as we experience and remember actual life. It has a multiple texture, like the texture of life itself. Immediacy is of the utmost importance. The writer must imagine, not invent. She must efface herself. She must see and become the characters or the objects she wishes to represent. There is a letter to Dorothy Brett in which she talks of contemplating a duck or an apple or a character until 'you are *more* duck, *more* apple, or *more* Natasha than any of these objects could ever possibly be.' It is what she calls (in the same letter) 'that divine *spring* into the bounding outline of things.'[27]

An example of the kind of authenticity achieved is Stanley Burnell's dash for the water in 'At the Bay'. The scene is early morning:

> A few moments later the back door of one of the bungalows opened, and a figure in a broad-striped bathing-suit flung down the paddock, cleared the stile, rushed through the tussock grass into the hollow, staggered up the sandy hillock, and raced for dear life over the big porous stones, over the cold, wet pebbles, on to the hard sand that gleamed like oil. Splish-Splosh! Splish-Splosh! The water bubbled round his legs as Stanley Burnell waded out exulting.

There is a very subtle mixture of precision and involvement there. In one sense the imaginative involvement is total. She has run every step in imagination—and the word that makes you feel it most clearly is 'staggered'—'staggered up the sandy hillock'. It slows up the momentum of the sentence, not because Burnell is exhausted—in a moment he will be 'racing' again—but because despite his efforts to keep up the pace, his feet are sinking, the harder his strong legs drive them, into the soft dry sand. But there is at the same time a cool eye looking from outside on this figure 'racing' (and the conventional phrase seems to belong to him) 'for dear life' in his 'broad-striped bathing-suit'.

Here style is of immense importance, not for its own sake, but because through it we receive a direct transmission of the author's sense of life. As the passage continues the character of Stanley Burnell is conveyed to us directly in every word she uses to represent his actions and the thoughts and feelings racing through his head. He wades out 'exulting'. He 'swoops' to 'souse' his head and neck, delighted with himself for being first in the water again. Then he hears Jonathan's voice and realizes that he is not first in after all, and we get a succession of small explosions occurring inside his head. 'Great Scott! Damnation take it! . . . Why the dickens didn't the fellow stick to his part of the sea? Why should he come barging over to this exact spot?' Stanley gives 'a kick, a lunge'. To escape from Jonathan's conversation, which he thinks of as 'piffle' and 'rot', he turns over on his back and kicks with his legs till he is 'a living water-spout'. Coming direct through the language is the characterization—Burnell's energy, his confidence, his childlike delights and disappointments, his conventionality, the limits of his understanding. This is the same Stanley who will punish his wife by going off in the morning without saying goodbye, suffer all day for it, and arrive home full of remorse to find that the omission has gone unnoticed. We can describe him in abstract terms, which is what the lesser fiction writers would do, inviting us to do their imagining for them. Katherine Mansfield doesn't describe in abstract—she presents; and this can be seen even in the grammar. Its tense is almost exclusively past historic which, because it makes each action finite and exclusive, is hardly different in effect from present tense narration. There are no summaries, no imperfect tense which is the characteristic tense of a great deal of narrative. If any action is representative the grammar doesn't tell us so. We make that only as our own assumption. To put it another way, the author is not present in the grammar. Compare the Mansfield passage with one from R. L. Stevenson's *Weir of Hermiston* (also about a family holiday):

Thus, at least, when the family were at Hermiston, not only my lord, but Mrs. Weir too, enjoyed a holiday. Free from the dreadful looking-for of the miscarried dinner, she would mind her seam, read her piety books, and take her walk (which was my lord's orders), sometimes by herself, sometimes with Archie, the only child of that scarce natural union. The child was her next bond to life. Her frosted sentiment bloomed again, she breathed deep of life, she let loose her heart, in that society.[28]

Stevenson is a great story-teller and that is the story-teller giving the life of his characters in summary before he narrows his focus on to a particular scene. We hear it as a voice. Someone is telling us all this. Someone has made this summary and may at any moment step in during the action and direct our judgement. In the Mansfield by contrast, rather than being related the events *occur*. Immediacy is achieved by a combination of imaginative involvement and intellectual detachment, a combination which Frank O'Connor, for example, admires and yet is shocked by—precisely because explicit judgement is eliminated, the author will not intervene directly. Of the scene in which the duck is beheaded in 'Prelude' O'Connor says 'For me this is one of the most remarkable scenes in modern literature.' But he is shocked by it because it seems to him to be 'written in a complete, hypnotic suspension of the critical faculties.'[29]

I described the method of 'Prelude' and of 'At the Bay' as accretion because they both follow a sequential time line but that line is not in itself significant. In terms of plot nothing is added on. 'Prelude' is organized around the departure from one house and the settling in at another. 'At the Bay' follows the doings of the family during a single day of their summer holiday. Both are divided into twelve sections, and each section is itself a small fiction offering a view of one character or relationship. In both it is the female characters who hold the centre of the stage, and the two pieces together might be called 'The Four Ages of Woman'—Kezia the little girl, Beryl the young woman on the brink of experience, Linda Burnell the young mother sinking under the oppression of repeated child-bearing, and the Grandmother, the survivor. Stanley Burnell is the characteristic Mansfield male, the 'pa-man'—bluff, successful in his work, vigorous, simple, warm-hearted, generous, loving, but also demanding, uncomprehending, insensitive, slightly ridiculous, above all less subtle than the women who surround him and who suffer his benevolent despotism because convention and circumstances require it. Put together, 'Prelude' and 'At the Bay' make up a portrait of a marriage as subtle and complete as you are likely to find in fiction. There is about the relationship a feeling of pathos and inevitability. It is unsatisfactory though by no means a disaster. No one is to blame, there is nothing to be done. Linda loves her husband despite her clear-sighted recognition of his limitations; but her love has been complicated by fear of child-bearing, and fear sours the marriage for her and makes her want to escape from it. In her consciousness of the proximity of death she is joined in 'At the Bay' by Jonathan Trout, a male figure very different from the Mansfield 'pa-man', sensitive, artistic, a man who is wasting his talents and his life in clerical work for which he has no appetite and no aptitude. How much subtle female psychology there is folded away in Linda's final dismissal of Jonathan from her mind ('he is like a weed') is a subject one would not presume, or dare, to embark on.

These are the central relationships and themes of the two stories. But they come into clearer focus in 'At the Bay' than they do in 'Prelude'. 'Prelude' has been sharpened in the process of being cut down from the longer version, *The Aloe*. But there is still, I think, especially in the early sections, an impression that the writer is feeling her way, that she is not quite sure where the centre of her interest lies. In 'At the Bay' the writing is surer and the focus narrower—and it is significant that whereas the writing of 'Prelude' was spread over two and a half years, 'At the Bay' was completed in a matter of a few weeks. When she returned to that material a second time she demonstrated that she had learned how to handle it.

'Prelude' is the first story in the 1920 collection, *Bliss and Other Stories*.

The second is 'Je ne parle pas français', and it is here she discovered the method I called circumlocution for producing an extended fiction. At least in its potential I think this is an advance on 'Prelude', though the technique is not something that could be applied simply by an act of will. It depends both on fullness and on singleness of imaginative identification. Whereas in 'Prelude' and 'At the Bay' Katherine Mansfield is entering into the lives of characters who existed in her childhood and discovering what might have been the truth of their feelings and relationships, in 'Je ne parle pas français' she is creating a character, discovering him as she writes herself into him, extending her consciousness of him day by day; and it is in this articulation of the character of the Frenchman, Raoul Duquette, that the interest lies.

Once again, however, we need to disengage the story from the Mansfield mythology. Following Murry's lead again the commentaries have tended to see it as a piece of thinly veiled autobiography, with Mouse as Mansfield, Duquette as Carco, and Dick Harmon as Murry. 'The fate of the Mouse,' Murry writes, 'caught in the toils of the world's evil, abandoned by her lover, is Katherine's fate.'[30] No approach is more likely to kill our interest. If Mouse is the centre of attention, and Mouse is Mansfield, the story must inevitably seem tedious and self-indulgent.

First let's consider Mansfield's own description of it as 'a cry against corruption'. This influences the commentaries and leads to some very heavy moralizing about the character of Duquette, whose 'peculiar depravity', Sylvia Berkman says, the story 'is shaped to illuminate'.[31] But internal evidence suggests that not more than a third of the story was complete when Katherine Mansfield wrote the letter which Murry treats as her final word on the subject. In fact she continued to write to him day by day as the story progressed, and it is clear that her attitude changed. On 3 February the story was 'a cry against corruption'. Exactly a week later she is describing it as 'a tribute to Love',[32] which does not at all suit Murry's simple distinction mentioned already, in which 'Je ne parle pas français' represents the negative pole of her fiction. She had in fact swung from a negative to a positive state of feeling in the course of writing it; and I think one can feel that in the story itself. Her letters show a growing excitement in the technical aspects of the story; and that excitement in turn invades the whole conception, including the characterization, so that Duquette ceases to be simply corrupt and becomes something subtler and more complicated. Sexually equivocal, a gigolo, self-absorbed and full of falseness and posturing, he is nevertheless gradually invested with Katherine Mansfield's own sense of comedy, her capacity for euphoria, her eye for the absurd, and this extra dimension, not present in the initial conception, in turn affects the view we have of the English couple, Dick Harmon and Mouse. Of course their suffering is real; but they are also absurd; and it is

Duquette's mixture of mannered detachment and equivocal involvement that permits both the comedy and the tragedy of their situation to receive simultaneous expression. But the chief interest remains all the time in the character of Duquette himself. The story opens from that centre— Duquette and the café whose atmosphere is used to express his feeling about life in general—and it returns there.

Why did Katherine Mansfield write after finishing 'Je ne parle pas français' 'I feel I have found an *approach* to a story now which I must apply to everything'?[33] What was the technical advance she had made? In 'Prelude' she had achieved immediacy, she had made 'that divine *spring* into the bounding outline of things', and she had broken the dominance of narrative in fiction; but the events were still arranged in a linear sequence. The real achievement of 'Je ne parle pas français' (and it is something she repeated in 'The Daughters of the Late Colonel') is that it establishes a central point of reference and then moves in circles about it, going back and forward in time. The result is a further thickening of texture. Duquette's consciousness is real to us because it is a shifting thing, quite distinct yet difficult to pin down as it ranges about. We begin at the café at a certain point in time which I will call the 'present'. We go back to an earlier moment which is nevertheless later than the time of the principal events of the story. We come forward to the 'present'. We go back to Duquette's childhood. We move forward to his becoming tenant of a bachelor flat, which is before the principal events of the story. We come forward to the 'present'. He orders whisky and this reminds him of Dick Harmon. One third of the fiction has been written before Harmon is mentioned. From that point on there is something pretty close to a narrative sequence. But the sense of richness, of a texture, has been established. And into the narrative sequence are slotted elements which are in no sense at all part of the 'story', but are simply further extensions of the portrayal of Duquette's character. His confrontation with the concierge, his escape to the metro, his encounter with the lady who has flowers on her 'balcony'—none of these advances the narrative at all. They are not in any way significant to the outcome; but they add considerably to our sense of Duquette.

There is more 'story' to 'Je ne parle pas français' than to 'Prelude', but it is only an excuse on which to hang the fiction, or a way of winding it up, and if we pay too much attention to it it may leave us confused. There is a very fine, subjectively drawn line between richness and confusion. 'Je ne parle pas français' begins as a cry against Duquette's corruption and becomes something like a celebration of it. The fiction is as equivocal as the character; and we may decide that this is a good or a bad thing according to mood and appetite. But the brilliance of detail, and the gusto, are beyond dispute; so, I believe, is the fact that technically the story represents a step forward into greater complexity.

The work most closely related to 'Je ne parle pas français' in content and method is 'A Married Man's Story' published as an unfinished piece in the posthumous collection *The Dove's Nest and Other Stories* (1923). Both these stories have a first person male narrator, a man who is in some degree cynical and at odds with the world. Both move in circles from a central point, going back and forward in time. But 'A Married Man's Story' is darker, less ebullient, steadier in tone and purpose; it is probably the most sombre of all Katherine Mansfield's fictions; and it suggests a further range of feeling she might have been expected to explore and develop. Murry puts the two stories together, but once again it is according to the positive-negative classification already described, which he related to the progress of their marriage, 'Je ne parle pas français', and 'A Married Man's Story' belonging to periods of estrangement and doubt, 'Prelude' and 'At the Bay' to periods of peace and love.[34] For this reason the exercise of attempting to date 'A Married Man's Story' and to plot exactly where it comes in Katherine Mansfield's writing is particularly interesting.

During May 1918 she wrote regularly from Looe in Cornwall to Murry who was then in London. Once again they were friends apart. On the 28th she mentions a new story she is writing; and in his 1951 edition of her letters Murry footnotes this remark saying he believes the work referred to is 'A Married Man's Story'.[35] So far as I know there is no evidence other than this footnote for dating the story from that time; but every critic and commentator who gives it a date gives May 1918.[36] Murry had, however, twenty-eight years before he published that footnote, dated the story differently. In his introductory note to *The Dove's Nest* (1923) he listed it among stories written 'Between October 1921 . . . and the end of January 1922'; and since this note went on reappearing in the *Collected Stories,* two contradictory pieces of information continued to be available after 1951, though it was a contradiction no one appeared to notice.

In fact, as might be expected, Murry's earlier dating, not the later, was nearer to being correct; but even it was significantly inaccurate, suggesting the story was not written until after *The Garden Party* stories were complete, whereas in fact it belongs among them. Among papers deposited in the British Museum by Violet Schiff on the death of her husband Sydney there are letters from Murry. On 23 August 1921 Murry writes from the Chalet des Sapins in Switzerland:

K. is in the middle of the longest and last of her stories for her new book which is to be called (I believe, though this is confidential) 'A Married Man' and other stories. It's the married man she's in the middle of now. I think it's an amazing piece of work.[37]

Thus 'A Married Man's Story', the darkest of all her fictions, belongs not to a period of estrangement but to the second period of sustained marital harmony. More surprising, it belongs to the same month in which 'At the Bay' was being written, and seems even to have interrupted the writing of 'At the Bay'. The sequence of that extraordinarily productive period seems to have been as follows: She is writing 'At the Bay' on 8 August.[38] By 14 August she has set it aside and completed 'The Voyage'.[39] On 23 August she is well into 'A Married Man's Story'.[40] She becomes ill and lays it aside.[41] After the illness she returns to 'At the Bay' and finishes it somewhere between 5 and 22 September.[42] She makes several false starts on new stories, and then early in October writes 'The Garden Party'[43] which becomes the title story for the new collection. 'A Married Man's Story', being incomplete, remains unpublished until after her death, when Murry locates it first (1923) as coming after *The Garden Party* stories were complete, then (1951) as coming before they were begun.

'A Married Man's Story' is the strangest and most impenetrable of her fictions, and one of the most compelling. It has a remorselessly sinister quality. Its central character is negative in a way that throws up, when the comparison is made, all that is positive and life-affirming in Raoul Duquette. What the central idea was to be is not fully revealed. Something has happened 'last autumn' which has turned the marriage sour and brought out the dark side of the narrator, causing him to revive the horror that hangs over him from childhood. The horror springs (I am now re-sorting the elements into something like a narrative) from the memory that his mother, who had been bedridden throughout his childhood, came to his bed-side the night she died (he was thirteen) and told him his father had poisoned her. Whether this really happened or not he doesn't know. The father was a chemist who sold a fivepenny pick-me-up to young women whose 'gaudy looks' and 'free ways' fascinated the child. There is something sinister about this pick-me-up and the women who take it. The father's manner in selling it is 'discreet, sly, faintly amused and tinged with impudence'. After the mother's death the father consorts with some of these painted young women. He is an alien and frightening figure and the child thinks of him as Deadly Poison, or old D.P.

Some time after the mother's death the child, or young man, has had an experience which makes him feel that everything has changed, 'the barriers [are] down', he has 'come into [his] own world', he is no longer alien. He has turned, however, not towards human kind, but towards his 'silent brothers'; and this, the last phrase in the story as it stands, seems to refer back to the wolves, described earlier as his 'fleet, grey brothers'. So as a young man he has discovered his identity, not in human brotherhood, but in a sense of absolute alienation from human kind. This separation has been concealed, and for a time he has lived a normal life, has married and earned the love and affection of his wife. What is it then which 'last autumn' has changed it all, brought his subtle, submerged cruelty to the surface, and made his wife feel his coldness and the gap that exists between them? It must be, I think, the birth of the child. This must be the central idea, which remains incompletely expounded. He has become a father and now must act out the role of the father as he conceives it from his own experience. Symbolically, he has begun to poison his wife.

It is not a pretty story and it is easy to see why Katherine Mansfield laid it aside and never returned to it. But it is a gripping and impressive fictional exercise, and one whose symbolism takes hold of the imagination. It is also fascinating because it is once again an eruption of her central preoccupation—the male seen as the destroyer of the female in a sexual relationship.

I made the point early on that Katherine Mansfield worked largely by instinct. If I ask myself what it was an instinct *for*, I can only answer that it was for the real fiction, which comes from the exercise of imagination, rather than for the imitation which the constructing intellect can so obligingly produce when the imagination refuses to do its job. And it is this which places her among the moderns and makes her contemporary, in a meaningful sense, with Pound and Eliot.

If there is one discovery at the heart of the Modernist revolution of sixty years ago it is that there is something which is 'poetry' as distinct from anything else, and that this is not a form but a quality. Further, the fragments which exhibit this quality, if they come from the same man at the same period and out of related preoccupations, will naturally cohere, without structural linking. In fact the structural elements are almost always non-poetic, and are better dispensed with. This is one of the lessons of Pound's editorial exercise on the manuscripts of 'The Waste Land'.

The earliest influences on Katherine Mansfield, when she was still at school, were the aesthetes; and her first regular place of publication was A. R. Orage's *The New Age*, where she must have read some of the theorizing that lies behind the revolution that was going on at this time in all the arts.[44] In music, in painting, in poetry and fiction, every accepted structural principle was being questioned; and although Katherine Mansfield was only intermittently of a revolutionary disposition, she was aware of what was going on, and influenced in her practice by the feeling that the artist's job at that time was to 'make it new'. Her work, not considered as a number of discrete pieces of finished writing but rather as a movement towards something, demonstrates that fiction, too, is a quality, not a form. The items of 'Prelude' and 'At the Bay' cohere without narrative linking. And individually they are most successful when they are not forced to make a point. When she pushed herself, when she tried to write virtuously, when she worked too deliberately to shape the fictional fragment, of whatever length, to make a point or to come to a conclusion, she produced her weakest work. In her later writing she is still learning to be content to be fragmentary, learning that it is part of the writer's job to engage the reader's imagination by leaving gaps as often as by filling them, learning not to interfere with the creative process once it has completed itself. Murry describes 'A Married Man's Story' as 'unfinished yet somehow complete',[45] and in that he is right.

Where did it come from? With many of her stories the identification between life and fiction is so close her chief problem is that of shaping family and personal history into art. But for 'A Married Man's Story' I can see no source in her life except a few physical details suggesting her Wellington childhood. The story is like a dream, a nightmare, a necessary eruption from the unconscious.

In 'At the Bay' Linda Burnell comes to accept the negative elements in the relations of the sexes and to affirm the whole process, even by implication the early death she seems to feel threatening her as a consequence of repeated child-bearing. Section VI, where she discovers the love for the new baby she thought she was incapable of; and the magnificent passage in section X when the beams of the sunset remind her, not of death, as they usually do, but of 'something infinitely joyful and loving'—these constitute something which feels very close to a resolving of that dilemma observed right from the earliest of Katherine Mansfield's stories. It is a fascinating thought that in order to achieve it she had to lay aside 'At the Bay' and pour out the old horrors in the form of 'A Married Man's Story'. The result was a fragment as genuine and compelling as anything in her collected work.

FRANK SARGESON:
TWO SMALL TRIBUTES

ON THE PUBLICATION
OF FRANK SARGESON'S NOVEL
'MEMOIRS OF A PEON'

The Grub Street dogs are yapping after their tails.
Someone has made the books they said were dead
Get up and talk in Auckland.
Frank, you always grow the best tomatoes,
The fattest peppers. Only your book makes clear
Why, coming through your hedge to get my share
I have to bow so low.

Written in London in 1965 and first printed in *Landfall* 78, June 1966.

A LETTER TO FRANK SARGESON

Dear Frank,

Robin Dudding has asked me to write something about you for the occasion of your seventy-fifth birthday but how could I do it? As soon as I stop and think about you as a 'subject' I feel swamped by it. You have been such a large part of my literary life any thought I have about what might be suitable soon grows into a piece of autobiography, a memoir, a book. I will write it one day, if I live long enough, but not now. I would have to go through all those letters we have exchanged during the years when I have been overseas; and the notes that shot back and forth across the harbour during the sixties before you got your phone; and think my way back into scenes and conversations that deserve more than a casual sentence or paragraph at an inconvenient moment. The fact is that for twenty-four years, since I first started visiting you, you have represented a particular atmosphere. To do anything like justice to it there would have to be tomatoes and peppers and beans and pumpkins as well as books and manuscripts and conversation; your haversack would have to be 'in' it—and certain gestures, and rituals, and preoccupations.

There is a whole book, a novel perhaps, to be made out of just one year, 1955, when Kay and I lived in a glassed-in veranda right on Takapuna beach, Janet Frame was writing *Owls Do Cry* in the hut behind your house, and you were working on your plays. I remember one occasion when the four of us went swimming together. We took a bus to one of the remoter bays. When we were in the water some guns went off—the military were practising on the headland—and Janet was terrified. You wreathed yourself in seaweed, took up a short stick for a pipe, and did a Pan dance. That too is an atmosphere, life imitating art, reality moulding itself to the colours and shapes of your own fiction.

On my desk at this moment I have an essay by a research student

Written for *Islands* 21, March 1978, celebrating Frank Sargeson's 75th birthday.

troubled by the fact that your fiction doesn't represent New Zealand as it really is. Isn't this the inevitable next step when for so many years you have been plagued by the goodwill and praise of critics who have found New Zealand perfectly represented in your work? I know the sociologist-critics have always made you uneasy. It isn't that a fiction writer is licensed to misrepresent; but there is such a difference between 'represent' and 're-present'. We are the inheritors of Keats' dictum: 'I am certain of nothing but of the holiness of the Heart's affections and the truth of Imagination'. Imagination is not some unbridled Ariel, wayward and arbitrary in its inventions. But if we 're-present' what we know, we present ourselves along with it. It is that magical foreshore between subjective and objective, dream and reality, to which the Romantic imagination has exclusive riparian rights. This is something you have always understood; and it is in this understanding that you and Allen Curnow meet (though I don't think you have met in 'reality' since 1955, when you told him in the street that the pohutukawa's 'spectacular blossom' has stamens, not petals, and his bus came along before he could think of an answer. Did you think his Ariel was getting above itself in his brilliant poems of that year?)

As for 'reality' as the sociologist measures it—what we measure we cannot know by measuring. All we know are the measurements. To know, we have first to imagine. That is a paradox I won't pursue into infinity, Frank; but I will just add before leaving it that in the last few years I have seen you acquire three or four friends more like Sargeson characters, and in that degree more 'unreal', than any in your fiction. One was the man who sent your firewood down from Kaukapakapa once a year, and whom you seemed to 'know' before you had met him. When he turned out to match your idea of him it crossed my mind that you might have been feeding on honey dew and drinking the milk of Paradise, because there seemed no other explanation possible than that you had conjured him into being.

If I wrote about the care you have taken reading my poems over the years, and the things you have noticed in them that have gone unnoticed everywhere else (at least so far as I know) I would be writing partly about myself. And ideas—the subjects on which we have agreed, or agreed to differ—they seem relatively unimportant. It is observation and anecdote (seeing and shaping) that seem most to matter when I think of you—and I recognize as soon as I put down those pairs I have brought myself back to that foreshore where the tides of the imagination wash over shells so real they can cut your feet:

> the sea
> Levels its lucent ruins underfoot.

Again I'm letting it run away with me, but I can't resist the thought that it was there we swam with Janet and Kay in 1955.

Your fictions are composed of anecdotes, just as poems are composed of images. The skill is to make them seem to flower from one centre, not to look like washing strung out on a line. The anecdote is the image. In your conversation long ago the knife slashed at the lily leaf on the pond and the frog vanished and then the little severed frog-hand floated to the surface— just as you had seen it happen in a Remuera garden. Later it happened on one of the pages of *Memoirs of a Peon*. And the big toes I had seen tied together in the morgue refrigerators at the Auckland Hospital when I worked there as a student—how many years after I described them to you was it they turned up in one of your novels?

I don't think you will mind being called an 'atmosphere'. That is something breathed. Some part of my creative life has lived off it these twenty-four years. This is pretty heavy stuff to lay on you on your birthday (when you turned seventy we bought Chinese takeaways) but this is a public statement and maybe calls for a little of the truth we skirt around shyly in private. Anyway, although now is not the moment for me to embark on that memoir, I don't want to miss the celebration. Like many others who will be contributing to this special issue of *Islands*, I count your living and writing up to the age of seventy-five as part of my own good fortune.

SYLVIA ASHTON-WARNER: LIVING ON THE GRAND

Katherine Mansfield was born in 1888, Sylvia Ashton-Warner in 1908, and Janet Frame in 1924—three New Zealand women each of whom has achieved some measure of literary fame or reputation outside the country in which she was born. They have in common that they have worked uneasily in (and always breaking out of) the fictional mode. The fictions of all three are forms of autobiography while autobiography tends towards fiction. It is the self they are struggling always to define, or to create, and the self is founded on fact but not exclusively composed of it.

All three gain and lose by being New Zealanders. Mansfield escaped from the colony, as it was then, only to live and die severed from her true subject matter, too often dressing it up in middle-class clothes, smoothing its colonial rough edges for her English readers first and foremost of whom were the Bloomsburies who thought her vulgar. Janet Frame suffered early in life the New Zealand repression in its medical form whereby (as she puts it in her latest novel) 'dis-ease is classed as disease', and she has since lived as a recluse in New Zealand, with frequent travel abroad. Ashton-Warner lived all her working life until the age of sixty in New Zealand, often in her fiction speaking through the persona of a foreigner (Anna Vorontosov in *Spinster*, Germaine de Beauvais in *Incense to Idols*). As a writer she did not receive her due in New Zealand, and after the death of her husband she spent most of a decade abroad (a good deal of it as a teacher in North American universities) chanting over to herself with satisfaction 'I'm no longer in New Zealand'.

What these writers gained from being New Zealanders, I think, was the

A review for the *London Review of Books*, 7 May 1981, of *I Passed this Way* together with re-issues of *Spinster* and *Teacher*, with supplementary notes for addition to this book.

same in each case—the lack of any profoundly etched social identity, so that the raw, untrammelled, human personality and intelligence is overlaid with very little and breaks out easily into full abundant self-expression. They are not hidebound by forms and decorums and literary convention. In the writing of each at its best there is clarity of vision, an uncommitted intelligence, a capacity both for passion and detachment; and the detachment is never far removed from a sense of comedy which is a form of revolt against all prevailing pieties. Anna Vorontosov in *Spinster*, visited by the senior Schools Inspector who brings with him two distinguished academic visitors, records:

... he ... introduces me to the others; Mr This and Mr That. They're both modestly dressed men. ... Indeed the smaller of the two might well have been some roadman who had just helped the larger out of a drain. (*Spinster*, pp.218-19)

—which is very close to the note of Katherine Mansfield's comic deflations of the masculine order, such as the occasion when she feels faint at an exhibition of Naval photographs in 1918 and is assisted by 'two Waacs and a Wren':

They asked me ... whether I had *lost* anybody in the Navy—as though it were nothing but a kind of gigantic salt-water laundry.
                                        (Penguin *Letters and Journals*, p.125)

Mansfield and Ashton-Warner have a histrionic quality which the more retiring Frame lacks. They are both chameleons, ventriloquists, with a perfect ear for the speech of others, and the ability to cast themselves into a role. Both were troubled from time to time by this habit of role-playing, though it was part of their fiction, and Ashton-Warner fairly early sorted out for herself what was essential and inessential in it:

After that concentrated think I feel a good bit better, I've finished playing a role. Now I'm *me*. There's an incredible tendency in this last shaking year to imitate those I admire. God Almighty, I saw it! Patterning myself on other people ... where would I get and what would I be? A carbon copy of other people? I'm determined to stay how I am and be damned.   (*Myself*, p.201)

That was written when she was thirty-four, the age at which Mansfield died.

The role of the artist had (I suppose has for every artist) to be played before it became quite real, and both these women chose it for themselves before they chose to be writers. Mansfield thought at first she would be a cellist, and might equally have been successful as an actress and singer; Ashton-Warner veered between piano and paint before settling for the pen. Socially Mansfield the expatriate had to conceal 'the little colonial' under some suitably respectable literary persona; while Ashton-Warner had to bring her native flourishes down to the space New Zealand society permits for individuality—never enough to swing a cat in. Since both were unsuccessful in these required acts of self-limitation they were both victims of the kind of malice that can be illustrated by Frank O'Connor's description of Mansfield as 'the brassy little shop-girl of literature', or by Virginia Woolf's complaint that she 'stank like a civet cat'—the latter (if it requires translation) recording simply that the Woolf nose judged the Mansfield perfume to be insufficiently expensive. These, I suppose, are examples of a peculiarly British snobbery; but that a parallel repressive malice has operated against Ashton-Warner in New Zealand ('cutting him/her down to size' it's called) must simply be recorded without examples.

Both these women sustained their ambitions and carried themselves over obstacles by dreaming, and the dreams were opposite and exactly complementary. Ashton-Warner's dream was of freedom, the life of the artist in Paris and London, a studio, intellectual friends ('artists, musicians, writers') and lovers—all of which Mansfield had. Conversely Mansfield's dream was of health, a stable marriage, children, a garden, an outdoor life ('the earth and the wonders thereof—the sea, the sun')—all of which Ashton-Warner had. Together they make up the two faces of a common (but not, of course, uniquely) New Zealand syndrome. More interesting perhaps is that they are the two faces of the modern woman who wants both kinds of self-fulfilment—which I think Ashton-Warner finally achieved, and which Mansfield would probably have achieved too if there had been antibiotics to cure her T.B. They were perhaps fortunate, however, in being born early enough to discover their individual needs without benefit of feminist theory. Neither woman wasted energy in trying to eliminate the emotional and psychological consequences of sexual biology.

Their backgrounds were markedly different—Mansfield the daughter of a wealthy merchant and banker and an ailing mother, Ashton-Warner the daughter of an invalid father and a schoolteacher mother who worked to feed and clothe ten children. In their teens the differences become more marked—Mansfield sent 12,000 miles to a private school in London, Ashton-Warner riding ten and more miles on horseback each day to a back-country high school. Even so, the differences may be less significant than the likenesses in the earliest and most formative years—middle position in a large family, love and rivalry among female siblings, early musical training, and space in which to grow, the discovery of the self set free, not in society, but in a benign yet challenging landscape.

All her life Ashton-Warner has been protesting, inwardly at least, that she is an artist not a teacher. But as the child of a working mother she was inside a classroom from her earliest years. As a teacher she took her own babies into the classroom. Her husband was also—and always—her head-master. And when he died and she went abroad to satisfy a lifelong ambition to escape into a fuller artistic life, she was soon working in North American universities as a teacher of teachers, remitting money to New Zealand to help support a daughter who had been widowed young, and grandchildren. At the centre of much of her work there is the figure of a teacher who is at once brilliant and erratic, reluctant and original, failing to satisfy the pedestrian requirements of a system which itself fails to foster the true individuality and needs of the growing child. When her grading marks are low (as they always are) she wants to resign; and the artist in her is always chafing to be free of the classroom. Yet she can write (it is Anna Vorontosov in *Spinster*) of the end of the summer holidays:

. . . my arms have become itchy on the inside to hold children. From the wrists on the inner side along the skin right up to the shoulders and across the breast I know a physical discomfort. If ever flesh spoke mine does; for the communion of hands, the arms stretching round my waist and black heads bumping my breasts. It amounts to deprivation and I realize . . . how wild were my thoughts of resigning last year when the grading came out. The truth is that I am enslaved. I'm enslaved in one vast love affair with seventy children.   (*Spinster*, p.188)

During the period of her training as a teacher her future was balanced between two dreams—one of the artist's studio, the other of conventional love and marriage. Everything fostered the one and obstructed the other. She married a fellow-teacher, moved with him to a sole-charge school in the remotest part of the country, and bore three children. After the second birth she was asking to be allowed to teach again. Her husband objected but she won out (he would later repeatedly talk her out of resigning) and the pattern of their life together was established—he headmaster of small remote schools teaching predominantly Maori children, she mistress of the infant room where she evolved the reading method based on what she calls a 'key vocabulary'.

The best insights are simple and hers was that her Maori infant pupils were failing to progress in reading because the imported books (usually *Janet and John*) bore no relation to their lives and emotions. She discovered that for each child there were certain key words related to their day-to-day lives and to their feelings. Find one of his or her key words and the child who had taken three weeks to learn and forget a phrase from *Janet and John* would learn it in a few seconds and retain it. (A typical list for one of her Maori infants reads 'butcher-knife', 'goal', 'police', 'sing', 'cry', 'kiss', 'Daddy', 'Mummy', 'Rangi', 'haka', 'fight'.) She wrote and illustrated her own reading books for Maori children, making multiple copies one at a time by hand. The story of how these books developed, proved successful in the classroom, and failed to gain the recognition of the New Zealand Department of Education (which also inadvertently burned the final master copies she submitted to them) is one of the saddest, and most sadly convincing, she has to tell. Maori frustration and violence, she believes, begin in the infant room and in the slowness or failure to read, which puts many Maori children behind their pakeha schoolfellows. Gang violence, and the disproportion of Maoris in New Zealand jails, follow.

The books she put together and the stories she told in the classroom were mostly drawn from the children's accounts of their own lives, and written in the kind of English they spoke:

> I see in a current supplementary for primers the conversation of Quacky the Duck—
> 'I do not like the pond. I do not want to live there.'
> Has the compiler never heard of the word 'don't'? . . . In grown-up novels we enjoy the true conversational medium, yet five-year-olds for some inscrutable reason are met with the twisted idea behind 'Let us play'. As a matter of fact, Maoris seldom if ever use 'let' in that setting. They say 'We play, eh?'
>
> (*Teacher*, p.71)

Among the illustrations to *Teacher* are some of the stories her infant pupils wrote for her as they progressed:

> Mummie got a hiding off Daddy. He was drunk she was crying.

> I went to the river and I kissed Lily and I ran away. Then I kissed Phillipa. Then I ran away and went for a swim.

> Our baby is dead. She was dead on Monday night. When Mummie got it.

> When I went to sleep I dreamt about the war. The Chinese never won. The Maoris won.

And a parallel example from *Spinster*:

> Last night . . . I felled out of bed. So Daddy told Mummie to shiff over.

But words were not her sole medium. Paint, music and dancing were equally important. Her aim was a classroom in which the creative spirit would be fostered and violence correspondingly defused. Her idea of education was less to put in than to draw out. As a trainee she had observed a successful and worthy teacher who achieved those high grading marks that were never to come her way, who kept order without using the strap, and whose class was generally happy. But no mind developed there

as a personally operating organ in its own right. . . . What you came up with was
sixty small imprints of Miss Little. . . . It was the kind of schooling that produced
efficient rather than interesting people, promising to supply a fine army one day
. . . and a subservient people.   (*I Passed this Way*, p.159)

By comparison Ashton-Warner's classroom was to be unpredictable but
bursting with life. Sometimes, listening to her play the piano, her children
would one by one lay aside what they were doing and join in a spontaneous
dance. This was for her a moment of collective inspiration. At her best
(and she has recorded her failures) she created a medium in which the
individual wills and talents of the children could meet and join and find
expression, while each remained itself, unique and untrammelled. Community and not conformity was her aim.

Meanwhile she was writing, recording in diaries her successes and
failures in the classroom, her relations with her husband and with her passionate friend 'Opal', her attempts to create the conditions in which she
might write more purposefully, and something of the progress of her first
(unpublished) novel, *Rangatira*. Some of these diaries (in which 'Opal' is
given the male identity of 'Dr Saul') were reshaped and published in 1967,
more than twenty years after they were written, as *Myself*, a piece of fictional autobiography or autobiographical fiction as worthy of reprint as
anything she has published.

Of the three books under review *Teacher* was the earliest written. Half of
it is a straight account of her theory and practice in the classroom. The
second half is a diary 'Life in a Maori School', which brings the theory to
life with a series of observations and reflections taken from day-to-day experience. Both sections are excellent, and indispensible to the fullness of
the picture; and those who have thought of Ashton-Warner as a woman all
heart and of small intellect (she sometimes writes of herself as if this were
true) should look in particular at her straight expository prose which has
the clean sharp efficiency of a first-rate mind.

Teacher was completed about 1953 and for ten years Ashton-Warner
tried unsuccessfully to have it published in New Zealand. *Spinster* was
written in part to give fictional form to her account of how she had found
ways of teaching her Maori pupils to read. It was published in 1958 in
England and America, her first big success as a writer, reprinted numbers
of times and filmed with Shirley MacLaine in the leading role. It became a
point of reference in discussions of educational theory, but still no one
would publish *Teacher* in New Zealand where she most wanted it to have
its effect, and she at last allowed the book to be published abroad. It came
out first in 1963 and like *Spinster* it has been through a number of reprints
including a Penguin edition.

In *Spinster* (reissued now with a rather prim introduction by Fleur Adcock) Ashton-Warner puts her spinster-teacher Anna Vorontosov in the same 'pre-fab' classroom with the same Maori pupils described in *Teacher*. Into the school comes a young teacher, Paul Vercoe, confused in his feelings and confusing to Anna, who seems to believe that she is holding him at arm's length while we as readers, hearing the events in direct first-person narrative from her, nevertheless recognize what she fails to see, that it is she who wants him, while his primary attentions are directed to a Maori pupil who bears him twins which die at birth. It is this illegal love affair and its imminent consequences and not, as Anna imagines, his relationship with her, that seems to lead to his suicide—an event rendered with a curious comic gusto which I suspect signifies that half way through the book Ashton-Warner's imagination had had enough of this somewhat conventional fiction and wanted to get on with something nearer to the heart of her own experience.

So there is a perceptible fault-line between *Spinster* as documentary and as plotted fiction, and this is more clearly recognized because we have in *Teacher* the autobiographical material which reveals how far the classroom scenes are drawn directly from life and even from Ashton-Warner's day-by-day records of it. Anna is supposed to be a virgin and it is often not the character but the novelist whose broad knowledge of life gets into the writing (as when she speaks of 'the physical conversation of love-making', and 'the fear-and-joy . . . of the labour-ward'). *Spinster* deserves its re-issue as a 'modern classic', but as a novel it is less unified than her next, *Incense to Idols*.

But *Incense to Idols* was too much for her readers in New Zealand. It was not just the heroine's sexual freedom and her determined worship of Baal but (I think) the wit and extravagance of it all that was found offensive. (Told that God loves her Germaine de Beauvais observes that the Traffic Superintendant seems pretty interested too.) A novel which included a scene where the heroine and her doctor-lover admire a tiny foetus in a wine-glass aborted at eight weeks, of which he may or may not be the father (she's not in a position to be quite sure), he referring to it as 'she', she insisting on 'he'—this, Ashton-Warner wryly observes, 'weeded out my fans overnight'. She had done something as original on the page as she had done in the classroom, and her 'grading' in literary circles sank correspondingly low. Towards the end of the 1960s when Dennis McEldowney, in the periodical *Landfall*, made the one serious attempt to consider all her work, he was publicly rebuked for it by *Landfall*'s former editor, Charles Brasch, who declared Ashton-Warner unworthy of such attention.

That is not the end of the story, however. More books have followed including a novel set in London, *Three*, which is as economical as *Incense to Idols* is copious, and which is, I think, Ashton-Warner's most successful working of autobiography into the fictional mode. The recent presentation of the New Zealand Book Award for non-fiction to her autobiography, *I Passed this Way*, perhaps signals Ashton-Warner's return to favour in New Zealand, where she now lives in retirement.

In a passage central to an understanding of New Zealand (and no doubt other Commonwealth) literature, Maurice Duggan's teenage rebel Buster O'Leary, driving a Ferguson tractor on Puti Hohepa's farm with lines from Coleridge's 'Kubla Khan' running through his head looks up to see Fanny Hohepa sitting on a fence playing her ukulele and singing. How is he to reconcile Puti's 'ruined acres' with the 'twice five miles of fertile ground' of the poem? Or Fanny and her ukulele with the 'damsel with a dulcimer'? There is, Buster observes, a 'discrepancy between the real and the written'.

This 'discrepancy' is acute during the colonial phase, but it continues insidiously, long after. It is there in the infant room with *Janet and John*, and later with poems and stories in which fruit trees blossom in April, snow falls at Christmas, and the sun goes around to the south. That Maori children can't cope with it is an important fact, but not more important than that European-New Zealand children who can, do so at some cost to their sense of identity.

Meanwhile the education system, expressing our national insecurity, works hard to impose uniformity. If we have no confidence in a collective identity we can't be permitted one as individuals. It is not the depth of the social imprint that produces fear of rebellion but on the contrary its shallowness.

Most of her life Sylvia Ashton-Warner has been in the classroom which is, I think, the furnace in which the new society is forged. There, as in her writing, she has offered passion, style, extravagance, a lavish public expenditure of the self, as her form of rebellion against the uniformity which comes from fear and uncertainty.

Further Notes

In conversation Sylvia Ashton-Warner confirms that the character of Dr Saul in *Myself* is the same as Opal in *I Passed this Way*—i.e. that the man in her life in *Myself* was really a woman. (Short pause when the question is put, and then 'I thought someone would catch me out sooner or later'.) This explains what is otherwise implausible—that her husband would so sanguinely have tolerated the passion between these two.

However I don't agree with Ashton-Warner when she says in her introductory note to *Myself* that the character of Saul unbalances the book. He gives it a puzzling or slightly unreal quality in parts, at least until the 'facts' are recognized. But the centre of the book is not Saul. Nor is it 'the story of a school' as her note suggests. Its centre is the freedom of the creative spirit, the making of a space, a privacy, in which it can live and breathe, the guarding of that space against invasion, the balancing of life, which is to be the material, against art which is to be the product. It isn't art that matters so much as the *life of art,* the process. *Myself* is not even a book about the writing of a book. It's a book about the preparation for the writing of a book. And meanwhile life whirls on—the war, the threat of a Japanese invastion (the year is 1942), the family, the school, the love affair with Saul, and the escapes into the haven of 'Selah' which represents the privacy of the creative self. Her prose is like a flight simulator—it takes you right inside the experience of her life day by day, including its bumps and spins. And when all goes well the most commonplace domestic or rural events are elevated and have about them the excitement you expect only special and obviously thrilling events to have. Mansfield is the only other New Zealander I can think of whose writing has from time to time this peculiar lift—'painted with a brush of stars'.

*   *   *   *

Sylvia Ashton-Warner is still terribly undervalued in New Zealand. There was McEldowney's excellent article on her in *Landfall* 91 (1969) but that drew a rebuke from Charles Brasch. The only reference to her in *Essays on the New Zealand Novel* edited by Cherry Hankin (1976) is a passing swipe in Allen Curnow's essay on Bill Pearson's *Coal Flat.* Curnow's complaint is that Anna Vorontosov lacks 'precise orientation within a world whose limits are known, and known to be established objectively'—something which, he argues, Pearson gives his spinster schoolteacher, Miss Dane. But this is one of those points that can be put into reverse. Replace the word 'objectively' with 'subjectively' and the argument can be turned against Pearson and in Ashton-Warner's favour. Miss Dane has a setting—yes; but does she exist as a fully realized character, the product of an imaginative commitment by the author as full as that Ashton-Warner has made? A point like Curnow's could be made (is in fact, in McEldowney's discussion of the problem of 'grounding'), but only within the limits of a proper recognition of what Ashton-Warner has achieved in *Spinster.* Instead it uses her work (a partial knowledge of it) as a leg-up for *Coal Flat.*

J. C. Reid (in G. A. Wilkes and J. C. Reid, *The Literatures of Australia and New Zealand,* 1970) uses the terminology with which many things 'female' (his word) have been traditionally put down: 'hectic', 'highly emotional', 'neurotic' (twice), 'highly-strung', 'cranky', 'self-indulgent', 'hysterical', 'turgid', 'pretentious', 'rattling feminine style', 'chip-on-the-shoulder feminism', 'undisciplined', 'fanciful', 'romantic'—all of this on less than a page, which tells us more about traditional academic responses to literature than about Sylvia Ashton-Warner.

When W. H. Oliver reviewed Charles Brasch's *Indirections* in the *Listener* in 1980 he described it as (approximately) the best / most sustained / most distinguished autobiography by a New Zealander. Apart from the oddness of rating Charles Brasch's literary pancake ahead of Sargeson's autobiographical trilogy there is the total absence of any reference to, or thought of, Ashton-Warner. I don't suppose Oliver had read *I Passed this Way*, or thought it necessary, although by that date Keith Sinclair and Mary Ronnie had awarded it the 1980 New Zealand Book Award for non-fiction.

Fleur Adcock's introduction to the re-issue of *Spinster* partakes of stock attitudes and is especially inexcusable because it dismisses (by implication) work which it's quite clear she hasn't read. She finds Germaine de Beauvais 'embarrassing' and says of *Bell Call* 'none of the characters engages us'—a statement which makes me wonder whether she read beyond the first few pages. There is no mention of *Myself, Greenstone,* or *Three.* And what sense of propriety is there in an 'introduction' to an author which is so luke-warm, so half-hearted?

Of our other critics Winston Rhodes has always been friendly to Ashton-Warner; E. H. McCormick praises *Spinster*; Joan Stevens is cautiously admiring, but recoils from much she finds 'unpleasant' in *Incense to Idols*, which James K. Baxter, on the other hand, defends (see note below).

The most interesting general observation generated in such critical discussion as there has been of Ashton-Warner's work is one by Dennis McEldowney (one which I think connects with my own observations about Mansfield's discontent with the conventional forms of fiction):

It has been remarked before that in the writing of New Zealand novels many of the barriers have been broken by women. . . . Their discoveries have been made not so much through intellectual contemplation as through intensity of feeling. This has exposed them not only to the dismay and sometimes hostility of their contemporaries but to the danger of overburdening their writing. . . . The central problem for all of them as for Sylvia Ashton-Warner, although she is technically far more proficient than any except Janet Frame, is that of embodying emotion in an acceptable form, or any form at all; as it were, of grounding it. . . . Male novelists more often face the opposite problem, of generating enough emotional steam to set their intellectual perceptions in motion. (p.235)

*   *   *   *

It's true that the Frenchness of Germaine de Beauvais in *Incense to Idols* is not convincing; but if she is considered in the context of the whole oeuvre as another incarnation of the Ashton-Warner persona she can be enjoyed as perhaps the most liberated, the largest, the most extravagant of them. Fleur Adcock finds her 'embarrassing'. James K. Baxter, on the other

hand, described *Incense to Idols* as 'the fullest, clearest, most precise document of a woman's interior life yet to appear in New Zealand literature'
(*Comment* 7, Autumn 1961). I think it's a novel about style—style as a life
force, a blast of fresh air, an insurrectionary drive. It has an intellectual
structure as well as elements of plotted melodrama; but I think its comedy
predominates—if you can take it. 'Humour goes hand-in-hand with creativity' Ashton-Warner says in *I Passed this Way* (p.111), 'and creativity
belongs to freedom of the mind'.

I'm sure a lot which comes to Ashton-Warner as comic is taken as melodrama because her readers are not prepared to believe she is black-hearted
enough to be asking them to laugh at matters so grim and serious. The
foetus in the wine-glass is an obvious example. So I think is the
remembered death of Germaine's husband, who staggered from the con-
ductor's rostrum with a heart attack and pitched dead among the first
violins, while Germaine continued playing the concerto. In *Bell Call*, Dan,
the writer who is in part an Ashton-Warner persona, listens to Tarl's account of a harrowing scene of domestic violence. Dan loves it. He's not
heartless, but he can scarcely contain his pleasure at being spectator to the
human drama. Tarl is speaking of her little son Ben:

'Oh it was dreadful . . . *dreadful!* Bennie started vomiting near the gate all over
Gavin and [Gavin] had to put him down. He was practically unconscious. Sobbing
. . . a jerky sort of moaning.' Demonstration. 'He crawled away like a wounded
animal on his hands and knees into the long grass. He's still lying there now. His
little wrists are raw. The inhumanity of it. What d'you think of a man like that?'

Dan is so grateful for all this that in moving about getting the coffee and the cups
ready he is making far too much excited clatter. The scene is suffering from it. An
audience should be quiet. (p.102)

There is so much in Ashton-Warner where her role as novelist is like
Dan's. She is not without compassion, but she has a large appetite for life
in all its phases. Because she has a stronger stomach than many of her
readers she is credited either with bad taste (worse because she's a
woman—if she were Balzac it might be different), or with too much sensibility, as if she had been weeping and wringing her hands over what is in
fact comically presented.

In *Spinster* Anna's 'affair' with Paul Vercoe has been all in the mind and
it's becoming tedious to the reader when the author, with a characteristic
flourish, rids her book of it by having Paul commit suicide. The first news
the reader receives of this death is pure Ronald Hugh Morrieson:

'We've been the whole morning,' cries Parent Number One sensationally at my
back door, the next afternoon, Sunday afternoon, 'cleaning the ceiling! Been
through buckets of water! And we've burnt the scrubbing brushes! Really Oi never

knew a man had so much blood in him! Look, without a word of a loi, Miss Vorontosov, there were bits of heart on that ceiling! You can ask the others!' (p.165)

At the graveside while Whareparita screams ('She must be enjoying
that', Anna thinks) there are only Anna and Canon Maui to fill the grave:

> It's easier to fill in than dig out. Thud goes the first clay on the coffin. There you
> are, Little One, you settle down. Thud, thud. Now you go to sleep and be a good
> boy. Thud. You did the right thing. We're making good progress, brown Canon
> and I. Thud, thud. His white surplice will have to be washed again after this.
> Scoop, grunt, thud. There . . . there . . . look at my sweet boy. I'll look after you.
> Puff, puff. Why ever didn't you comfort yourself with Whareparita, the loveliest
> thing this side of the . . . puff . . . river. 'So quick, so clean an ending.' Filling up.
> 'O that was right, lad . . .' thuff, thuff . . . 'that was brave.' Thuff, thuff. 'Yours was
> not an ill . . .' scoop . . . 'for mending'; . . . lift, strain. ' 'Twas best . . .' spread,
> spread . . . 'to take it . . .' smooth, smooth . . . 'to the . . .' sigh, rest . . . 'grave.'
> (p.167)

Where has all Anna's tremulous feeling gone? Dead and buried. In the
fiction as distinct from the documentary, this is for me the high point of
Spinster. It has verve, vitality; it jolts the sort of mind that likes to cruise
through the middle latitudes of fiction; it assaults the pieties and rides
rough-shod over solemnities; it affronts the precious.

One of the nicest jokes in Ashton-Warner is the story of Germaine de
Beauvais' early life—which is funny in itself, but takes on an extra dimension when one is in a position to see it as a parable about Ashton-Warner
herself, who has spent most of her life in the classroom, beginning when
her teacher-mother took her there as an infant, but who insists she is not a
teacher. Germaine explains (it's that shocking scene with the wine-glass
again):

> 'My mother died when I was born you know, at birth. They gave me to my father a
> minute old. He was at the piano playing. He put me on top of the pianoforte and
> went on playing. And that's where I stayed all my babyhood waking and sleeping. I
> lived on that Grand; I heard every note. There was no woman there, he cared for
> me himself. The sound of the music has not left me till this day. I hear music all the
> time. . . . I'm not a real musician; I don't really love music. It's music that loves
> me.' (p.139)

*　　　*　　　*　　　*

Both *Spinster* and *Incense to Idols* have an intellectual/imagery structure of
a kind Janet Frame also likes to give her books, a technique which, if it
isn't handled carefully, can give the fiction a feeling of abstraction.
Spinster's is of birth and still-birth—Paul Vercoe's twins to Whareparita
are still-born, Anna's reading books are also twins, a live birth. *Incense to*

Idols has the structure of content versus style, the worship of God versus the worship of Baal. In the end Germaine is defeated by the puritan ethic, loses her style, is persuaded she is worthless, and destroys herself.

If I have a reservation about *Incense to Idols* it is a certain thinness of texture, a lack of 'grounding' (McEldowney's word) in the realities of small-town life. They are there, but sometimes I feel there are too many words for too little substance—that the words are not being worked hard enough. This is another way of saying the book is a little too close to a conventional fictional construct. What redeems it and makes it valuable is precisely those elements in it which were found offensive when it first appeared —the sense of a real life, a living personality, that comes through the wit and extravagance of Germaine de Beauvais. The more extravagant she is the more the fiction comes to life.

But it would be quite wrong to give the impression that Ashton-Warner's style is generally wasteful in its use of language. All her novels imitate the repetitiveness of life. The same events recur with minor variations. The movement towards any sort of conclusion or resolution is slow. But a good test of her economy is to look at her dialogue. Her characters get their sharpness of definition partly from speaking straight to the point and without wasting words. And she doesn't nudge us adjectivally and adverbially, as most fiction writers do.

In the following passage from *Bell Call* Dan has just told Tarl, who won't send her children to school, that he won't give evidence to support her in Court:

Astounded. 'But all he wants you to say is . . .'
'I don't take direction from your lawyer.'
Hands pressed to cheeks, poised on one foot, one heel forward, staring at the floor. 'But all he wants . . . you said you would stand up in any court in this country to defend the right of the one to be different.'
'I did. But I've never said I'd take sides between a man and his wife. There's a distinction.'
'But all he wants . . .'
'I don't argue.'
'I'll give him a ring. He's waiting.' When she returns, 'You could be subpoenaed.'
'What's that mean?'
'Cookies, Mummie, cookies,' from Homer. Dan passes him the tin. 'Eat them outside, little boy.'
'It means if you are summoned to court you've got to come.'
'Oh? There's always the hazard I might not say what your lawyer has arranged.'
(p.184)

Compare that with—well, let the reader choose: any passage of dialogue by almost any run-of-the-mill novelist will make a distinction apparent which is in fact a distinction of *mind*. Ashton-Warner knows not to let authorial commentary repeat what the dialogue has already conveyed; and on the other hand that authorial commentary will not put into it what the naked dialogue lacks in point and drama.

★   ★   ★   ★

In *Three*, in the final obscure and terrible dust-up between mother (a nameless Ashton-Warner persona), son Julian, and daughter-in-law Angélique, the mother accuses the young couple of blaming her for the fact that their friend and lodger, Carlos, did *not* commit suicide. In her confused and hysterical state she has spoken as if all agree that his suicide would have been a good thing: 'He did have it in him to do this but he couldn't. He's utterly wrecked the plot.'

This mother figure is a writer, and it appears she has confused what is desirable in the real world with what is shapely in fiction. Her fictional world also perhaps held some kind of future for herself with Julian and Angélique. In reality there is no such future once their need of her is past, and the book ends with her departure. Life refuses to satisfy her appetite for the vivid and extravagant; but she remains vivid and extravagant herself. The style is sober and penetrating, and the book unnervingly—and beautifully—'real'.

★   ★   ★   ★

'Precise orientation within a world whose limits are known, and known to be established objectively.' This, which Curnow asserts *Spinster* lacks, it has. The classroom, the school, the surrounding landscape are as much as anything in our literature ever could be 'the regional thing, the real thing' (to use another of Curnow's phrases). The problem, insofar as there is one, is perhaps a lack of adequate extension, so that the picture fades off into unreality, into the fictional abstract. That is true also of *Incense to Idols*—not true of *Bell Call* nor of *Three*. I'm prepared to take the edges of the picture as fictional 'givens': 'Let's pretend there was a woman called Germaine de Beauvais who came from Paris in pursuit of her former teacher . . .'

But again it would be wrong to concede too much, even on this question of 'subjectivity' and 'objectivity'. Ashton-Warner has a view of reality which is hers and no one else's (so has Henry James, so has Dickens, so has every good novelist). But there is a special and important sense in which she has greater objectivity than any other New Zealand fiction writer.

In writing about R. A. K. Mason's poem 'Be Swift O Sun' in 1963 I concluded

However remote such a poem may be from fiction, there is nevertheless a lesson in its triumph over subjectivity which I believe most of our active fiction writers have yet to learn. Its charity may begin at home, but it does not end there.

What I meant by this was that our fiction writers most typically *take sides.* There are good characters, who are usually outsiders, with whom the writer identifies; and bad ones who are insiders, and who persecute the outsiders.* Even Janet Frame falls into this pattern. I don't deny that our society promotes it. But I think the fictionist imagination ought to produce images which are at least distinguishable from the moralist's, and this hasn't always, or often, been the case in New Zealand. But it is the case with Ashton-Warner. McEldowney writes

A faculty in Sylvia Ashton-Warner which makes her almost unique among New Zealand novelists, achieved in spite of the fact that she is as dedicated as any to the ideal of spontaneous living, is her ability to appreciate and convincingly create characters within rather than outside regulated society. She can find among such people those who are living, and living through, not in spite of, their social function, when it is more usual to declare that they are all dead. (p.237)

He has *Bell Call* (1969) particularly in mind. It is a novel that appeared perhaps ten years too soon. Tarl Pracket is a young woman of a kind well-enough known in the 1960s I suppose; but her Eastern view of life, her love of the unregulated, her resistance to institutions, and her fierce independence from, and (ultimately) rejection of, her husband, the father of her four children, make her a vivid contemporary figure, a sort of feminist friend-of-the-earth. What is marvellous in this book is the way Ashton-Warner presents this central character, from the point of view of those dealing with her, as preposterous, selfish, irrational, sometimes cruel, a damn' nuisance, and at the same time as brilliant, appealing, a survivor, a good mother, and *successful.* Tarl's theories even work in practice; and her children, who are permitted every licence, emerge just as beautiful as the theory says they should. No New Zealand novel presents a moral problem so thoroughly in the round as *Bell Call* does. Dan the writer, observer of it all, protests

'But God damn it, everyone's too convincing in this drama, from the magistrate through Blondie and Ric right down to Benjamin himself. They're *all* not only able in their subjects but their passions are contagious. I agree with each one utterly till

---

*A Swedish journalist asked me whether in Samoan society the moral distinctions were so clear and obvious and simple as Albert Wendt's novel, *Leaves of the Banyan Tree,* made them seem. I replied that I didn't know Samoan society, but I recognized in the novel a moral/sociological pattern which I thought Wendt had picked up from New Zealand fiction.

the next comes along. A writer is on everyone's side. His response is a multiple response. It's life that's upsetting me—not they. Reality. Every time they arrive life breaks new records in reality.' (p.131)

Late in the story Dan commits, out of jealousy, an oblique and clever act of malice against Tarl by making money available to her which he knows she will use in a way that will land her in trouble with the law. But it is not, I think, this act, since it springs from frustrated love, which leaves a shadow over him, but rather his self-preservation at the end, when he turns Tarl away in favour of his own writing. He has early on faced the question whether his work is more important than hers (he is a famous writer, she an unknown painter) and concluded that it is not (p.178). In the end he is seen with sympathy, with gentleness and charity; but I think he is seen to fail. Fiction has become for him a haven from that intolerable degree of 'reality' which Tarl's delicious invasions bring. He has 'served his time in heartbreak a lifetime ago' when his wife died, and can't stand any more.

At this point the ghost of his long-dead wife, who has been the shadowy narrator, abandons him to the loneliness of his fictional world. It is the final irony. His rejection of Tarl is a rejection of the life which that ghostly presence craves. The artist has vanished into his art. There is nothing left to tell.

JOHN MULGAN:
A QUESTION OF IDENTITY

I begin with an occasion when I had dinner in a house in the bush at Karekare on Auckland's west coast. We sat around an English coal range the couple had hauled by means of a wooden-track bush railway to the top of the hill on which they had built their house. On a nog in the unlined room was propped an old photograph. It was the young woman's grandparents with her mother and uncle as infants. The grandfather was Alan Mulgan, the mother Dorothea Turner (author of the Twayne series book on Jane Mander), and the uncle John Mulgan.

I mention this as one example of the ways in which I find myself repeatedly 'meeting' the author of *Man Alone*, though he was dead some years before I had heard of him; and because I have in mind something Allen Tate argued in one of his essays on Poe: that because the circumstances of our relation to an author are a conditioning element in the nature of our response to his work there are times when it helps definition to lay all our cards on the table. It is not, in such a case, or ought not to be, a matter of identifying with the author; where there are overlaps the differences can be as useful to definition as the likenesses. In the Poe essay Tate writes as a Southerner of a Southerner:

. . . in discussing any writer, or in coming to terms with him, we must avoid the trap of mere abstract evaluation, and try to reproduce the actual conditions of our relation to him. It would be difficult for me to take Poe up, 'study' him, and proceed to a critical judgment. One may give these affairs the look of method, and thus deceive almost everybody but oneself . . . Poe surrounds us with Eliot's 'wilderness of mirrors', in which we see a subliminal self endlessly repeated. . . . It is not too harsh, I think, to say that it is stupid to suppose that by 'evaluating' this forlorn

First published in *Islands* 25, April 1979.

demon in the glass, we dispose of him . . . he is with us like a dejected cousin: we may 'place' him but we may not exclude him from our board. This is the recognition of a relationship, almost of the blood, which we must in honor acknowledge: what destroyed him is potentially destructive of us. Not only this; we must acknowledge another obligation . . . of loyalty to one's experience: he was in our lives and we cannot pretend that he was not.[1]

If I were to write John Mulgan's biography (something I have no wish to do) I could write a large part of an early chapter with little or no research. It would describe simply the physical environment in which he grew up from the age of five, when his father took the literary editorship of the Auckland *Star*, to the age of fifteen when he was sent for a brief period as a boarder to Wellington College before returning to Auckland to enrol at Grammar. I know for sure where he would have played as a child, which fields on the slopes of which volcanic cones would have offered blackberries and bracken and caves. I know the route he would have taken to school, the houses he would have passed, the infant school rooms (recently demolished) in which he learned to read and write. I think it was during 1917 that my mother's father began landscaping two quarter-acre sections on a corner near Maungawhau School in Mt Eden and building a house there. The young Mulgan must have passed that corner every day on his way to and from school, and might well have noticed the bearded foreigner obsessively building stone walls and laying out gardens. Three decades later both Mulgan and my grandfather (who died before I was born) would be dead, and I would be reading *Man Alone* in that same house and writing stories in which hunted heroes escaped capture by slipping aboard foreign ships on the Auckland waterfront.

I came on the book in the Mt Albert Grammar School library in 1949. That was the first year of its reprint, the London edition of 1939 having made little impression before stocks were destroyed in the blitz. No one recommended it to me and I don't recall having heard it discussed. New Zealand writers were not mentioned by teachers of English and at that time I don't think I had heard of any apart from Katherine Mansfield (she had long ago figured on a set of Weet-Bix cards of 'Famous New Zealanders'), William Satchell whose *The Greenstone Door* a primary school friend had once shown me a copy of,* and Frank Sargeson, whose photograph on the dustcover of *I Saw in My Dream* I had stared at in Whitcombe and Tombs, imagining that as an author published in London he must be very wealthy.

I once wrote in a poem that I had read only two novels before puberty. This exaggeration for comic effect was far from the truth. However it

---

* Satchell was another I have since discovered was very nearly a neighbour. He lived close to Landscape Road where the Mulgans lived.

wasn't until secondary school that I read novels regularly—I suppose on average about two each week. It is difficult now to remember titles and authors but it was mostly conventional English stuff—school stories, murder mysteries, P. G. Wodehouse, Charles Kingsley, Rider Haggard, John Buchan, the Baroness Orczy, Conan Doyle, R. L. Stevenson— together with Americans like Poe, Fenimore Cooper, Edward S. Ellis, and Zane Grey. I remember very clearly my first Scott (*Rob Roy*) and my first Dickens (*Oliver Twist*). After reading the Scott I wrote an essay in which the first sentence ran on for two pages; but though they excited me greatly neither of these books set me writing narrative. Mulgan did. He had delivered up to me large pieces of my own experience in the stylized form of fiction. His book was the first to close for me what Duggan's Buster O'Leary calls the 'discrepancy between the real and the written'.

Every fictional mode is a stylization of experience, and every stylization is in its way, I suppose, a romanticizing. It is only the degree and kind of romanticization we quarrel over and which constitutes the critical issue between literary fashions. If I had read Alan Mulgan's *Spur of Morning* in 1949 I would have been interested, no doubt, but I could hardly have felt that I had moved very far out of the sphere of what I called above 'conventional English stuff'. In John Mulgan's novel I had stumbled by chance on something which was simultaneously 'modern' and New Zealand. On the imagination of a sixteen-year-old already engaged in writing it inevitably had a powerful effect. But in my imitations (there were probably only two or three) there was a difference: my hero, escaping along the wharves to the waiting foreign ship, left behind him a woman with whom he was in love. In this I was showing myself more conventionally 'romantic' than my model; but I was also perhaps writing unconsciously (everything was un- conscious) a criticism of *Man Alone*. Johnson, its hero, does not exist as a sexual being, and to this extent a mature reader can scarcely believe in the involvement with Rua which precipitates the important action.

Alan Mulgan, father of the author of *Man Alone*, called his autobiography *The Making of a New Zealander*. He was not made a New Zealander by being born here (in 1881) but almost, one might feel, by a process of elimination. In the end there was nothing else to be, and once that had been recognized and accepted the local stratum of his loyalties and affec- tions was given freer rein and became predominant. But that was achieved late. Most of his writing life was spent attempting to resolve what I once described as a 'tension . . . in the mind of every New Zealander between "here" and "there" '. Why the tension should have been so extreme in his case must have been partly a matter of personal temperament, partly a reflection of the peculiarities of the Katikati settlement into which he was born.

Katikati and Te Puke in the Bay of Plenty were settled in the 1870s by Northern Irishmen brought out by Vesey Stewart. They brought with them their anti-Catholic prejudice (Alan Mulgan denies this), their political conservatism, their hatred of the idea of Home Rule for Ireland and their consequently exaggerated loyalty to London, the British Parliament and the Crown. 'English-mail day, once a month, was an event', Alan Mulgan writes of his boyhood.[2] 'It was a joy to me to be allowed to ride down for the mail. Letters came to settlers with news of relatives and friends left behind, of life in a deep-founded and well-ordered society. . . .' The description of the society left behind by his parents—'deep-founded and well-ordered'—expresses his sense of the inferiority of the colony, something he never entirely lost. This may be characteristic of the first phase of colonization, but in the case of Vesey Stewart's settlement it seems to have been stronger and more durable. To the north of them the Auckland settlement was one generation older, the North Auckland settlement, two. A few miles south in the Bay of Plenty the Tauranga mission had been established in the 1830s, and a great-great-grandfather of mine was settled as Church Missionary Society catechist across the range in Te Aroha in the same decade. Among the already assertive colonials the Ulster Johnny-come-latelies clung to their separate identity and sense of superiority. I have met even third-generation descendants of that settlement, born half a century later than Alan Mulgan, who seemed still to combine as he did a deep attachment to the New Zealand landscape in which they grew to consciousness with a sense that the 'Home' society was superior and that by some special licence they still belonged to it. Alan Mulgan's writings are full of the awkwardnesses, contradictions, confusions of snob and cringe, which stem from that inheritance.

Alan Mulgan must have had some of the endearing qualities of the Ulsterman too. He was (in Yeats's phrase) 'a foolish, passionate man', a victim of surges of strong feeling (he records that he could not trust himself to read 'Lycidas' aloud 'for fear of breaking down').[3] In his novel *Spur of Morning* he describes Philip Armitage, who is clearly a self-portrait, as 'exciteable'; and I noticed that when I asked Frank Sargeson what he remembered of Alan Mulgan Sargeson used the same word. He had a pendulous lower lip, Sargeson recalled, which moistened as his talk became animated and which he mopped from time to time with a large handkerchief. Sargeson's attention was drawn constantly to the state of that moist lip, and to the application of the handkerchief, so that he found it hard to attend to what the man was saying.

In his autobiography Alan Mulgan mentions his struggles with a speech impediment, describes the anguish still caused in old age by memories of boyhood failures on the cricket field, describes himself as having been an unhappy and self-doubting child, admits to the boastfulness of the unconfident, and records how, after a promising start as a pupil, he failed repeatedly to win the scholarship that would have taken him from Grammar to University. Clearly there was no lack of intelligence. Something else stood in the way. His son John, perhaps inheriting a more general competence from the mother (she was a graduate, having won the scholarship which Alan Mulgan failed to achieve), must have seemed the fulfilment of all his father's hopes and perhaps something of a balm to his hurt pride. Rugby player, cricketer, boxer, yachtsman, school prefect, cadet N.C.O., scholarship boy, member of the Students' Executive in Auckland and the Bodley Club at Oxford, winner of an Oxford 'first', soldier (rising to the rank of Lieutenant-Colonel), guerrilla fighter, winner of the Military Cross, survivor—and in the end he took his own life. There is an enormous and bitter irony here which I do not pretend to explain or do justice to by quoting Yeats's nevertheless apposite lines:

> Soldier, scholar, horseman, he
> As 'twere all life's epitome.
> What made us dream that he could comb grey hair?

John Mulgan belongs to the literary generation of Sargeson, Curnow, Fairburn, Glover, and it is a commonplace that, like their contemporaries in England, they were in revolt against the generation which preceded them, one of whom was Alan Mulgan. But the nature of the revolt has proved difficult to describe with precision. In poetry, where these things tend to receive clearer definition, it was expressed (here as in England) as a 'modern' revolt against 'Georgian' romanticism. That is how Auden is usually placed in literary history, which in turn places (for example) Curnow and Glover. Each movement in New Zealand is a reflection largely of its counterpart in Britain. Just as the English Georgians wrote cosily about an England of cottages and country lanes, so their New Zealand counterparts wrote cosily and prettily about New Zealand. (I forbear to quote Alan Mulgan's lines on Auckland as example.) And as the Auden generation turned a cold eye on this romanticizing, describing power-houses and gasworks and urban squalor, so Curnow and his contemporaries deflated the myth of a South Seas paradise and depicted New Zealand as a country of mean cities and mortgaged farms, 'a land of settlers / With never a soul at home'.

Put thus the history looks a little simpler than it is. In England the Georgian movement (its favourite word was 'little') had begun as a reaction against the Victorian and Edwardian grandiose; it had been capable (as for example in some of the poems of W. H. Davies) of social realism; and it had thus contained within it the seeds of that further movement towards truth-telling, the war poetry of Wilfred Owen and Siegfried Sassoon. One can argue that it is not so much a question of Georgians and moderns as of good and bad Georgians; or of Georgian realists and Georgian sentimentalists. Technically a poet like Auden learned only a little from the great American Modernists, Pound and Eliot, and I believe he and his contemporaries can quite properly be seen as inheritors of the Georgian realist tradition.

The Mulgan revolt, son against father, might be similarly described, and the differences between them are as much political as stylistic. The sentimental England of thatched cottages and country lanes implied a desirable order and nothing major to be done; the England of gas-works and cloth caps implied a need for change. So in New Zealand the cosiness of Alan Mulgan's vision is conservative in nature and motive, while the emphasis on ugliness and squalor in *Man Alone* is correspondingly (and opposingly) political. Anyone who studies John Mulgan must be in Paul Day's debt for the work he has done and the facts he has brought to light.[4] That acknowledged, I proposed to do nothing but complain of Day's emphasis, and if there is one complaint I would make above all others it is that he depoliticizes *Man Alone*, a novel which is basically Marxist in structure. Its account of New Zealand society is economic and the implied consequences are political. Mulgan's hero is innocent of politics, but his novel is not.*

At the time when the new literary movement which would very largely swamp his reputation was gathering momentum, Alan Mulgan must have felt he was enjoying his most notable successes. 'Success' meant first and perhaps most importantly, publication in London. In 1927 *Home*, his account of a visit to England, was published. In 1932 Dent brought out his long poem, *Golden Wedding*. Then in 1934 and 1935—chiefly, it seems, because son John was now on the spot to negotiate with London publishers—came the novel *Spur of Morning* (published by Dent) and a travel book, *A Pilgrim's Way in New Zealand* (published by Oxford). Day relates that the son was already out of sympathy with the father's style, and that the last-named book must have been particularly distasteful to him because he never mentioned it to his wife who only learned of its existence after his death.[5] In fact it is possible to see the germ, not of *Man Alone*, but of John Mulgan's method of entry to his novel, occurring in direct reaction to *A Pilgrim's Way in New Zealand*, which takes the form of an address to a potential visitor to New Zealand. John Mulgan also begins by bringing an Englishman—his hero Johnson—to New Zealand; but it is made clear we will be shown the sober truth, not the Georgian romance. Here are some samples from early pages, taking father and son in turn:

---

* Mulgan himself was aware of this. In one of his letters he wrote 'I didn't think anyone had heard of *Man Alone* except my family and left-wing friends'. Quoted by Day (Oxford), p. 26.

It [the Waitemata Harbour] is a pleasant place to come in to, and I hope you will not be disappointed. There will be low green hills to take the morning sun as you watch; away in the west a higher range of dark bush mountains where the sun sets at evening. The city will be gay with its miles of red-roofed suburban homes, and nearer to the wharves, which you approach, a sky-line of tall buildings will show that this is a city well advanced from the pioneering stage.

A Pilgrim's Way in New Zealand, p. 7.

What he saw then was the brightness of red iron roofs straggling down to the shore on two sides of a land-locked harbour and clustered together on one side the steel-grey cranes and advertisement-plastered buildings of the port and the city.

Man Alone, p. 7

Here, within this strip of land buffeted by the wide-ranging might of the ocean, is every variety of landscape save desert—fertile plains and peaks of perpetual snow, drowsy land-locked bays and long surf-beaten sands, mountain-encircled lakes of marvellous beauty, pastoral areas of almost English tidiness and sweeps of tussock and scrub, active volcanoes, great glaciers and fiords, hot springs and ice-cold rivers, lovely mountain flowers and superb sub-tropical forests. It is as if Providence had organized in one little country an exhibition of Nature's beauty and strangeness. . . .

Some of this, perhaps, a returning New Zealander may tell you as you lean over the rail on this last night at sea. He may even say that, distant though it is, he can already smell the land, the sweet tang of his home. If he is sentimental about the scent of tea-tree on a hundred hills, forgive him, for it is a pleasant land and much beloved by its people. *A Pilgrim's Way in New Zealand,* p. 4.

Johnson leant on the rail, watching the shore and the small boats that went by. The deck was full of luggage and people moving and talking. Beside Johnson, a returning New Zealand soldier, still in uniform, spat carelessly into the water. The tide from the upper harbour moved swiftly down tugging at the ship. The warm mist of a day's rain that had lifted hung over them. The soldier turned and said to him:

'That's Auckland, mate—the Queen of the North.'

'The what?'

'The Queen of the North. That's what they call it—in Auckland. This is God's own, this country.'

'It looks all right.'

'It's not a bad little town—nor a bad little country neither.'

Man Alone, pp. 7-8.

Throughout Chapter I of *Man Alone,* in which the 'homey' Johnson arrives in New Zealand, the tone is cool, neutral, and steady (quite the reverse of Alan Mulgan's exciteable prose), but the details chosen for noting are cumulatively negative. At the end of the voyage a 'stale tiredness' hangs over everyone. The New Zealand soldier Johnson speaks to on deck has a face that is 'shrunken and pock-marked and unhealthy-looking'. Ashore in the bar, 'no one got merry with the drinking. There was a quietness and sickness over everything'. Johnson eats his meal 'almost alone in a large room with a fat, white-faced, dark-haired waitress to serve him'. In his room the water in the carafe smells bad, but when he tries to order tea the girl looks at him 'disfavourably' and says 'We don't serve after half-past nine'.

This emphasis on negative qualities has a number of motives. Partly it is an attempt to correct, not merely the father's picture of New Zealand, but a false way of seeing the world which the sentimental Georgian cosiness encouraged. This in turn merges with the political motive. It is as if the writer were saying, in a tone and with a purpose that owes a good deal to W. H. Auden,* 'The world is *not* beautiful—all is *not* well. Let's look at it squarely and perhaps we will begin to understand why.'

But finally, as I suggested earlier, every stylization of experience—even a negative one—is a kind of romanticizing. The steady eye that does not flinch at what it sees, the cool tone, the laconic speech—all are part of a convention that is not solely negative in effect. Spender's pylons and Auden's slag-heaps are not only symptoms of the evils of industrial society; they are also beautiful in their ugliness. The dark satanic mills are also dark romantic hills. The 'Ern Hem' character who reveals little emotion and less thought is only a whisker and a clean suit away from Clark Gable and the strong silent Hollywood hero. All these elements go into the making of *Man Alone*. It is a dour picture of the New Zealand of that time, and a truer one than that found in Alan Mulgan's work. It has a political dimension with international implications. But it is in its way also a romantic view of New Zealand, a piece of frontier mythologizing—and this aspect gathers strength especially in the three chapters dealing with Johnson's escape into the Kaimanawas.

The accepted picture of John Mulgan's political development goes something like this: product of a conservative household he had little occasion to think about the realities of poverty until his experiences as a student special constable during the unemployed riots in Auckland in April 1932. That experience, however, brought a quick realization of the plight of the unemployed, and in reaction to what he had done Mulgan 'penned an acid editorial'[6] in the May 10 issue of the student newspaper, *Craccum*. That editorial marks the beginnings of his political awakening. As Dan Davin puts it, 'awareness swiftly succeeded ignorance and his honesty reflected on what his experience as a Special Constable taught him'.[7] When a controversy blew up in Auckland in 1933 over the freedom of academics to ex-

---

* Mulgan exactly echoes the tone and point of view of the Auden group when he writes to his parents in April 1938 that for the moment the important thing to be done is 'persuading as many people as possible in the short time that's left which side they should be on.' Quoted by Day (Twayne), p. 41.

press opinions on public issues Mulgan supported the free speech cause, and this cost him the nomination for the Rhodes Scholarship. From that time onward he was always sympathetic to the Left in politics, though never an extremist.

This picture is, I believe, misleading in a number of ways which it is important to correct if we are to place *Man Alone* in the stages of Mulgan's political development. In the first place I doubt very much that John Mulgan was any sort of a leftist while a student at the Auckland University College—and I am pretty sure he was no martyr to the cause of free speech. Second, however, I believe he did swing to the Left, much more radically than Day allows, but that this happened at Oxford. Day's fault is first to over-dramatize Mulgan's reaction to his role as a 'special'; and second, to let the wise detachment of *Report on Experience* (written 1944-5) represent Mulgan's political viewpoint throughout, as if it had been consistent over a period of a decade or more. In fact I think if a biographer should try to plot Mulgan's political development more accurately and less blandly than Day has done, he would probably find a slow but decisive swing to the Left reaching an extreme point in Oxford in 1937-8 (the time when *Man Alone* was written) and then a slow return during the period of the war—though not of course, a return to where he had begun.

It seems clear that as a young man at Auckland University College John Mulgan was very much the middle-class 'establishment' figure his father would have wanted him to be, though capable of sufficient detachment and lucidity to make him seem at times a radical in his family. A great deal has been made of his reaction against his own role as a 'special'; but it is surely as deserving of note that his first response to the unemployed riots, whatever his second thoughts were going to be, should have been to join the forces of order.* Nor was the reaction afterwards as clear-cut as Day, Davin, and Bertram have made it seem. Certainly the 'acid editorial' was no exercise in breast-beating. It is, in fact, to anyone who goes back to the files and looks it up, somewhat obscure coming from a student who had himself been sworn in as a 'special'; and the main force of the argument seems to be, not that students should not have offered themselves, but that too many who did so saw their job as being to confront the unemployed belligerently rather than simply to 'protect property'. It was legitimate to protect property; and if that was his attitude he must have felt it was wrong of the rioters to damage it†—a view clearly different from the one we shall

---

* So did Bertram and Curnow. They too, one might guess, were exhibiting family reflexes —as I suppose Maurice Shadbolt and I were two decades later when as first-year students at the College we became (separately) involved on the side of the unions in the waterfront strike of 1951.

† This exactly coincides with Alan Mulgan's view as expressed in his novel *Spur of Morning* and in his autobiography—see *The Making of a New Zealander*, p. 160.

find governing the account of the riots in *Man Alone*. My point is that Mulgan's political 'awakening' in 1932 by no means provided him with left-wing convictions of the kind he was later to admit to and display in his writings.

That he remained basically conservative is illustrated by his refusal to join the *Phoenix* venture in 1932 (Allen Curnow recalls that he was once urged by Mulgan to steer clear of the group)[8] and by the 'strong disapproval' he expressed in 1933 (in a combined meeting of the Literary Club Committee and the *Phoenix* Committee on the subject of *Phoenix*) at 'the use of a university publication for purposes of political propaganda'.[9] It is impossible to imagine that five years later in Oxford he would have voiced such a complaint about a comparable periodical.

That leaves, in support of his early political radicalism, only his signing of a circular in 1933 (at the time of the free speech controversy) in support of a candidate for the College Council who believed academics should be free to speak out on public issues—the action which it is said cost him the Rhodes Scholarship. Again, too much has been made of this by Day and others, and I will show (in part three of this article) why I believe it was not this action which cost him the Rhodes nomination.

I have no doubt that the young Mulgan was politically open-minded enough to shock or at least surprise his father from time to time, but not, I think, to alarm him. And I can find no evidence to suggest that he acquired his Marxism in Auckland.

But acquire it he certainly did at Oxford. Between 1933 and 1938 he must have moved to the Left, more gradually than Day's account suggests, but also more decisively, not (I imagine) into full membership of the Communist Party, but certainly close to it ('there wasn't anywhere else to go' he was later ruefully to reflect)[10] where he would have experienced the euphoria of those first successes of the Republican forces in the Spanish Civil War, the disappointment of Franco's victory, and the disillusionment of the Hitler-Stalin pact of 1939. Beyond again lay the realities of the war in Greece, where the Communists he had to deal with were to prove both more impressive and more distasteful than the abstract argument on either side might have suggested would be the case.

Mulgan's political position by 1938 is clearly marked by his editing of *Poems of Freedom* for Victor Gollancz, publisher of the Left Book Club series. No one could appear at that time under that imprint without tacitly declaring himself a Marxist, and this is confirmed by the engagement of W. H. Auden to write an introduction. Obliquely but unequivocally in terms of the political debates of the day Auden and Mulgan make their position plain and suggest a contemporary political sense in which all the poems in the collection should be read. Auden writes in his introduction:

Avenge, O Lord, thy slaughtered saints, whose bones
Lie scattered on the Alpine Mountains cold

was what Milton felt about the Albigensians, but it is equally well what we feel
about the Basques. . . .

Of course it was not what everyone felt about the Basques—it was what
'we', the Left, felt. Auden quietly marks out his position in relation to the
Spanish Civil War, which in turn, in the context of the events of those
years, defines a general political position. So too does Mulgan, with an
oblique reference to the British policy of non-intervention:

We could quote, too, all those poems of the early nineteenth century, written at a
time when a British Government was playing a part in Europe as destructive of
liberty and democracy as we see it playing to-day, and demonstrating just as clearly
that axiom, that class is thicker than blood. . . .

I do not think this anthology will appeal to those who cannot, for example,
understand why men are prepared to fight for a principle of international law, or in
defence of democracy, or for social betterment, but not merely to preserve imperial
dividends.

This is fighting talk. And to accompany it the youngest poets included in
the anthology were Auden, Spender, Day Lewis, Rex Warner—and
R. A. K. Mason, whose 'propagandist' editing of *The Phoenix* Mulgan had
objected to five years earlier in Auckland. Auden was represented by eight
verses from a poem given the title 'Brothers', but which originally had
been called 'A Communist to Others'; and Mulgan's trimming of a lot of
characteristic Auden jokiness made it a more serious-seeming political
statement. Mason was represented by 'Youth at the Dance' which Curnow
has described as a 'revolution-cry . . . the one poem by Mason which may
be read as a direct expression of the political passions of the "thirties" ';[11]
and the anthology concluded with Spender's tremulous and lyrical call to
revolution, 'It is too Late Now':

Oh young men oh young comrades
it is too late now to stay in those houses
your fathers built where they built you to build to breed
money on money. . . .

Nineteen thirty-seven to nineteen thirty-eight probably represents the
extreme point of the young Mulgan's leftward swing—and this is reflected
in brief passages quoted by Day[12] from letters to his parents at this time,
letters which to anyone who has studied the Auden group of the 1930s, are
immediately familiar in tone and content:

At times I've looked forward with a sort of gloomy pleasure to the destruction of
this country and its selfish intolerant ruling classes. As it comes nearer I can see

how much that might have been enlightened and fine is going to be lost. As you
look back to 1935, saw how they sabotaged the League—rather than risk com-
munism in Italy—how things have got worse ever since, how the democracies
throughout Europe feel themselves betrayed, the Americans turning away
disgusted, the splendid fight that the Spanish people put up going for nothing—it
isn't any real satisfaction to know that all these people will destroy each other.

(February 1938)

Not only in argument and tone, but even sometimes verbally, he seems
to echo Auden:

... this seems the time of the pamphlet and the article where the importance of
things is the importance of a political meeting, of persuading as many people as
possible in the short time that's left which side they should be on. . . . These do
seem to me to be crisis years. (April 1938)

As a way of characterizing the drabness of the time and its prevailing sense
of political necessity this suggests much in Auden, and particularly his line
in 'Spain 1937' about 'the flat ephemeral pamphlet and the boring
meeting'.

Man Alone was written during 1938 and so belongs to this phase of
Mulgan's political development. It opens with a reference to the Spanish
Civil War—as much a point of definition for the politics of the thirties as
Viet Nam was to become for the politics of the sixties—and it contains, I
believe, an essentially Marxist analysis of the period of New Zealand
history from 1919 to 1932. It is not surprising that this should be so, only
that it should have been so little remarked upon. It is at this point that the
two aspects—political and literary—of the revolt of Mulgan *fils* against
Mulgan *père* come together. *Man Alone* explodes not only the terribly
literary cosiness with which New Zealand is written about in *Spur of Morning,* but also the comfortable middle-of-the-road politics which that novel
puts forward as the right path into the future.

Leaving aside for the moment Part II, which was written as an afterthought at the request of his publisher, Part I, the major portion of the
book, itself divides into two sections—the first nine chapters reaching their
climax in the Queen Street riots of 1932 and Johnson's escape to the country; the remaining eight dealing with Johnson's affair with Rua, the death
of Stenning, Johnson's ordeal in the bush and his escape from New
Zealand. It is the first of these two sections that follows a pattern of
economic history with political implications. Chapter I has Johnson arriving in New Zealand in 1919. It covers a period of perhaps two days,
establishes the dour tone and drab atmosphere that is to predominate, and
quickly gets him on the move to his first farm. Then there is an accelera-
tion of the fictional time scale, which, closely looked at, is so extraordinary

one might argue—at least in abstract—that no novelist could get away with it.

Chapter II (Blakeway's farm) occupies three years; Chapter III (Thompson's farm) adds a further year and a half; Chapter IV takes us up to 1930, which means a further six years have gone by. Page forty-three[13] in Chapter V mentions it is twelve years since Johnson's arrival. From page eighteen to page forty-three—in twenty-five pages—we have covered twelve years.

Conversely, Chapters VI and VII deal with one night, and Chapter VIII adds a day—thirty pages to cover just a couple of days.

Chapters I to VI are really a piece of economic and social history. They cover the period from the end of the War until the Depression and the Auckland riots of 1932. They pretend to tell Johnson's story but Johnson is merely standing unchanging in the foreground while all the change and development—the real narrative—is going on around him. The subject is not Johnson but New Zealand, its 'good years' (which were the years of John Mulgan's childhood) and the subsequent decade. Historically the sudden plunge Mulgan describes is 'true'; but one has the impression that he felt it deeply and personally, as if the broader collapse was paralleled within himself by some awakening to a sense of loss:

That was the last of the good years, though Johnson didn't know it at the time—1930, when everyone had money and the war was long over and never coming again. *Man Alone*, p. 39.

They were easy years, and after they passed, from the time of the depression onwards, we were caught up in events that never allowed us to move with the same sense of freedom that we had then.

The shadow of the depression ended this golden summer. 1929 was the last of the good years. *Report on Experience*, p. 9

The social history, it seems to me, is suffused with a melancholy which is personal, and which gives *Man Alone* its special and yet intangible quality. The book is a lament for something lost.

In fact the image of New Zealand throughout that period does not match the description of it as 'the good years'. Blakeway's farm is dreary, Thompson's worse. The period on Peterson's scow, however, is something of an idyll, and this allows for the sense of sharp decline when the Depression comes. What Johnson loses chiefly is freedom—the ability to work where he likes and leave when he has had enough.

Throughout these years Johnson has evaded the pressures of orthodox capitalism, but not because he is master of himself and has a consistent sense of an alternative and better ideal. It is true that when he is under pressure to marry Mabel and buy land he is not excited by the prospect;

but it is Scotty who gets him away on to Thompson's farm. And even then Johnson only drops the idea of sending for Mabel* when he sees the hut they are to live in.

In Chapter IV, when Peterson urges him to buy a boat, his resistance has become more conscious. His sense of the freedom the country offers has developed:

'There isn't any better country than this, not where a man can go about and get work, and stop when he wants to, and make money when he needs it, and take a holiday when he feels ready for one.' (p. 36)

But this freedom of the spirit is dependent on an economic freedom which is precarious. When that goes, everything goes with it, and the man who (unconsciously or by design, it makes no difference) has resisted capitalism is now its victim.

Chapter V, the most directly 'economic', traces the decline into the Depression. Johnson works at various jobs. Prices are dropping on the world markets, Wall Street plunges, there is talk of Social Credit and a farmers' government, there are attempts to create a mood of buoyancy (the marvellous image of 'Cheer Up Week' in a small Wairarapa town), but the slump goes remorselessly on. Johnson and Scotty arrive in Auckland out of work. They are soon out of money, in the food queue, on relief work, and finally in the relief camp for the unemployed, building what is now the Scenic Drive through the Waitakere Range.

Chapters II to V are the social/economic survey of a period of history; they bring us to the point of the author's own awakening to political realities. Chapters VI to VIII are the consequences in dramatic action.

The chapter on the riots is vivid—partly, no doubt, because it draws on Mulgan's own experience (though that is not to say he saw at first hand the Queen Street scenes he describes); but more important because the violence is presented as the inevitable consequence of the economic realities which precede it. Johnson is only one of many who have declined capitalism or been thrust aside by it and are now being squeezed. And the structure of the chapter is quite deliberately Marxist, building on a contrast between the feeling expressed on pp. 53-6 that the men were 'going forward together', and the loss of that sense on pp. 56-7.

In the grimness and tenseness of that mass of men a new spirit came over them. It was a very silent procession that marched, without bands or songs or shouting. Johnson going with them felt this change. He lost the sense of waste and frustration

---

* There are very few women in this novel and two of them are called Mabel, Johnson's repulsive brother's repulsive wife being the second. I feel sure this is accident not design, Part II having been added to the novel as an afterthought. But it is clear that Johnson's brother was as unfortunate in marrying his 'Mabel' as Johnson has been fortunate in escaping from his.

that had been with him. Instead he felt that he had a part in something. What it was he could not have said, but only that he was with men who shared his lack of fortune, who were the same as he was and had the same purpose; that they were going forward together, where, he could not say, but only that they were going somewhere and would be together. (pp. 53-4)

At this early stage in the march Johnson 'could not say' where they were going. Later, when they have been stopped at the Town Hall and 'the little man' who gets up to address them is knocked down by police, 'then at once men seemed to know where they were going'. (p. 55)

Thus the first surge down Queen Street with its consequent smashing of windows is included in the framework of 'men moving together'. Johnson is driven by the crowd 'knowing that it no longer mattered what happened while the whole street moved forward with him' (p. 56). But once this first revolutionary surge, this sharing of their sense of 'waste and frustration' (p. 53) and 'overwhelming . . . anger' (p. 54), is over, unity is lost, and with it purity of impulse and of motive. The men become individuals again, each for himself instead of for the group:

It was curious to him at this moment, as the crowd rushed from place to place, to feel himself coming back again and to know what he himself was doing. He could see the same feeling grow on men's faces as they looked at one another, and wondered suddenly who was watching them at what they did, and knew that they themselves as single men were breaking and looting and no longer all together. (p. 57)

The sense of being part of something in which men are 'moving . . . together' will not be recovered until the final chapters of the book, when Johnson is gathered into the International Brigade to fight on the side of the Republic in Spain. Just as, in the early chapters, Mulgan has created a vivid sense of the movement of social and economic history (often the driest and most boring kind of history) out of a sequence of close-ups of men at work on the land, so in the riot scene he creates something which is both psychologically convincing ('It was curious . . . to feel himself coming back again and to know what he himself was doing') and which at the same time is like the concrete realization of a piece of abstract political theory. The revolutionary action is pure and self-sustaining while it is truly collective—a spontaneous eruption out of a 'revolutionary situation'. As men lose their collective identity and become individuals (men alone) purity of action and of motive is lost.

Man Alone flounders in its middle chapters. The first impulse—to explain 'the good years' and their loss in the political terms he had acquired at Oxford during the mid-thirties—had carried him too fast to a conclusion. If there was to be a novel there had now to be something else—a 'story' which would spring out of human relationships. Mulgan might well have developed as a novelist but at this stage he was good on states of mind (Johnson in the riots, Johnson in the Kaimanawas) but poor on the interaction of characters. The chapters dealing with Rua and Stenning stumble along, not altogether convincing in human terms, and seeming to lack direction, as if Mulgan is uncertain where the story is taking him. Once Stenning is dead and Johnson has made his decision to escape, the momentum gathers again, but this time it is something different, something regional rather than international.

Already, if the Rua-Stenning chapters have been slightly weak in human terms, the sense of place has been strong. Now, with Johnson the 'man alone' pitted against bush and mountains, the novel moves confidently again. Writing in England, Mulgan's recall of his own experience in such places was accurate and unfaltering. The writing is spare, efficient, the tone is right, there is once again a proper narrative momentum and a proper fictional density. The suffering is real; Johnson's psychological state and his physical condition are convincing. The journey out only stretches credulity as far as exciting fiction should and no further; it is remarkable for its physical quality and for the sense of reality achieved. In these three chapters (XIV-XVI) Mulgan has bodied forth something that I think is part of the New Zealand consciousness. The bush is not merely (as Day implies) a hostile force. It threatens Johnson's life yet it also protects him from the worse threat of human society. In those chapters Johnson enacts what I called (writing partly under Mulgan's influence) Smith's dream. He escapes social and political responsibility and earns his freedom by surviving the rite of initiation which loneliness and physical hardship impose. Once again he has achieved purity of action and motive, not this time in the sense of 'men moving together' but, quite the reverse, as a 'man alone'. This contradiction in the novel's fabric of ideas is not resolved—merely patched over. I doubt whether it can be resolved honestly in New Zealand fiction so long as it remains a contradiction fundamental to our sense of ourselves—so long, that is, as our collective sense of identity is something imported, while our individual sense is shaped in childhood in direct relation to the particular physical environment of these islands. Alan Mulgan had done his best to work this problem of identity out consciously. John Mulgan did better, coming at it obliquely, one might almost argue, unconsciously—but through the operation of the imagination rather than the intellect. If our sense of ourselves is inevitably contradictory, at once local and 'received', that is precisely the identity which *Man Alone* catches.

At one point I think it is possible to see Mulgan attempting to cement over the crack between the two sections into which Part I has fallen. How is the death of Stenning and the subsequent escape story related to the

economic and political history of Chapters I to IX? In Chapter XVII
Johnson talks to Peterson and reflects on how Stenning came to be killed:

> 'I didn't shoot him,' Johnson said sombrely. 'He shot himself. I didn't want to
> shoot him. I liked him all right. There was a reason why it went like that just the
> same. I've been thinking about that. It came with working away there on the farm,
> just the three of us, and no pay. None of us had any pay. You couldn't get away.
> You couldn't do anything but go on working. I've been thinking about that and the
> way things were there. It wasn't any life.'
> 'You're not much better than one of these reds,' Peterson said. (p. 182)

Peterson's reply is faintly improbable. It does not follow very directly or
obviously from what Johnson has said. It is there, surely, as a pointer to the
significance of Johnson's 'reason why it all went like that'. His 'reason' is
economic and hence by implication political; and so a structural link is cast
back to pull the two parts of the story together—not a very convincing link,
because after all economics do not determine when and whether wives are
unfaithful and husbands jealous (unless one cared to argue that affluence
provides time and opportunity)—but clearly Mulgan has emerged, like
Johnson from the bush, with the sense that there was an initial 'reason' for
the novel itself, and he had better get back to it if the whole thing is to hang
together.

Part II reinforces that initial Marxist intention, broadening the picture
so that Johnson's life lessons take him, not by a process of reasoning or of
conscious political theory, but out of his wish to recover his sense of unity
with working men, to the Republican side in Spain:

> There were memories of men he had known and liked, men, black and clay-stained
> on the New Zealand roads, sweating on steamer decks, paint-blistered, dirty, and
> lice-ridden in the seamen's camp at Panama, tough, sceptical on New York docks.
> There was a desire in him now for a life that would give warmth and meaning to
> these memories before he grew too old, for a life active, but with good food and
> good drink, and men moving, making something together. (p. 196)

And as he goes off in the train towards the Spanish war that theme of
'doing something together' (p. 205) echoes again.

To put it extremely, *Man Alone* is two fictions, related yet distinct,
joined to make a novel. If the joining is less than perfect, it is good
enough—it holds together as a single work.

The first of these fictions is basically economic history as narrative, nar-
rowing upon a consequent and violent action; it is a story of men collec-
tively, in which each character stands for a social category (dairy farmer,
farmer's wife, casual labourer, returned soldier, etc.) among whom
Johnson is not even an observer but merely a travelling object, an excuse to
keep the camera moving and a point of focus. The second fiction is one in
which Johnson becomes the subject, not as a 'character' nor as the

representative of a social category, but as something much more universal. He is Man (I will suggest, in a moment, basically the New Zealander) contending with the bush and the mountains. In Part II, written at the publisher's request (and they were right to ask for more) the novel is brought back to its original preoccupation: collective men and political action in a time of crisis.

But the two fictions are not as disparate as I have made them sound. They have a common preoccupation. Mulgan was trying to establish in his own mind the identity of the New Zealand he had left behind—at one level socially and politically, at another (one might say) mythically, existentially, even metaphysically. This effort at definition is a great advance on his father's because it is undefensive and leaves out all those rationalizings and subjective comparisons with which choices are bolstered or necessity made palatable (I live in England because I can go to the theatre; I live in New Zealand because I can go to the beach). Another fault of Paul Day's account is that it takes the discussion back into that very area of naïve comparison which the novel ought to have rendered irrelevant. He does this partly by minimizing the novel's political dimension, and partly by seeing it as what might be called *Mulgan's Revenge*—a revenge on New Zealand for denying him the Rhodes Scholarship.

Day achieves this first by over-emphasizing what it seems to me the novel very largely forgets—that Johnson is an Englishman; and second, by writing as if everything negative in the picture of New Zealand implies something corresponding and positive in what with Alan Mulganish circumspection he calls 'older societies'. Thus in his Twayne book on John Mulgan:

A representative of an older civilization . . . Johnson is a good type of reflecting mirror in which . . . New Zealand life can be seen for what it is. (p. 97)

. . . the mountain . . . is a symbol of the non-material values which Johnson stubbornly expects, coming as he does from an older society where some values transcend those of economic advantage. (p. 108)

[Johnson] has a kind of civility which inhibits him from throwing himself into the work and speculation fever which he finds gripping the New Zealanders, enslaving them and denying them freedom and maturity. He sees the land with the vision of an inhabitant of an older culture. (p. 116)

It is necessary to unravel Day's confusion if only because he is almost our sole critic of Mulgan's work. When Johnson is introduced in the first sentence of the novel it is as one who, like the narrator, comes from New Zealand:

I met Johnson on the quay at one of those fishing villages in Brittany which everybody paints, and got into conversation with him, first of all, because we both spoke English, and afterwards, because we found we both came from the same country, which was not England.

Two pages later it is revealed that Johnson is English-born, that he went to New Zealand as an immigrant after the war. But that initial identification hangs over him, all the more, I think, because Mulgan draws so much on his own experience in creating the character, and identifies with him in times of crisis. We are told Johnson is an Englishman, but we are never made to feel that he is. Quite contrary to what Day suggests, Johnson never compares what he sees in New Zealand with what he might be supposed to have experienced in England. He has no background except a nebulous 'farm' which he says he was 'brought up on' (p. 16). He exhibits no class consciousness or class traits and it would be impossible, if one believed in that 'farm', if it had any fictional density, to decide whether he had been the son of the owner, of the manager, or of a farm labourer. As the novel advances he seems more and more the prototype Kiwi (or the fictional stereotype)—practical, inarticulate, unreflective, resourceful, unemotional, egalitarian, pragmatic—very much like the New Zealand soldiers as Mulgan describes them in *Report on Experience*. And when he returns to England and to farm work he is in fact quite alien, much more so than would be the case if he were returning to his point of origin:

[Johnson] represented a foreign and unknown quantity, something alien among the corn. The eyes that met his were without hostility but without friendliness. Johnson closed the gate carefully after him and went on down the road. (p. 194)

There is no passage where Johnson is made to feel as deeply alien in New Zealand as he does here—and that it is homesickness he feels is subtly hinted by the echo of Keats:

> Perhaps the self-same song that found a path
>   Through the sad heart of Ruth, when, sick for home,
>   She stood in tears amid the alien corn.

Once again it seems Mulgan has simply transcribed his own experience and attributed it to his character.

Johnson is thus nominally an Englishman but imaginatively a New Zealander; and in neither form does he possess the marvellous critical detachment attributed to him by Day. If he thinks it would be good to climb Mount Ruapehu he is hardly, in that, manifesting something especially characteristic of a member of an 'older society'; nor is Scotty's and Stenning's lack of interest in the climb characteristically Kiwi. And if the New Zealand Johnson travels through reveals itself to be progressively in the grip of economic anxieties and the 'acquisitive bourgeois compulsions'[14] of capitalism, it is shown in that to be *like* those 'older societies', not different and inferior. In fact what is characteristically 'New Zealand' in Mulgan's view is represented by those 'good years', the 'golden summer' before the economic realities of a larger and harsher world caught up with the country of his youth. On this, Patrick Evans is a better guide than Day:

The advent of the Depression in New Zealand inevitably drew the attention of local observers overseas, for it proved that this country was no more insulated from the world economic virus than any other had been, and scenes which were occurring the world over occurred here. To thoughtful observers like Mulgan, New Zealand was being steadily drawn into a world which was engulfed in an endless war—in which the conflict of 1914-18 had been followed not by peace but by the economic warfare of individuals and classes which marked the 'twenties and by the general collapse of the world's economy which occurred after 1929. In such an interpretation, the riots [in Queen Street] and the rise of Hitler were aspects of a single phenomenon. . . . Our social structure and economic system had not been sufficiently unusual to prevent our catching the economic disease.[15]

This is much more accurate, and truer to the spirit of Mulgan's novel, than Day's emphasis: 'Throughout the book we are constantly reminded that *in this country* economics provide a grimly constricting rule over human destinies.'[16]

The tone of *Man Alone* is dour, the image of New Zealand on the whole drab—and there are no doubt many elements in the drabness that can be identified as peculiar to this country. But that is a product of the realism with which a whole generation of writers, here and abroad, were treating their experience—not because something better existed elsewhere. Just as those *Kowhai Gold* Georgians had sentimentalized New Zealand so they had sentimentalized England (Alan Mulgan's *Home: A New Zealander's Adventure* is the prime example) and John Mulgan rejected it all:

We can dispense now with the legend which tradition fostered for us of a benign England, the staid old mother of the seven seas. . . . England was Tilbury on a raw November morning, streets of tenement houses crowded with pale, flat-capped working men who obviously had no work.[17]

Asking why Mulgan should have turned to the writing of a novel at the time he did, Day writes:

The answer to this question is to be found in the beginnings of Mulgan's life in New Zealand, in his family background, and in the qualities of his own character.
The principal fact which is relevant to Mulgan's departure from New Zealand was that he had been rejected. However it had happened, the Rhodes Scholarship which, as every sane person who knew the facts would agree, he well deserved, had been withheld from him. More, this miscarriage of justice appeared to derive from Mulgan's outspoken espousal of the cause of free speech and social justice. A provincial society had revenged itself on an intellect more keen and a vision more clear than was customary. . . .

So, in implied disagreement with his father's optimistic complacency, in bitter recognition of the remorseless malice of New Zealand society towards himself, the book was begun, and completed by April.[18]

Though some credit is no doubt due to him, it is exaggerating Mulgan's 'espousal of the cause of free speech' at this time to call it 'outspoken', particularly when it is remembered that he complained of Mason's 'propagandist' editing of *The Phoenix*. It is also misrepresenting the refusal to nominate him for the Rhodes Scholarship in 1933 to call it 'the remorseless malice of New Zealand towards himself'. And above all, it is trivializing his novel to imply that it was written as an act of retaliation for this apparent slight. *Man Alone* is something more serious than an act of revenge.

I have admitted to a sense of kinship with Mulgan of the kind Tate describes when he writes of his 'cousin, Mr Poe'. Such feelings are in one sense irrelevant, and may even cause impatience or offence; but I think where they have provided structure and motive for criticism they are better acknowledged. It is still strange to me that the first New Zealand fiction writer to make an impression on me (and it was a strong and durable impression) should later be found to have had so many areas of experience in common with my own. Separated by twenty years, we attended the same primary school, and the same university college; both, as undergraduates, were involved on the perimeter of violent political action, which influenced our political thinking—he with the riots of 1932, I with the 1951 Waterfront strike.* Those local events were joined in our political thinking to a civil war abroad which became the point of political focus for a phase of history—in his case Spain, in mine Viet Nam.† Without pretending to be novelists, we both wrote novels (I partly under his influence) attempting to pull these political elements together into our consciousness of New Zealand. Both novels have two endings; and if I write now about the problem of ending *Smith's Dream* it is because the continual putting of questions on this subject by teachers and pupils has forced me to analyse the problem in a way which I have come to think is relevant also to *Man Alone*.

Briefly, my first idea was that Smith should be killed at the end of the novel, and it was not until I reached the final chapter that I felt compelled by what I took to be a very strong 'artistic impulse' (not, I was sure, a sentimental one, or the wish for a 'happy ending') to have him survive. When

* Patrick Evans is right when he says '*Smith's Dream* is in fact a heightened account of the 1951 period in New Zealand's social history as much as a glimpse into the future . . .'. *Landfall*, March 1977, p. 17.

† There is an interesting irony in the fact that one of New Zealand's most hawkish journalists in Saigon during the sixties was Nicholas Turner, grandson of Alan Mulgan and nephew of John. The family politics, it might be said, had gone full circle.

the novel was first published some readers liked it but complained of the nebulous ending. And I had myself begun to see why it was that Smith ought to have been killed. The novel offered a fairly simple moral proposition. That you can escape political and social responsibility by getting away and being a 'man alone' in the bush is the old New Zealand dream—Smith's dream—and it is false. There is no escape. Smith tries it but life catches up with him in the form of Volkner's Special X. To have him drift off alone at the end of the book was to contradict its whole moral point. So now my original intention seemed undoubtedly right; and when a paperback was planned for 1973 I changed the end. From that time on, through a large number of reprints, Smith has died on the last page.

Most politically conscious people approved of the change; but I am told by Peter Smart that classes divide sharply on the question. I notice too that some I regard as readers of acute literary sensibility prefer the earlier version—and I think I can now see why. Smith is like Mulgan's Johnson (derivatively he lacks a Christian name) in being fairly characterless. He is perhaps the modern fictional type, a bundle of responses rather than a character. But he is not totally without definition. He thinks that he is a political animal but discovers he is not. He is a *survivor*, a modern Crusoe. Each time his life crumbles around him, he re-makes it. At Coromandel, at Rotorua, and then at Coromandel again, he creates a routine. There is something in him which keeps going.

In the penultimate chapter a reason is offered, in the old headmaster's speech, for opting out of the political battle. It has turned purely destructive. 'Life' in a fuller sense exists outside it. Whether the girl on the beach was a satisfactory image or not (probably not) she represented that fuller, more affirmative life—and it was towards her that Smith walked at the end of the first version. Two views of life are clashing here, the political and the existential, there is the justification for both in the novel, and so a contradiction, and a justification for either ending.

Coming back to *Man Alone* with all this in mind I was struck by its concluding sentence: *'There are some men, this fellow said, you can't kill.'* That was the spirit in which I wrote *Smith's Dream*, and the justification for its first ending. What, then, does this Johnson, a man you 'can't kill', represent? I think there was confusion in Mulgan's mind, just as there was confusion in mine about Smith (the imagination works properly only when the rational mind is uncertain). Johnson in Queen Street, with the sense of 'men moving together', Johnson going off to the Spanish Civil War, is a political animal (though not a rational one). Johnson in the Kaimanawas is existential Man. Is it good to be a 'man alone' or not? Mulgan's conscious position, insofar as he has one, is (as it was mine) that it is not. On his way to Spain Johnson echoes the 'men moving together' theme of the Queen Street riots:

'I've only felt like this sometimes, . . . going somewhere with people I liked, *doing something together*. It's a fine feeling. Most of the time a *man* spends too much *alone.*' (p. 205. Italics mine.)

Yet the novel—and Johnson—are at their best in the Kaimanawas. Mulgan's second ending (the addition of Part II) was necessary because the novel had moved too far from where it began. It had to be brought around again to its initial theme. That the two views of life and of New Zealand, the political and the existential, remain side by side in it unresolved is a fact, and an imperfection, but not one disastrous to the novel.

'What destroyed him,' Tate wrote of his 'cousin, Mr Poe', 'is potentially destructive of us.' Lieutenant-Colonel John Mulgan M.C. had survived action in the Western Desert in 1942. In September 1943 he had been parachuted into occupied Greece where he took part in a guerrilla campaign that lasted until the German withdrawal. In January 1945 he returned to Greece as commander of a force set up to compensate Greeks who had suffered in helping the Allied war effort. That mission successfully completed, he returned to Cairo. His war was over. He was a survivor— 'one of those men you can't kill'—and then he took his own life.

I have written of a sense of kinship, of overlap. Yet I could hardly be unaware of the differences. Mulgan's short life was so much the success story, from school, through university, to Oxford, to the war. At corresponding ages we passed through the same system, were subjected to similar pressures, and were both, in our very different ways, 'successful'. Yet I had always the sense that the system (as distinct from the landscape) was foreign, or I foreign to it, and although this could be a source of pain at times, it was also liberating. Though the Swedish/German grandfather whom the schoolboy Mulgan very likely observed building stone walls died before I was born (he sailed off to the New Hebrides and died of malaria) his authority pervaded the house and affected my sense of identity. So in a different way did my father, who was an official in the Labour Party, of largely Irish Catholic descent (though lapsed himself) and quite outside the 'Home' oriented society represented by Alan Mulgan. My antecedents were so mixed the elements could cancel one another out leaving me free to choose or to invent. Although such literary culture as I acquired was predominantly English and rendered England a mythical place (and the B.B.C. London crackled nightly through static) the Pacific islands where my grandfather had sailed and worked and where my mother had spent much of her childhood were more present to my imagination. My mother and grandmother talked about them endlessly; and the house was full of photographs of sailing ships, palm-fringed lagoons, and men in white suits and pith helmets on wooden verandas surrounded by bronze workers bare to the waist. It was the atmosphere of R. L. Stevenson and Joseph Conrad rather than of Georgian poetry.

All this, and my father's politics, made it possible for me to stay largely outside the required orthodoxies of the time without too much discomfort. To take only the example of the military: by the time I was in the sixth form (1949—the year I read *Man Alone*) school cadet training designated the enemy as 'Red', and on the grounds that this was political and that my affinities were with the Left, I declined to do it. (As a result various coveted honours were denied me.) My only experience of the army was the absurd compulsory military training of the fifties, where again my politics set me against the system instead of in step with it.

What has all this to do with Mulgan? It is just that there is a sense in which everything conspired to make him an established figure, the expression of a current orthodoxy; and I suspect this laid upon him an identity which may have been alien to his nature, and left him little freedom to discover what his own nature was. Even as he rebelled against the politics of his family it was an orthodox rebellion, sanctioned by undergraduate Oxford as he found it in the 1930s—and in *Report on Experience* one can feel him moving cautiously back (as Auden did) with the return swing of the pendulum, already looking back on his politically radical days with detachment and irony. Even his war turned into an expression of his Oxford politics. It was a war Mulgan could commit himself to seriously, whole-heartedly, and in which all his various skills and talents found outlet.

What caused him to commit suicide must always be something of a mystery. Certainly his experiences in Greece, however unsettling, are not sufficient explanation. Nor, though he writes so eloquently on the subject,[19] does James Bertram convince me that some sad penetrating lucidity about the future of Western civilization explains it. No doubt the suicide requires at least in part a medical explanation; and there is a poem in *Kiwi* 1932 signed J. M.* which if (as I assume) it is by John Mulgan, suggests

*The Friend Who Died

I have just come from meeting death.
I heard his voice chill as the breath
Of unknown winds, whisper to me—
'Your friend whom you have loved, is dead.'
Turning I could not see
The speaker, only knew what he had said;
And knew that he was gone and then
I felt a lonelines as when
One comes into an empty house:
But could not say
If I was lonely having lost a friend
Or because Death had gone away.

an underlying sense of estrangement from life and a consequent death-wish many years before he took his own life.

No one explanation is going to be sufficient. But there is, it seems to me, a melancholy in every sentence he wrote, which may well have been the melancholy of a man who was travelling further and further down a wrong road. He asserted that he was not really an artist yet proved he had it in him to be one. But apart from the peculiar eruption which produced his novel he lived out a life so entirely orthodox one can only imagine a continuation of the same pattern: expatriate, public, much-honoured, but to the man who wrote the Kaimanawas chapters and had tasted a little of what Frank Sargeson calls 'the life of the imagination', deeply unsatisfying. I don't mean to suggest that Mulgan saw all this clearly (had he done so he might have altered the course of his life)—only that the identity he had forged for himself and which he believed belonged to him gave him nothing he could look forward to with pleasure or with hope. Intellectually he had shaken off a great deal that was false in his father's sad dualism, but still it seems to me he was, in the life he led and in the history he was obliged to live through, its victim.

II

Alan Mulgan's novel *Spur of Morning* was published in 1934, only five years before *Man Alone*. Like *Man Alone* it is in part a journalist's use of the fictional mode to survey a period of New Zealand history. Also as in *Man Alone*, the novelist goes back to memories of his early years—but Alan Mulgan in his fifties was looking back to the first decade of the century; John Mulgan, writing in his twenties, went back to the period 1919-32. Both novels involve politics; both reach a point of crisis in a riot (A. M.'s in Wellington, J. M.'s in Auckland) and in the reaction of the hero to that event.

But I do not think *Spur of Morning* had any influence on *Man Alone*, apart perhaps from a determination on John Mulgan's part to do otherwise, which is hardly significant. What does seem to me possible is that the youthful career and character of John Mulgan may have influenced his father's writing of *Spur of Morning*.

Alan Mulgan's hero is Mark Bryan. He comes from a working-class background; but apart from that difference, he has much in common with the young John Mulgan. He is academically brilliant, athletic, a great rugby player, blunt, somewhat dour, and a radical—all this standing in deliberate contrast to the character of his friend Philip Armitage who is plainly Alan Mulgan's self-portrait. Philip is conservative, a rugby enthusiast but not a player, uncritically loyal to England and the Empire, and naïve. He is also a writer. From time to time we hear he is writing a poem, and at the end of the story he has had a novel accepted in London. He has a great deal to learn about the world, and learns it partly through journalism, partly through the influence of his friend. It is clear that Alan Mulgan is importing back in the direction of his early years a liberal understanding he would not have possessed in the years of which he is writing. But the novel is not in the least radical in its politics. Just as the conservative Philip Armitage has to learn that there is sometimes right on the workers' side and corruption in high places, so the radical Mark Bryan has to discover that a Governor can be a good man (he becomes a regular visitor at Government House) and that there is corruption among Liberal-Labour politicians. On all scores (Left versus Right, New Zealand versus 'Home', the pride of wealth versus the prejudice of the workers) the novel comes down programmatically in the middle. The very conventional Jane Austenish plot is resolved when the young radical Bryan, deprived of his seat in Parliament by the machinations of the wealthy landowner, Feldon, playing upon the prejudices of the Labour movement, gives up his political career, disillusioned with both sides, and marries Sylvia, Feldon's daughter, who by this marriage also rejects her traditional loyalties. The novel's 'good' characters join in a group on their own, disdaining active politics in favour of the life of the intellect, literature, conversation, and picnics on Auckland's west coast.

The impression of Auckland in the early years of the century is interesting: for the rest, the novel is pretty trivial stuff. But what is of special interest to the reader of *Man Alone* is the riot sequence and its consequences. Mark Bryan has been brilliantly successful as a Labour politician. He is the youngest cabinet minister in the Empire, but in the later chapters, though still young, he is learning moderation and so being accused of losing his fire, of becoming conservative. When a group of strikers attack a warehouse in Wellington,* smashing windows and resisting the police, Bryan, the appropriate minister, is asked to sanction the calling in of the army. This he agrees to without a moment's hesitation; and the ponderous tone of the writing at this point makes it clear that we are to see his decision as right. The strikers have been provoked; but property must be protected against 'lawless elements' (p. 279) and the young cabinet minister congratulates his troops—'big picked men in the prime of life and the pink of condition' against whose 'disciplined attack' 'the mob . . . had no chance' (p. 281).

It is this noble act which Bryan's political enemy Feldon employs against him. Already Bryan is suspect with the Labour movement. Now Feldon

* Called Wellesley in the novel. Auckland is called Eden. 'The colony' is unnamed.

pays a Labour man to stand against Bryan as an independent. This splits the Labour vote, and Bryan is defeated.

One of the devices Alan Mulgan uses with varying point and effect is literary echo. There are echoes at various points of Pope, Arnold, Landor, and no doubt others I have not noticed. The chapter (Book Five, Chapter V) dealing with the Labour party turning against Bryan is called 'The Mutable Many', a half-concealed echo of Act III Scene i of Shakespeare's *Coriolanus,* where the too noble young Roman, refusing to bow to the will of the people, who are being encouraged by the tribunes to drag him from power, thunders:

> For
> The mutable, rank-scented meiny,* let them
> Regard me as I do not flatter . . .
> I say again
> In soothing them, we nourish 'gainst our Senate
> The cockle of rebellion, insolence, sedition. . . .

This echo serves, as John Mulgan's of Keats cited above, to place a character without being too explicit. Bryan is the headstrong but noble un-compromising hero against the 'mutable many' now bent on pulling him from power. It is unobtrusive; but it leaves no doubt, if there were other-wise room for any, where the novelist stands. The liberalism of the novel has been skin-deep, its conservatism fundamental.

There can be no doubt that in many ways Mark Bryan is Alan Mulgan's ideal, and that the idealization is complete only when Bryan has learned moderation and disengaged himself from the politics of the Left. But Alan Mulgan could not conceivably have created a hero who was politically radical twenty years, or even ten years, earlier. It is surely the political cir-cumstances of the 1930s together with the influence of his own son that ex-plain the character. To have a son successful in all the ways he himself had wanted to be yet at the same time given to some (at that time acceptably moderate) degree of political radicalism, must have made the creation of Mark Bryan possible.

But what had the young Mulgan done when riot occurred in his city? He had allied himself with the forces of order, to 'protect property'; and it is impossible to imagine that this was not in the older man's mind when he wrote the chapter in which Mark Bryan does the same. So it must have seemed to him that he was right in the middle-of-the-road political future he outlined for his radical hero.

But there is a final point. If the character of Mark Bryan was built partly

* Mulgan's edition of the play would probably have read 'many'.

on observation of the son, was not the son's career built equally on the father's ideal which is expressed in the character? This young man Bryan, of physical and intellectual prowess, headstrong in his youth but capable of learning, one who 'had never finally failed in anything important' (p. 303) is precisely the image John Mulgan lived up to for most of his life, and yet which may (as I suggest above) have been alien to his deepest nature.

III

John Mulgan was the Auckland University College nominee for the Rhodes Scholarship in his second year as a student, 1931. He was unsuccessful, but seemed to come away from his interview at Government House, Wellington, with an impression that he would win the scholarship if he applied again.[20] In 1932 he was not nominated; and by way of explanation Day quotes Alan Mulgan's account which suggests that the Professorial Board's use of a new preferential voting system produced a result no one expected or intended.[21] By 1933 John Mulgan had completed his B.A. and was enrolled for an M.A. (which he did not complete). It was confidently expected, at least by the Mulgan circle, that this would be his year. In the meantime, however, he had signed the statement in support of a free speech candidate for the College Council, the action which it has been said cost him the scholarship. Two other students and not Mulgan received the 1933 Auckland nomination, E. P. Haslam and L. W. A. Crawley. They were not successful (though Haslam won the scholarship in 1934) and in fact that year no Rhodes Scholarship was awarded.

I have already quoted Day's opinion that 'every sane person who knew the facts would agree' that Mulgan deserved the scholarship; that 'this miscarriage of justice appeared to derive from Mulgan's outspoken espousal of the cause of free speech and social justice'; and that this 'remorseless malice' of a 'provincial society' towards 'an intellect more keen and a vision more clear than was customary' prompted Mulgan to write *Man Alone*. Day offers little real evidence for his view of what happened, but it is the stuff of which literary mythology is made, and James Bertram, for example, echoes it in his article in *Comment*, 39 (cited above).[22]

If I am now to question this comfortable mythology it is not because I wish to suggest that Mulgan was not academically first rate, nor to whitewash the Auckland University College. Mulgan's Oxford 'first' leaves no doubt about his academic competence. And as for the Auckland University College—the story of Mulgan suffering from signing the free speech document is perfectly believable as something that *might have happened*. My belief that it did not is based on the only evidence I can find (but it is probably the best)—the academic records of Mulgan and the two candidates who were nominated for the scholarship in 1933.

Crawley was a year ahead of Mulgan, Haslam a year behind. Of the three, Haslam's record at Auckland University College is clearly the best. Comparing their performances in each of their undergraduate years (i.e. Mulgan's first year, 1930, with Haslam's first, 1931, and so on) I find Haslam ahead on aggregate marks and on his average percentage per paper. Further, in every case where Haslam and Mulgan took the same unit (e.g. English I, History I, Economics I) Haslam earned higher marks. Finally, Haslam's average increased in each of his undergraduate years (and his lowest average was higher than Mulgan's highest), while Mulgan's declined, so that year by year Haslam's superiority was more clearly marked.

The comparison with Crawley is a little more complicated; but on the whole his performance was superior to Mulgan's, and by 1933 he had the distinct advantage of having completed an M.A. with first-class honours.

Mulgan's performance in his third year (1932) was mediocre. Though he passed all three units he sat (English III, Greek III, Latin II) his mark on two of his papers was less than fifty per cent and his average over eight papers was a fraction under sixty-two per cent. The academic case for him was therefore weak. Other criteria would have to have been cited in his favour by anyone wishing to support him. In the case of the Rhodes Scholarship, however, these further criteria are irrelevant to the purpose of the scholarship, which is to provide the scholar a means to postgraduate study. Sport is generally considered important—but should one give the opportunity for advanced study to a man who is academically inferior but physically faster or stronger? And how does one assess a candidate's qualities of 'leadership' and 'manliness', which are mentioned in the terms of the award? The academic quality is the only safe one on which to base a nomination, and if I had been on the Professorial Board that year I find it hard to imagine how I could have voted for anyone but Haslam.

Of course it is possible that some members of the Board might have intended to vote for Mulgan and then decided not to because he was associated with the free speech side of the controversy which had raged during the year. But if that happened (and so far no one has produced any evidence) it was still a case of doing the right deed for the wrong reason. Haslam clearly deserved the nomination.

In a recent review article in the *New Zealand Journal of History* Keith Sinclair mocks the predominant Oxford orientation of a generation of New Zealand writers and intellectuals and cites the continuing enquiry into why Mulgan failed to get the Rhodes Scholarship as an example. Sinclair is right. The Rhodes Scholarship was seen as something more than a means to further university study. It was an entry to Oxford, and an accolade in itself, like a military decoration or a Queen's Birthday Honour—something to be mentioned forever after in connexion with the name of the winner. Worse, it was for many years one of the most insidious forms of colonialism, by which good academic brains were skimmed off from New Zealand, exported abroad, Oxford groomed, and usefully absorbed into English intellectual life, while second-rate Britons were sent out to fill the gaps which those Rhodes Scholars might have been expected to fill in New Zealand. If a Rhodes Scholar returned to New Zealand he was felt to have done less well than those who stayed in England, not quite to have fulfilled his promise, and so his position in the academic hierarchy was usually second-in-command to one of those British exports who filled the top positions. The system was obviously self-perpetuating, and explains why colonialism lasted longer in the universities than anywhere else.

Mulgan had to make his own way to Oxford where he evidently worked harder than he had done in Auckland. He received his 'first' and went into the Oxford Press, where his successor after the war was another New Zealander, Dan Davin, a Rhodes Scholar who has remained there ever since.

It is clear from Alan Mulgan's note quoted by Day, and from the emotional tone adopted by Day on this question, that it was felt by Mulgan's family that he had been denied his due when the college failed to nominate him in 1933. That the nominees of that year might have had stronger claims does not appear to have been considered. This feeling is only a further manifestation of the 'Home'-oriented atmosphere which surrounded him (and surrounds the discussion of his work) and of which he was indubitably the product. He was one of the remarkable men of his generation; but his successes and achievements would not deserve more than a paragraph thirty and more years after his death if it were not for the fact that in 1937-8, in a brief and almost secret deviation from the path of an otherwise entirely orthodox career, he had written *Man Alone*, not a great novel, but one which in its rare dour sober truthfulness enacts a phase in our national history and catches certain truths about our national identity.

POSTSCRIPT

This article drew a number of letters in the following issue of *Islands* (number 26). James Bertram seemed determined to believe that Mulgan was a martyr to the cause of free speech, victimized by the College Professorial Board, and that my article was some kind of loyal whitewash. One of the very few new facts to emerge from this correspondence, however, was J. A. W. Bennett's recollection that Willis Airey (himself a life-long Marxist, and a Rhodes Scholar) 'was emphatic that political or parochial prejudice played no part' in the decision not to nominate Mulgan for the scholarship.

It is quite true that the Governor General, Lord Bledisloe, favoured Mulgan—and my article never disputed that fact, for which there is evidence in the papers of Sir George Fowlds. It is also true that the atmosphere of the College at that time was intensely politicized and divided, especially on the issue of academic free speech; and it is entirely conceivable that Mulgan's signature (his mother's name also appeared) on the 1933 circular letter supporting a 'free speech' candidate for the College Council might have set illiberal members of the Professorial Board against him. My point was that there was no evidence of victimization of Mulgan by the College on political or any other grounds; and that there were on the other hand (and this had not previously been known) good academic reasons for putting other nominees ahead of him. I was well aware that academic considerations were not supposed to be the sole criteria; but they could hardly be ignored, and Mulgan's academic performance had declined during his three undergraduate years. Bertram in his letter complained that academic records which I cited 'were supposed to be confidential'. The Mulgan mythology would, of course, have been better served by their continued suppression. But that mythology involved a slur on the names of other scholars (notably Haslam) who were supposed to have won the nomination unfairly; and that being so it seemed (and seems) to me appropriate to make public a summary of the records.

Since my article appeared Keith Sinclair, who is writing a history of the University of Auckland, has completed a draft of his chapter on this period, and I have done some further investigations of my own. From Sinclair I learn that a sub-committee of the Auckland Professorial Board set up to consider six possibles for the Rhodes Scholarship in 1933 assessed them on three criteria. In sport all were rated good. In administrative ability all were rated satisfactory. In academic achievement they were put in order of merit, and three were rated ahead of Mulgan. This appears to confirm my supposition about why he was not nominated by Auckland in that year.

But that rating of all nominees equal on all criteria but scholarship seems to require interpretation. Sinclair says the sub-committee consisted of two conservatives (on the free speech issue), one liberal, and one waverer. It may be that they agreed to put aside all questions except academic ones because both sides knew that to introduce assessments of character and public involvement would engage their own political preferences and those of the Professorial Board to which they were recommending. Whatever the reason, it was clearly a procedure which ruined Mulgan's chances.

I don't think there can be any final answer to this question. How, in the end, does the Professor casting a vote for or against know, even inside his own head, whether his motives are entirely 'pure'? And what kind of mythology might there have been room for if, for example, Mulgan, with lower marks but supported by the Governor General, had received the Rhodes Scholarship, and Eric Haslam had written *Man Alone*! If there was prejudice against Mulgan he had certainly played into the hands of those who were prejudiced by neglecting his studies. I was right at least to put to the test of a few new facts that mythology which Day and Bertram had gathered out of the air of the time and enshrined in their writings on Mulgan.

Bertram in his letter to *Islands* also takes issue with me for saying 'I doubt very much that John Mulgan was any sort of a leftist while a student at the Auckland University College'. But Jean Bartlett in the same correspondence writes 'Karl Stead has deduced, and I can confirm, that John was never a Marxist while he was in Auckland.' This was a development which occurred in Oxford. J. A. W. Bennett questions whether he was ever a Marxist at all; but by 'Marxist' Bennett appears to mean Communist, and my guess in the article was that even in the 1937-8 period Mulgan did not join the C.P.

Denis Glover's contribution to the debate was to suggest that my attitude to the Rhodes Scholarship was one of envy: 'Had Stead had the necessary qualifications,' Glover wrote, 'I hazard he would have been in boots and all'. I don't dispute this. In the 1950s there were not many scholarships about, and we were scarcely freer of that 'colonialism' of which I wrote than in the 1930s. But I should add in self-defence that of the 'necessary qualifications' I no doubt lacked the most crucial was celibacy. I had married while still an undergraduate, and the terms of the Rhodes Scholarship precluded not only those unnatural creatures women, but also men who had apparent and licensed commerce with them.

RONALD HUGH MORRIESON:
THE MAN FROM HAWERA

A Professor of English who has some pretensions to being a writer of poetry and fiction spends his summer reading certain classics he is conscious he ought to have read before. They include collections of stories by Chekhov and Isaac Babel; Moravia's *The Time of Indifference*; three of Balzac's novels (*Père Goriot, Cousin Pons,* and *Eugénie Grandet*); Dostoevsky's *The Brothers Karamazov*; Dickens' *A Tale of Two Cities*; Stendhal's *Le Rouge et Le Noir*; and Flaubert's *Madame Bovary.* On the advice of a friend the Professor then reads two novels by a man who lives in Hawera.

I am writing of myself. The friend is Frank Sargeson, the Hawera novelist Ronald Hugh Morrieson, his novels *The Scarecrow* and *Came a Hot Friday.* I should make it clear that I am not working myself into position for a thundering declaration that Mr Morrieson is the equal of Dostoevsky, Dickens, Balzac, etc. I first had in mind that it was a measure of his talent that his novels succeeded in engaging the attention of a reader who had so recently lumbered himself with all those daunting reminders of the greatness possible to the mode of fiction. I think now the proper point to be drawn is rather that having read the works listed I was better equipped to see merit in Mr Morrieson than if I had spent my summer reading a dozen of the slickest and most successful novels of the past decade. This is something I would like to explain, at least to myself. The little I have to say about Mr Morrieson will therefore have to be approached by a circuitous route.

If I say that Ronald Hugh Morrieson is less of a stylist than (to take an

First published in *Landfall* 98, June 1971, together with an article by Frank Sargeson on the same subject. At this time Morrieson's work had had no serious public attention in New Zealand.

obvious example) Maurice Duggan, I wonder whether I have said anything at all. A Russian will tell you that Dostoevsky is inferior to Tolstoy because he is less of a stylist. A Frenchman will say the same of Balzac as compared with Flaubert. In each case a point of a kind is made, but can the value judgement be made to rest on it? In the English tradition we are not, so far as I know, in the habit of making the same point about Jane Austen at the expense of Dickens—I suppose because we accept that the degree of success achieved in a work of fiction doesn't depend on style in the narrow sense. It depends on the ample articulation of a vision of life.

It is the word 'style' that is confusing. It can mean simply the apt and felicitous use of words, and the perfection of sentences. But we can give to it, if we choose, a much broader meaning. Are not Balzac's crude energy and Dostoevsky's frenzy aspects of style? Without them, how could the vision of either be articulated? A certain niceness of phrase is essential to the delicacy of Chekhov's vision, just as blood, sweat and ecstasy are necessary to Babel's. That is not to say that Chekhov is more of a stylist than Babel but that he is a stylist of a different kind.

Out of all those classics read during the summer only *Madame Bovary* disappointed me. It was certainly the most carefully composed and orderly of the group. All the others (with the exception perhaps of *Eugénie Grandet*) are uneven in quality and in one way or another would surely flout any general rule of order one might care to propose for writers of fiction. In all of them the unevenness seems to mark the waxing and waning of energy and imagination as the writer struggles for something that exists within and beyond himself. In Flaubert the struggle is altogether different and less appealing. The author is in no doubt about what he has to say. He is not labouring towards a discovery but sits patiently buffing his artistic fingernails and holding them up to catch the light.

'Art is but a vision of reality' Yeats says. It is not objective reality nor subjective vision but the mutual accommodation of the two. We must know that what is being seen is in some way representative and real; and we must be given at the same time a clear impression of who is seeing, and how he sees it, and that his is a distinguished mind and a rare sensibility. In *Madame Bovary* we see a distinguished mind and a rare sensibility stubbornly feeding on a theory of life rather than on a vision of it, and the result, for all the care that has gone into it and the elegance achieved, is lifeless. Emma Bovary is never permitted to surprise her author by any action which does not accord with his disapproving view of her. He creates her only to punish and finally to kill her. As a personality she is faintly composed of sentimental and religious yearnings, weak egotism, and boredom. She has never a moment of free energy. Even in her waywardness she is entirely conventional and predictable. If she had been allowed to come to life her first positive action might have been to seduce her author. But

Flaubert preferred his theory to real flesh and Emma Bovary does not exist.

The comparison with Balzac is instructive. In his view of the actions of men and women within the accepted conventions of society Balzac's intelligence is anarchic and cynical. The great majority of his characters are marked by avarice, dishonesty, insensitivity, and viciousness. Yet even wallowing in filth to achieve money and social advancement they attain a kind of grandeur. Like God, their author breathes life into them, gives them their freedom, and loves them despite himself and despite the awful uses they put their freedom to. What does it mean, then, to say that Balzac is less of a stylist than Flaubert? No more than that Flaubert's sentences are executed with greater care. They ask to be admired and one admires them—as sentences. They are not the servants of a fictional vision but a substitute for one. Balzac's sentences, on the other hand, are engendered by the vision and exist only to express it.

This is heavy stuff for the man from Hawera, but the novels of Ronald Hugh Morrieson do, in their way, articulate a vision of reality, and therefore deserve whatever we can give them in the way of public notice. I wasn't at once drawn to either. I was slowly gathered in. I was conscious of lapses. The writing sagged in places. There was plenty of what I suppose might be called 'bad taste'. There were patches of dialogue which the author tried to render more amusing by representing it phonetically. (This phonetic dialogue became especially trying when the characters were drunk.) And there was, in both novels, a jokiness as of some beefy barroom bore cracking you over the head with lead-weighted witticisms and then nudging you in the ribs and saying 'Get it?' Reading Mr Morrieson's novels is like dining with the chef. He has excelled himself and he doesn't want you to miss a thing. I imagine a reader fresh from Updike or Powell or Wilson or Vidal might feel a certain embarrassment. If that is so it is time to remind ourselves that the tradition of the novel in English includes Fielding, Smollett, Sterne, and Dickens, all lapsers and nudgers who are likely to lose their cool at the onset of another bright idea. In Mr Morrieson as in them the crudeness is part of the energy, and that energy, as well as generating the total vision, can produce moments of astonishing verbal beauty and flashes of genuine wit. Mr Morrieson is not their equal but he belongs to the same tradition, and he has his own notion of style which he sets forth boldly on the second page of *The Scarecrow*. The novel opens as follows:

The same week our fowls were stolen, Daphne Moran had her throat cut.

On the second page the narrator remarks,

In Treasure Island I liked the sound of 'The same broadside I lost my leg, Old Pew lost his deadlights.' When I get around to writing myself, I decided, that is how I am going to sound. It is harder than it looks. The opening sentence of my story is as near as I can get.

There is style beyond the style the narrator is talking about. Only a true creative talent, warming to its task, feeling (as Matthew Arnold would have said) Nature taking the pen from its hand, would have dared to point out its own felicity.

I am not going to write in detail about these novels. To do that I would need to read them again, and perhaps again, and the summer, when university professors read for motives which are entirely pure, is over. Mr Sargeson will write another and better note. I will content myself with two examples of what Mr Morrieson can do, and with a final general observation.

The Scarecrow is the kind of book blurb writers might call 'spine-chilling' or 'hair-raising'. A long lean scarecrow of a man, a necrophiliac, drifts about a small town looking for young girls to murder and rape. He lurks in the shadows bearing a long knife. When he appears publicly he goes by the name of Salter the Sensational, a magician and something of a hypnotist. Before the story begins he has committed several murders. In the course of the novel he commits two more, and is only at the last moment prevented from adding the narrator's sister to the tally. If the novel's only effect were to make our flesh creep then I suppose it might be as nasty as a bald description of its subject matter can make it seem. But we are not (are we?) to decide on the merit of a novel by its subject matter. If we are, what is to be said of (for example) one whose central event is the beating to death of a greedy, lustful old man by the epileptic son he has fathered in raping an idiot girl known only as Stinking Lizaveta?* It is one of the freedoms of Art to linger over the horrors of human life—but only so long as the imagination and the talent of the artist can cope with them. Beyond that point there is no reconciliation, and no art.

Chapter Nine of *The Scarecrow* contains an event so appalling that in an age when books didn't go unnoticed this one might have been burned by the public hangman.† Sam Finn, the town idiot, discovers the Scarecrow at the undertaker's parlour in the act of having sexual intercourse with the dead body of Miss Mabel Collinson, a dipsomaniac music teacher who has broken her neck falling down the stairs that lead to her studio. Sam Finn protests at this outrage and is murdered. Put yourself in the place of the

---

* For those, like the Professor of last Spring, who have yet to come to Dostoevsky's master work, I confirm that I am describing *The Brothers Karamazov.*

† Though we no longer have the hangman we do have Professor Ian Gordon and the State Literary Fund Committee. I feel sure that if these novels had gone before Professor Gordon's committee they would have been declared unfit for public subsidy.

writer approaching such a chapter. It seems to me it would require the steadiness of hand and brain of a surgeon about to perform a difficult operation under a storm lantern in a ship on a high sea. Here are Mr Morrieson's opening sentences:

The stairway up to Mabel Collinson's studio was as sharp and quivering as a chord on a cool vibraphone. One step inside the doorway, one step along the passage, and bang!—there was the staircase, steep as a fire escape.

The high, narrow, box-like building was as old as the town itself. It was at the very end of the main street, on the dawn side of the elm. Mabel Collinson had lost all but six of her piano pupils through breathing gin fumes and cigarette smoke over them, and, at her lowest ebb, making daring suggestions to adolescent boys. She was a beautiful pianist, and had won an open scholarship when she was ten years old. At thirty-six, her body was still youthful and lovely like that of Dorian Gray, but her face was the tell-tale painting in the attic.

I can only say that in those cool sentences, and in the ones that follow them, there is such an instinct for combining the bizarre and the beautiful, I am entirely disarmed. And the account continues without faltering. We learn that Sam Finn has listened every night from the street outside to Miss Collinson playing her piano; that once, having followed her about the streets, he has lain naked in the wet grass while 'the music of her piano and the fine rain . . . [fell] on him like a benediction'; that on the night after her death he misses her playing and has some notion that if he stands outside Charlie Dabney's funeral parlour he may hear it there. This leads to his discovery of the Scarecrow at work—bravely but briefly described—and to the murder. The whole sequence puts Mr Morrieson's powers to the test and reveals how extraordinary they are.

The figure of the Scarecrow acquires—at least to a literary mind— something of a symbolic quality. He is Death the magician, clever and fascinating as well as horrible, stalking in the shadows and savaging his victims. The figure of evil in *Came a Hot Friday* is Sel Bishop, but he is as solid in the flesh as the Scarecrow is lean, 'a big beast of a man', representing everything that is coarse, ugly, and brutal in human nature. He is a character one might expect to find in the work of any one of a dozen New Zealand fiction writers, where he might stand as the intellectual's solemn reproach to our Kiwi culture. The situation which develops around him has, inevitably, large elements of melodrama. My second illustration of Mr Morrieson's skill is to describe the means by which he permits himself to exploit the climax of this melodrama without committing himself to it too solemnly.

Towards the end of the novel Bishop has three people locked in a closet under the stairs in his woolshed. They are Claire, the mistress he has grown tired of; Morrie, her drunken brother who has been Bishop's accomplice in crime and who seems ready to blab; and a young punter called Wes Pennington who has accidentally overheard an account of Bishop's crimes. Claire is distraught, Morrie dead drunk, and Pennington rendered helpless by the fact that his thumb has been caught and crushed in the closet door. Bishop decides to burn them in the barn and make it appear that the fire has occurred during a wild party. What he doesn't take into account is that the Te Whakinga Kid is watching him from the darkness outside.

The Te Whakinga Kid is a Maori and I don't know what Dr W. H. Pearson, who has written a properly censorious study of pakeha attitudes to the Maori in fiction, would make of him, except that he could hardly argue that he was the prototype 'Hori'. In fact I can think of no exact parallel in any contemporary fiction, and the nearest example of the type my summer's reading provides would probably be Jerry Cruncher, the body-snatcher in *A Tale of Two Cities*. The Te Whakinga Kid is a grotesque. He wears a cowboy suit, carries a cap gun, lives by the fantasy that he is a Mexican bandit, and speaks accordingly.* At the moment the Kid enters, Bishop has his trousers off and is making burns in them which he hopes will corroborate the story he intends to tell of how he tried to save his friends from the flames. The Kid picks up Bishop's rifle and orders him to unlock the closet. Part of the dialogue goes as follows:

'I am ze excellent shot, senor Bishop.'

This was a downright fib, the Kid having never had a real gun in his hands in his life. . . .

'You will release ze senor Pennington pleez,' said the Kid firmly, 'otherwise it will be my pleasure, to—ah—eliminate you.'

In a way this was the crowning moment of his life. To be actually using the fascinating term 'eliminate' in real earnest, face to face with the real thing, seemed like a dream to the Kid. It was an unexpectedly blissful turn of events, marred only by Bishop's size and proximity and the ferocious glare of his eyes. The Kid, swallowing, admitted to his immortal soul that there was a lot to recommend a seat in the stalls at the 'Bughouse' in Apuna.

Bishop laughed roughly.

'You blockhead. That gun isn't loaded.'

'Then, if you haf no objection, senor,' said the Kid, who was only half silly, 'I will pull ze trigger, yes.'

The explanation I make to myself of how this works in the total context of the narrative is as follows. The Kid's role at this point in the story (little guy bravely rescuing victims from big guy) is a cliché. But the Kid's fan-

---

* Can one dismiss the Kid simply as an unreal comic device? After completing this note I read of a young Maori convicted of armed robbery who, it was explained to the Court, lived by the fantasy that he was New Zealand's Ned Kelly.

tasy role as Mexican bandit makes him a parody of his actual role in the story. The victims are not rescued by a cliché, but from one, by an injection of comedy which mocks the rescue at the same time that it allows it to be satisfactorily concluded. The reader's innocent appetite for sensational narrative and his critical intelligence are simultaneously satisfied. To see this clearly one need only remove the Kid's fantastic garb, his Mexican accent, and the other comic associations that already attach to him, turn him into a Worthy Member of a Noble Race, and rewrite the passage 'straight':

'I'm a good shot, Bishop.'
It wasn't true, but Tui Porano knew there were times when a white lie didn't go amiss.
'Release Pennington. Otherwise . . .' He nodded at the rifle.
He was scared. Bishop was awfully big and awfully close and his eyes blazed ferociously. Tui Porano would rather have been watching it all happening at the 'Bughouse' at Apuna. He wasn't enjoying himself.
Bishop laughed roughly.
'You blockhead. The gun isn't loaded.'
'In that case,' Tui Porano said, 'you won't mind if I pull the trigger.'

As Mr Morrieson has written it the effect is totally different. It is as though the melodrama of (for example) Maurice Gee's 'The Losers' or 'The Eleventh Holiday' had been invaded by comedy. Evil is defeated, and not by Wooden Virtue out of Blind Faith, but by an eruption of rebellious imagination. Something rich and strange has been made out of a situation so trite in its possibilities that few writers with any pretensions would have dared to touch it.

E. M. Forster says regretfully (I quote approximately) 'Oh dear yes. I'm afraid the novel must tell a story.' Mr Morrieson enjoys telling a story and tells one at least as grippingly as any novelist we have had. I suspect, even, that he is only fitfully conscious of doing more, and that all the rest happens largely by instinct. It is this absorption in narrative that keeps him from self-consciousness and allows his imagination to throw up casually such delightful touches as the picture of a white horse and a black horse in a terrible storm which, in *Came a Hot Friday*, turns up half a dozen times as the sole adornment of half a dozen different rooms in the same town.

Narrative alone will not make a novel. Static fiction, on the other hand, even when it is as brilliantly executed as Joyce's *Ulysses*, is always in danger of affecting the reader like a woman who goes to a great deal of trouble to look beautiful and to preserve her virginity. What is the mystery by which a writer can make his river run faster at the same time that it broadens and deepens? The question is rhetorical. There is no 'technical' answer because there is no substitute for imagination and no way of making imagination work if it can't or won't.

I don't suppose it needs to be spelled out that even after everything that is snobbish in one's initial resistance to these novels has been swamped and borne away on the tide of narrative one is conscious nonetheless that many of the finer possibilities of fiction remain unrealized in them. They are not seriously to be measured against those master works which happen to mark the route by which I came to them. But neither are their merits to be accounted for solely by the word narrative. Each of them seems to grow organically and completely from a single germ of imagination, so that no part is extraneous, no part unconnected with or independent of its genesis. In this, as in their peculiar colour and texture, Mr Morrieson's novels are like the best of David Ballantyne's (*Sydney Bridge Upside Down* and *The Scarecrow* might have come from the same stable) and Mr Ballantyne is another writer whose talents have received less notice than they deserve.

This organic force gives a writer great confidence. It relieves him of questions and doubts, makes him happy to take up his pen and reluctant to put it down, and gives him something of the recklessness and daring of a boy on a powerful motorbike. The result is the kind of gusto everywhere present in Mr Morrieson's work—and as the word occurs to me I recall that it was the one Matthew Arnold used when he wrote in praise of Keats: 'this magic, this indescribable gusto in the voice'.

We are continually being reminded, and forgetting, that Art makes its own rules. I am grateful to the man from Hawera for reminding me again.

MAURICE DUGGAN:
LANGUAGE IS HUMANITY

If I have succeeded, as I think I have, in tracking down all of Maurice Duggan's published stories there were exactly thirty of them in thirty years (1945-75, dating them by their first appearance in print), twenty collected into his three published books, ten uncollected. The symmetry is misleading if it suggests a regular, plodding, dependable output, one story per year, which was not of course the way it happened. On the other hand, although Duggan's development was erratic and uncertain, beset by personal as well as by stylistic problems, he was fundamentally an orderly and methodical worker. There was always a tidiness, a symmetry, to his labours, so the pattern, however accidental, seems not inappropriate. And there is no unpublished fiction (apart from the unfinished novel, *Miss Bratby,* and a late fragment entitled 'Visiting Aunt Beth') because Duggan destroyed it all. When one writes about Duggan one writes essentially about what went into print.

Maurice Duggan was born in Auckland in 1922 and began writing at the age of nineteen, perhaps partly in compensation for the life of action which osteomyelitis and subsequent amputation of a leg denied him—action in the early 1940s and at the age Duggan then was meaning of course the war, 'active service overseas'. Though nothing gave him more satisfaction or contentment than writing, it never came easily—could not, because the demands he made upon himself were so large. In a letter undated but probably written in 1948, he told his mentor, Frank Sargeson, 'the vast gap between what I say and what I want even my conversation to mean is some-

This is the text of the introduction to Maurice Duggan's *Collected Stories* published by Auckland University Press and Oxford University Press.

thing that worries me'. Words could too easily be a substitute for perception and observation, drawing too much attention to themselves. He
learned (as he reflected in 1966, looking back on his early years as a writer)
that he had to find a subject which 'moved me strongly enough to force me
away from what had become a habit of rhetoric. If it was to be strong it had
to be simple; the language must be a focusing glass and not, as had up to
now been the case, a sort of bejewelled and empty casket'.[1]

Duggan's other problem was that he was not in the ordinary sense a story
teller. In conversation he was fond of quoting E. M. Forster's 'Yes—oh
dear yes—the novel tells a story'.[2] Narrative ('this low, atavistic form'
Forster calls it in the same passage) was the element in fiction which interested Duggan least. Modern fictional practice had shown that it could
be very largely dispensed with—and he was well aware of Joyce as a kind of
liberator. But narrative is not only a carrot to draw the reader on. It is also
for the writer a guiding hand, a determinant of what details are relevant
and what are not. It is the desire to get nearer to life as it really is that
makes the writer wish to shed it altogether, but the writer who dispenses
with it is like the sailor who navigates without charts or instruments. He
may make exciting discoveries—or he may simply lose his way.

Finally, and not unrelated to the question of narrative, there is the problem of length. That there is something called a novel, distinct from
something shorter called a novella, distinct again from the short story,
which in turn is not to be confused with a sketch—these are artificial
distinctions imposed largely by the conventions of publishing. Most
periodicals which publish fiction can use a short story but not a novella—
which is to say ten pages but not forty. Publishers want novels, but what is
the right length varies from one period to another according to the
economics of book publishing. For the writer, on the other hand, there is
the fiction he wants to write, and its proper length is determined internally. Like Katherine Mansfield, Duggan was always hoping to complete and
publish a novel. Like her, he never succeeded, and the failure can be seen
in both cases as a kind of artistic scrupulousness.

Style, narrative, length—these are Duggan's problems, I think, from his
earliest to his latest work. They are not matters which worry the writer
who is content to repeat the patterns and idioms laid down in the market
place and looked for by undemanding readers. But they are the fundamental problems of fiction if it is to be practised as a conscious art; and it is his
constant wrestling with them that makes Duggan something of a writers'
writer.

Although Duggan said in 1966 that the 'eight or nine pieces' he had
published before those that went into his first book, *Immanuel's Land*
(1956), were 'juvenilia' which deserved 'their deep obscurity in discon-
tinued publications',[3] it seems to me that all have merit and deserve

republication, the weakest being perhaps 'Notes on an Abstract Arachnid',[4] a story exhibiting the 'habit of rhetoric' he spoke of in his 'Beginnings' article, and the 'Conversation Piece' published in 1947 in which he guys Hemingway in a Hemingway style. Those nine stories show a slow and painstaking exploration of the fictional mode leading towards 'Six Place Names and a Girl', his tenth published piece, the first to go into *Landfall*, the earliest to be collected, which he clearly saw as a breakthrough because it taught him that in order for the language to be simplified, the subject had to be close to him. It was 'perhaps . . . less a story than a prose celebration of a topography and a time that, in rediscovery and re-creation, moved me strongly enough to force me away from what had become a habit of rhetoric'.

'Perhaps less a story than a prose celebration': there Duggan describes a good deal of his own fiction at its best. 'Six Place Names . . .' also taught him that there was no need to push the material falsely into the shape of a 'story'. Commending a review of Sargeson's in December 1950 he wrote in a letter '. . . the Lawrence quote I like, especially that about ". . . no consecutive thread. Only the laconic courage of experience." . . . That has always been my difficulty, solved in part by the *Place Names*, the problem of hanging whatever it is on the conventional peg, finding the machinery'. 'Six Place Names . . .', it is worth noting, is his first use of an experience which was re-used in 'Along Rideout Road that Summer'.

It seemed, then, that the material had to be in some way autobiographical if he was to achieve clarity of style, and it was this recognition that governed his writing during his two years in England[5] when he wrote most of the stories in *Immanuel's Land*. Like Mansfield, Duggan wrote some of his best fiction by using childhood in retrospect, the focus of a distant recall providing a principle of limitation, imposing shape. Like her he soon saw the possibility that such pieces, linked, might make a novel; and like her he had to recognize that to force the linkage would be to impose something artificial. His Lenihans, like her Burnells, compose a fictional world, the stories connected yet discrete. Brief pieces like 'A Small Story' and 'Race Day' show Duggan's earliest use of this family material. A longer story like 'Chapter' survives I think (hence the title and the lack of an enclosing focus) from the first of at least two attempts to make a Lenihan novel of prefabricated sections. 'Chapter' was in draft as early as 1951, but it appears first in print in 1955, signifying, I suspect, the abandonment in that year of plans for a novel, and thus finally releasing sufficient completed material to permit the publication of the first collection of stories which duly appeared in 1956.

Immanuel's Land contains the stories for which Duggan is probably still best known,[6] among them being some of the most perfect short fictions written by a New Zealander (my own choices would include 'In Youth is

Pleasure' and 'A Small Story'). The subjects—small agonizing crises and dramas in the family and school life of the child and adolescent—are of perennial interest; and in most of them there is no attempt to push beyond the limits of the short form. Inside those limits Duggan's focus is consistent and his control of word and nuance perfect. He achieves his moments of dramatic intensity without strain or falsification. These stories are lucid and utterly authentic.

One can see, however, that the brevity of the form and the narrow focus on childhood experience must have seemed constrictions he would sooner or later want to break out of. Only one item, 'Voyage', deals with fully adult experience, and it is nearer to a travel diary than fiction. Yet Duggan's problem was that his successes and failures as a writer thus far had more or less convinced him that his fiction if it was to succeed had to be a reworking of personal experience. Like so many of our writers (perhaps one should say simply, of modern writers) he suffered from what is no doubt a perfectly proper, but also distinctly limiting, inhibition about stepping far outside the bounds of his own first-hand knowledge; and this in turn made him nervous about using up what he referred to (deriving the phrase from Somerset Maugham) as his 'imaginative capital'.[7] If one used a particular life experience once he believed it would be difficult to use it again, and therefore the use had to be successful or the material would be wasted.

So for a time Duggan returned to that safely certain area of childhood experience, but attempting to make more of it. With his first book published he applied himself to the Lenihan material in the hope of quarrying blocks from it that would make a novel. It was even given the characteristically Duggan working title, *Along the Poisoned River.* There is a gap of three years from June 1955 during which nothing of his appeared in periodicals; then in July 1958 the story later called 'The Deposition' appeared in *Numbers* under the title 'Book One: A Fragment of a Work Abandoned'. 'The Departure' appeared in *Image* in April of the following year. It was not merely *Along the Poisoned River* that had been abandoned. With those stories Duggan's use of the Lenihan family comes to an end.

The second collection, *Summer in the Gravel Pit* (1965) is more various than the first. It prints the last of those Lenihan sections, together with three stories brought forward from *Immanuel's Land,* and some more recent stories. There is some truth in Duggan's statement that with the abandonment of *Along the Poisoned River* 'I ceased to be subject'.[8] It is only half true however. Though he allows himself freedom to invent, and a variety of disguises, Duggan and the events of Duggan's life are, I believe, somewhere recognizable in almost everything he wrote, the obvious exception perhaps being 'Blues for Miss Laverty'.

'Blues for Miss Laverty' was written during his most productive year, 1960, when he held the Burns fellowship at Otago University, and I am fairly certain I remember him telling me that it came to be written as follows. He was asked to address the Literary Society and prepared a talk in which he illustrated some of the problems of fiction by imagining an author writing about a music teacher, past her prime, who drank too much. As he thought out and expounded the problems such a fictional exercise might involve, and their solutions, he began to ask himself why the idea should be wasted. Why should he not write the story himself?—which he did.[9] It was published in *Landfall*, reprinted in *Landfall Country*, and chosen for Duggan's first London publication, his share in the Hutchinson New Authors collection *Short Story One*. Both there and in *Summer in the Gravel Pit* it was well-reviewed, singled out by at least two reviewers[10] as Duggan's best story up to 1965. This is not a judgement with which I can agree. Duggan's Miss Laverty is an advance on Mansfield's Miss Brill; but there is about both of them an air of contrivance. My own preference is for the works that are nearer to Duggan's experience, or which make room for the Duggan persona. In 'Blues for Miss Laverty' (as in one or two other pieces in the second collection) he shows he can turn his hand to what he called 'conventional fiction' with professionalism and polish; but there is something a little flat in the writing and a lack of total authenticity in the human material.

Much more remarkable in the *Summer in the Gravel Pit* collection is 'Along Rideout Road that Summer', a story which had a genesis not unlike that of 'Blues for Miss Laverty'. Duggan spent a brief period in 1959 at Auckland Teachers College and wrote for the 1960 issue of the College magazine, *Manuka*, an article entitled 'Only Connect (a presumptuous note on the teaching of English literature)'. It was a plea for a proper place to be given to the reading of New Zealand writing in schools. In other subjects, Duggan argued, teaching began with the known and the familiar. In teaching literature we began with works remote from us and consequently failed 'to establish the relationship between life and art', drove in fact 'a wedge between'.[11] Duggan recalled his own experience of lessons in English literature as 'a case of looking one way and rowing another', and described himself ('I over-dramatise, of course') 'dazed' as he staggered from school into a world which in no way matched the preparation those lessons had given him.

But after a time I did recover the use of my wits. I came to consciousness, to put it so, on Puti Huia's broken farm. I have clear memory of driving a battered old Ferguson tractor, in a paper chase of sea-gulls; and I can hear myself, now, chanting above the racket of the motor:

> A damsel with a dulcimer
> In a vision once I saw:
> It was an Abyssinian maid,
> And on her dulcimer she played,
> Singing of Mount Abora.

And the absurdity of it struck me. Twice five miles of fertile ground might have been Puti's wild dream; but the reality was something different—ruined acres, sagging fences, sodden ground. His inheritance and mine; for whatever it was that we looked upon, erosion and neglect, it was the reality, and to relate it to the English regional novel, to put Puti Huia, so to speak, into the gaiters and a hacking jacket and a peaked cap, was something I could not accomplish. The golden moments of English Literature, of nightingales and daffy-down-dillies paid no attention to this infestation of buttercup, these squabbling gulls, that hawk over the pasture.

Only connect, indeed! It was not easy. I looked up from my chanting, raised my eyes from the damsel with the dulcimer to meet the loitering figure of Maka Huia, bright ribbons trailing from . . . her ukulele.

Here is the outline sketch for, and the governing theme of, 'Along Rideout Road that Summer'. Puti Huia in the article becomes Puti Hohepa in the story; Maka becomes Fanny; Duggan becomes Buster O'Leary; and the Ferguson tractor, the gulls, and the lines from 'old S.T.C.' remain. Referring to the *Manuka* article in a letter written to me in 1966 Duggan said 'clearly Rideout Road began here . . . I . . . wrote the story the following year [1961] when I first began copy writing after coming back from Dunedin'.[12]

It will be worth lingering on this story because it contains so much that is central to Duggan's life and fiction. Three areas of experience are brought together: the sense of place, the experience of love, and the articulation of these through language. On all three the sense of self is constructed, a sense which may collapse if it is supported on falsifications. So many New Zealand writers have forced upon us that our dream of New Zealand is not true to reality (a section of Frank Sargeson's memoirs is called 'Third Class Country'), and Duggan is no exception. Here are not 'twice five miles of fertile ground' but Puti Hohepa's 'ruined acres'; no 'damsel with a dulcimer' but Fanny and her ukulele. Where Duggan differs from the brutal realists who preceded him—differs in some of his stories, anyway, and notably in this one—is the buoyancy, the gusto, the sheer pleasure he gets out of playing upon the disjunction between the real and the ideal. It is after all the ideal which is absurd. On Puti Hohepa's 'ruined acres' Buster O'Leary is to discover himself, to recognize the closeness to and distance from his father, and to experience love. It is a story about being 'almost happy' (the phrase is repeated at intervals) and the implication is clear: 'almost' is as near to 'happy' as we are likely to get.

The affirmation is strong. But the negatives are equally clear. For

Buster, 'a bookish lad', that 'discrepancy between the real and the written' is at once a torment and a sense of richness. For him there is an extra dimension to experience which those around him do not and will not recognize. ('Of course I understood immediately that these were not matters I was destined to debate with Fanny Hohepa'). For him the whole of the experience is cast in a golden glow which is at once the recognition that this is a kind of Eden he has stumbled on, and that, having already partaken of the fruit of the tree of knowledge, he has arrived there too late. Those commentaries which moralize the story, suggesting that it is meant to contrast Buster's moral failure with wholesome Maori values, misrepresent it by failing to catch either its central point or the full rich—and I should say *generous*—flavour of its governing tone.[13] Buster is young and unformed; but Duggan identifies with him and looks back on him with indulgence and nostalgia. It is sad that Buster must move on, but he must. Fanny is 'spontaneous and natural'; Buster is full of 'half-baked verbosity and conceit'—and in that contrast Duggan very likely had in mind the lines in which Yeats complains of his literary labours:

> The fascination of what's difficult
> Has dried the sap out of my veins, and rent
> Spontaneous joy and natural content
> Out of my heart.

She is 'too good' for Buster; 'too good by half'—it is his place to accept and repeat Puti Hohepa's judgement, which he does. It is ours to recognize that in some respects she is not good enough. He is already 'a bookish lad' when he arrives; and a society of almost total inarticulacy, though innocent and good in its way, is less than the fulfilment of one's humanity.

> Gooday. How are you?
> All right.
> I'm Buster O'Leary.
> I'm Fanny Hohepa.
> Yair, I know.
> It's hot.
> It's hot right enough.

—and so on. 'A genuine crumpy conversation' Buster observes; and in that gibe at a fellow-author (Barry Crump) Duggan dissociates himself from the line of New Zealand fiction which has gone in for the realism of inarticulacy.

It is the critics, not Buster, who have sentimentalized Puti Hohepa. What Buster observes and complains of is Puti's lack of speech. Buster is caught between the horror of his father's puritan eloquence ('orator-general to the dying afternoon') and Fanny's father's silence ('Maybe the chocolate old bastard was dumb, eh?'); between 'We were silent through dinner: we were always silent' at the Hohepas', and 'home where all hell lay between the soup and the sweet'. But what distresses Buster more is that when the Maori father does speak he reveals a lack of comprehension almost as deep as that of the puritan pakeha. He lacks the puritanism; but he is just as capable of unthinking pieties. 'A boy shouldn't hate his father'. In fact Buster has discovered love for his father—discovered it in the course of that incomparable scene (surely one of the richest in all New Zealand fiction) when Mr O'Leary empties his wrath upon the silent backs of his son and the Hohepas, and then departs:

> Silence. Light lovely and fannygold over the pasture; shreds of mist by the river deepening to rose. My father's hard leather soles rattled harshly on the bare boards like rim-shots. The mad figure of him went black as a bug out over the lawn, out over the loamy furrows where the tongue of ploughed field invaded the home paddock, all my doing, spurning in his violence anything less than this direct and abrupt charge towards the waiting car. Fanny's hand touched my arm again and for a moment I was caught in a passion of sympathy for him, something as solid as grief and love, an impossible pairing of devotion and despair. The landscape flooded with sadness as I watched the scuttling, black, ignominious figure hurdling the fresh earth, the waving arms, seemingly scattering broadcast the white and shying gulls, his head bobbing on his shoulders, as he narrowed into distance.

The Buster who finds himself capable of this 'impossible pairing of devotion and despair' hardly deserves the censoriousness with which the critics have treated him. Nor is there any justification in Duggan's tone for censure.

It would take many notes to unfold the literary jokes and references with which this story is peppered—and that would be to deprive readers of the pleasures of discovery. One example will serve:

> She is too good for you.
> It was said clearly enough, offered without threat and as just comment, while I was bent double stripping old Daisy or Pride of the Plains or Rose of Sharon after the cups came off. I stopped what I was doing, looked sideways until I could see the tops of his boots, gazed on *Marathon*, and then turned back, dried off all four tits and let the cow out into the race where, taking the legrope with her, she squittered off wild in the eyes.

The cowshed observations are exact and economical,[14] even down to the cow 'squittering' off down the race 'wild in the eyes'. To the Hohepas there is nothing odd about calling their cows Daisy, or Pride of the Plains, or Rose of Sharon, and they are not aware that these are faint echoes of a British pastoral tradition. But for Buster the whole cultural inheritance continues to reverberate around him, so that we have the authentic rural detail common in much New Zealand fiction given an added dimension.

Buster, looking sideways while he strips, 'gazed on *Marathon*', 'Marathon' being presumably the brand name on the top flap of Puti Hohepa's gumboots; and at the same time we are nudged towards remembering Byron's lines:

> The mountains look on Marathon —
> And Marathon looks on the sea;
> And musing there an hour alone
> I dreamed that Greece might still be free.[15]

The boy whose mind moves from the damsel with the dulcimer to Fanny with her ukulele moves here from her father's gumboots to Byron's romantic dream of a liberated Greece; and all this is laid over, or under, a story which makes perfect sense if the literary allusions go unnoticed—just as we may live in our society without recognizing all those details which form links back to its origins in the culture of Europe.

Again and again in his stories Duggan repudiates the inherited puritanism while at the same time affirming and celebrating those aspects of the parent cultures without which life and fiction both must lack a dimension. In 'Along Rideout Road that Summer' he rewrites the New Zealander's conventional rural idyll, investing it with a rare depth of feeling, and at the same time refusing to put behind him those literary/intellectual preoccupations which so many New Zealand writers have felt compelled to shed in the effort to achieve a true representation.

Duggan was born and brought up in New Zealand but from his earliest years he must have been conscious of his parents' alien accents and distant loyalties. A sense of being in some degree Irish (Catholic Irish, but he renounced the Catholicism) was something he never lost, and it becomes an important aspect of his major characters and of his prose as well. No one who was not of it could have characterized it so beautifully, or with such colourful, ambiguous malice:

The sad Irish bravura; the drear Irish Catholicism; the Irish syndrome—booze, melancholy and guilt; the pointless, loud pride—for what had they to be proud of, each man a Joseph in his coat of bright verbs?; the intolerance, the low superstition; the peculiarly Irish deceit.[16]

It would require an Irish accent to make the most of that, as it would to render the nuances of the exchange between Mr Lenihan and his new housekeeper in 'The Deposition':[17]

'What part of the old country is it you are from?' Mr Lenihan said.
'Belfast,' Mrs Byrne said.
'Belfast?' Mr Lenihan said. 'Now we're from another part, Mrs Lenihan and I:

nearer Dublin you might say, not to cross you with names that don't matter. I'm
the wrong one to want to revive dead squabbles. I hope you've no strong feelings
yourself.'

'I leave that to those that can afford them,' Mrs Byrne said, rather tartly, rather
obscurely. 'I never heard of much good coming of the thing.'

'Good.' Mr Lenihan said. 'We'll not cross words there then.'

The wage he offered her was generous and Mrs Byrne acknowledged it. He could
afford it, he told her, and smiled at the parody.

It is not surprising that two of Duggan's earliest published stories appeared in Eire in a periodical called *Irish Writing.*

Duggan indicates in his 'Beginnings' article that he left school at thirteen
(or perhaps fourteen, the statement is ambiguous), but if that is so he left
with some competence in Latin; and he was able to gain provisional admis-
sion to the university in 1947 and to pass with credit four units (eight
papers) towards a B.A. In that year he wrote for *Kiwi,* the literary annual
of the Auckland University College, and in 1948 he edited it, publishing,
as well as the usual student work, stories, poems and articles by a number
of established writers who had connexions with the College. By this time
he was married, recognized as a promising young writer, living on the
North Shore and included among the group there who gathered around
Frank Sargeson. At the end of the decade he went abroad for the two years
in England and Europe which were to be his only period away from New
Zealand.

For much of the fifties decade, after his precipitate return from Spain,
Duggan was a semi-invalid, recovering from tuberculosis. Once he was fit
for employment he went into advertising, which he hated and at which he
was brilliantly successful. But before that came the award of the Burns
Fellowship in 1960, which he never tired of saying was by far his most productive year.

So it was; but that is not how it felt at least for the first eight months during which, his letters show, he continued grinding away at his novel, *Miss
Bratby,* begun earlier (and to be taken up for brief periods during at least
six more years) without ever feeling that it was coming to life. In April
came the 'Miss Laverty' interlude described above—then back to what he
called in one letter 'the cold corpse of Miss Bratby', trying by desperate application to revive her, or to give her a kind of life she had never possessed.
By August he was announcing he had finished a first draft, but that he had
read it through 'in disgust and despair'. 'God knows where the draught is
coming from but it blows through the holes and gaps in the poor thin story
like a blast from the arse-end of a vacuum cleaner'.[18] At the same time he
was reading *The Backward Sex*, deciding that he was 'profoundly
uninterested in the conventional novel' which Cross's book represented,[19]
and fearing that that might be all he had achieved with *Miss Bratby*. What

he had so far written, he decided, was 'the frame only, and all the denseness, complication, only pencilled in'.[20]

It is in this state of despair with what he had achieved that he announced the beginning of something new, described as 'a sort of contrapuntal thing to Miss B.'[21] *Miss Bratby* must now 'lie and wait while I burst away down another cul de sac in search of the ineffable'.[22] By October he is able to say he has 'a dozen "brilliant" but obscure pages as a beginning to something at the moment indescribable, puzzling and strictly non-commercial'.[23]

Undoubtedly the piece described here as 'contrapuntal' to *Miss Bratby*, conceived in despair and in rejection of 'the conventional novel', is 'Riley's Handbook'. It is here that Duggan gets himself into the story in the best possible way—not by a literal recital of events, facts and circumstances,[24] but by the instrument of the living voice. Riley is a persona, preposterous, exaggerated, but a spacious enough character, and with a flow of language copious enough, to permit expression of the full linguistic and imaginative range of the writer Duggan was. The accumulated despair of months of wasted effort, and a sense of confinement in the merely conventional, were necessary for this breakout to occur. Riley may have been 'strictly non-commercial'; but it was surely an important new development in the history of our fiction.

That is very nearly the end of the story, as a study of the bibliography at the back of his *Collected Stories* shows. *Summer in the Gravel Pit* came out in London in 1965 but everything in it (with the possible exception of 'For the Love of Rupert' which I have not been able to date) had been written by 1961—and so had 'Riley's Handbook', which was not collected until 1970. In 1966 Duggan was awarded the Government Scholarship in Letters. He took time away from advertising, and although it did not give him a full year he must have found time either to write or to finish writing the two stories which were both published in *Landfall* during 1967, 'O'Leary's Orchard' and 'An Appetite for Flowers'. These were put together with 'Riley's Handbook' to make Duggan's third collection, *O'Leary's Orchard*, published in 1970.

The two stories of 1967 are nearer to the method of what Duggan called 'the conventional novel', and one may wonder why he retreated from what he had achieved in 'Riley's Handbook'. He had followed up the first person dramatic monologue style of 'Riley . . .' in 'Along Rideout Road that Summer', but in a much more open and available way. 'Riley's Handbook' was his most uncompromising fiction, seventy-five pages in length, and few concessions to that 'low atavistic' appetite for a story. It is not easy reading; it could never be a widely popular work. As Riley says:

It's the proper job we're after, here. It's enough, all said, to be sweating over making something out of nothing. I'm not in the amusement racket.

But I believe it is Duggan's most important and impressive work, and I think he himself must have known that it was. If he retreated from it, it may have been for no other reason than that he got little encouragement to repeat it.

I am far from wanting to suggest that 'An Appetite for Flowers' and 'O'Leary's Orchard' are unworthy companion pieces for 'Riley's Handbook'. They are both beautifully made and full of Duggan felicities. The novella 'O'Leary's Orchard' in particular is a good deal more than a comedy of manners, with its wry detached tolerant absolving view of the love of young girl and older man, and of the 'discrepancies of May and December'. Its observations draw hard enough on experience; and the pathos of the farewell of Gambo and Isabel is earned by all that has gone before:

> He had lied. He would miss her more than that. His life had been a preparation for a sense of loss. He had missed her often enough already, over the years. It would continue, an indulgence of himself, O'Leary's O of regret, unvoiced. It was what his life was fashioned to contain, this gentle fabrication, this bright figment.

Too much of our fiction, or of that part of it written by men, has lacked either the art or the will to deal with such subtleties of feeling. And if I am conscious in myself of some final critical affirmation held back from such a finely crafted story it is only perhaps because the Jamesian circumlocutions of the prose are not always and everywhere matched by a Jamesian complexity of situation, relationship, and feeling. In 'Riley's Handbook', on the other hand, the language is unwaveringly charged and supercharged with a sense of the character of Riley and with the rich reality of the pub he occupies and the people he shares it with.

As he was to do again in 'Along Rideout Road . . .', Duggan returned in 'Riley's Handbook' to some of that 'imaginative capital' which had in fact (contrary to his own notion of what was possible in fiction) been used before. The character of Riley is close to Duggan—the artist (Riley is a painter) with the tattered lung, one-eyed instead of one-legged, and with other qualities in common. In the Lenihan stories Duggan had already used more than once the subject of the traumatic death of a long-silent and melancholic mother, and her quick replacement by a hated stepmother. In 'Riley's Handbook' the desperate child-love that has turned to resentment and pain is directed in a wild comic/tragic frenzy against the corpse of Riley's long-dead mother, imagined resolving in its grave under the pines. What makes it so much more than rant (or that 'empty rhetoric' Duggan had laboured to be rid of) is the quality and force of repressed love that comes through it, making the most bitter abuse hurled at the dead 'Pegeen' seem shot through with beauty. The great crime he holds against her is to have given birth to him.

'Riley's Handbook' is a superlatively rewarding work to anyone who will give it the patience it deserves. Fully confronted, not skimmed or read with detachment, seen for what it is, it has the extravagance of genius on the brink of the abyss. It is a beautiful, funny, terrifying display. There is simply no work of fiction by a New Zealander in which the language (as Yeats might have said) is so packed in salt:

What was it? What dream of a fading glory and aristocratic demise prompted the siting of this pisgah pub, in the good old days when hope was dead and stinking, here, on the clay hillroad as it must have been. Spanned and straining the drayhorses dragging foot by foot from the dark, the flowerspiced dark, the torch, the carriagelamp, the gleam of brasswork, the Monday Wednesday Saturday news. Stovepipe hats in the stovepipe dark, hup, hupatit, over and on to new settlings over impossible roads. And doubtless, christ, the crying of the child waking neglected to the rumble and the horsesmell, the spice of darkened flowers and the dark like a coffining.

. . .

The reverend crow come to spoil my afternoon with his shadow, rapping like a discreet, a furtive coffinwood pecker at the side hatch for his twiceweekly bottle less the tenpercent tithing. Father Royle, dollman in his armozeen smock, dream pedlar in his driving gloves, the parish zephyr, holy purveyor of toy concepts and sugar-coated reassurances for ingrown adults afraid of their dark and their humanity. I'll say what I like. Hysteria and all. We don't care for each other, the strong conflict-ing odours. He sniffs at the reek of my early years and present fumings and I at the noisome hypothesis of his heavenly futurities and superstitions. I need no Royle rag doll father. Riley liealone. I'll settle, deep and in time, for the nothing that's coming to me. With pleasure.

. . .

Back through the millennia to the days and weepings of my youth, which is but another and the same, the dark head bent in darkness at the door, the shut door and locked, of a Pegeen raging in silent inconsolable melancholy. Did I imbibe my pres-ent at that past breast in the thirty seconds before she thrust me from her in repul-sion? Was I in that frequent vigil at that dark door listening to nothing less than a description—silence, breath, a smell of candlewax—of my future now all but past?

. . .

Nan, bigmatron, vastly embalmed in ciclatoun heaves into view, plumps slowly into the cane chair like a blancmange into its mould and on the shadowed inward corner of the verandah, newly visible because of the cant of my bed like a fucking precipice at the head, takes up the needlework recommended by medical wisdom as limbering to the finger and the fist. Her smile has gone cockeyed; her mouth has come unclipped at the corner. She swells, smiling as if at the morbid humour of it, above the folds of thread-starred linen, above the tonic therapy of wilful soft hands barely her own in their responses, embroidering her winding sheet.

Most of the last eight years of Duggan's life were used up in a battle against alcoholism which by 1973 he had finally, it seemed, defeated, but only in time to discover that he was suffering from cancer. ('And the nurse said "Drink this" ' had been the refrain of his 'Beginnings' article in 1966.) He had just begun to write again, and when he died in December 1974 he left behind a single item of fiction, unfinished perhaps yet curiously complete, 'The Magsman Miscellany', which seems a new and unexpected development, revealing Duggan's tenacious character as an artist, his capacity to force himself through narrow gaps into new and open territory.

> We sat together at one summer's end,
> That beautiful mild woman, your close friend,
> And you and I, and talked of poetry.
> I said, 'A line will take us hours maybe;
> Yet if it does not seem a moment's thought,
> Our stitching and unstitching has been naught.
> Better go down upon your marrow-bones
> And scrub a kitchen pavement, or break stones
> Like an old pauper, in all kinds of weather;
> For to articulate sweet sounds together
> Is to work harder than all these, and yet
> Be thought an idler by the noisy set. . . .[25]

Maurice Duggan always seemed a heroic figure, fighting on one front his battle with language ('the intolerable wrestle with words and meanings' Eliot calls it), and on the other the battle with life itself, made so much more desperate in his case by a succession of medical problems. I have described his development in technical terms because my impression is that that is how Duggan himself saw it. Each new story involved a high level of consciousness, of decision-making. But of course the results had to be such that the 'stitching and unstitching' did not show. A paragraph in the first section of 'Voyage' reads:

Sunk at its moorings a houseboat lay in water that covered all but one corner of the tilted gable and the top of a doorway, a dark rectangular cave. In the liquid shadow a striped pillow floated by a head of flaxen hair spread on tide. The damp hair weaved and shifted on the broken current. One waited some Ophelia, some Osyth reading her ancient book, embowered in that blistered paint, shrined in those waterlogged boards, to float from the dark with each shift of the tide. Brown leaves drifting enticed her out under the bare witchfingers of the hanging willows that plucked at her weeded hair. But only a rope end washed from the sunken doorway.

Could anyone, coming on that beautiful mixture of fact and fantasy (fantasy playing on fact, but the fact clearly distinguished) have guessed that the penultimate sentence 'took . . . three days, three days to get'?[26] The labour has been absorbed into the achieved felicity.

'Le style, c'est l'homme'. A conscious stylist beset by illness might suggest some frail aesthete, and again that would be totally misleading. Duggan was a big man, powerfully built, with a strong constitution, large appetites, recklessness, a sense of humour, high intelligence, a beautiful rich speaking voice (little of the obvious Kiwi in his accent), distinctly middle-class manners, and a kind of delicacy that was almost (in our old stereotypes) 'feminine'. He was a marvellous talker, great company while he remained sober and for some time after, the most modest and least prickly of all the writers I have known. All these elements of his personality find counterparts in his style. Language was his material as surely as the potter's is clay, and if he struggled with it it was always to get into it more and more of his own sense of life, which at its most heightened moments had somehow to mix the comedy and the pathos.

Much of New Zealand fiction before Duggan was devoted to a mixture of documentary and moralizing. These are legitimate pursuits, but the language of fiction can do other, and more. In a letter to a very young poet, written in the last year of his life, Duggan said:

I was intrigued by Mary's remark about students going to university (simply?) to learn a language, or two: I think she was teasing me. Because what other reason would there be for going, or in what else could a culture be embalmed, enfolded or expressed? Language is humanity; humanity is language. All knowledge has to have this framework; our vital myths are made of it. But you know this; all you have to do now is find it out.[27]

'Language is humanity'. No New Zealand writer has been more conscious of this, or more conscious that he worked in a frontier society where language and humanity were in danger of atrophying together. In the final separation of Fanny Hohepa and Buster O'Leary in 'Along Rideout Road that Summer' the full resources of Duggan's style are given to the pathos of a moment in which a great deal is felt but since nothing is said, the feeling itself becomes uncertain:

And in the end, beginning my sentence with a happy conjunction, I held her indistinct, dark head. We stayed so for a minute, together and parting as always, with me tumbling down upon her the mute dilemma my mind then pretended to resolve and she offering no restraint, no argument better than the dark oblivion of her face.

Duggan was not content to make language either a mirror, or a vehicle for ideas; nor did he want to put it to decorative use. If he worked at something we call 'style', attempting both to heighten it and at the same time to rid it of empty flourishes, it was because through style, and through it alone, was to be transmitted something approaching the fulness of the writer's sense of life.

DAVID BALLANTYNE: WHIMSICAL LOSERS

David Ballantyne is in his middle fifties and has published six books—five novels and a collection of short stories. Only three have been reviewed in *Landfall*. *The Cunninghams* (1948) was reviewed unsympathetically, although not uncharitably, by R. M. Chapman in 1949; and again negatively, even angrily, by K. O. Arvidson when it was re-issued in 1963. *The Last Pioneer* (1963) was reviewed coolly (I don't quarrel with that) by R. A. Copland in the year of publication. And in the same year his stories, *And the Glory*, were reviewed second to Shadbolt's *Summer Fires and Winter Country* by Winston Rhodes, who almost allowed himself to recognize that Ballantyne's was the more authentic collection, but evidently couldn't quite believe the report of his critical senses. After that came what ought to have been seen as a new breakthrough in Ballantyne's career—first *A Friend of the Family* (1966), then *Sydney Bridge Upside Down* (1968). They passed largely unnoticed.

Possibly Charles Brasch's greatest single merit as an editor was that everything worthy of notice (everything, that is, except Ronald Hugh Morrieson) was reviewed. Ballantyne has not been reviewed in *Landfall* since Brasch retired; and he has never been noticed in *Islands*. Of course it is possible an editor may feel protective towards a writer who has had more than his share of brickbats, and nervous of handing him over to unpredictable reviewers. But no one does any kind of service to an author by ignoring him. Better an attack than silence. At least an attack can be answered.

There are two large gaps in the spacing of Ballantyne's production. His first novel appeared in New York when he was twenty-three—about the same age as Katherine Mansfield when she published her first collection of

First published in *Landfall* 132, December 1979.

stories. Mansfield took nine years to produce her second book; Ballantyne took fifteen. In his case the gap is not surprising. He had used up his material and would clearly have to live some more before he would have more to write.[1] But the interval must have been painful; and the second novel is rather a leaden affair, a return to the same ground as the first, but without the urgency, without the sureness of focus, without the simple patient confidence *The Cunninghams* has that the characters are known and worth knowing, that the story is moving at its own pace to a conclusion which will be significant beyond the bounds of the novel's small-town social realism. *The Cunninghams* is a young man's simple anagram for time and death.

The other long gap is between what was, I thought at the time it came out, Ballantyne's best, *Sydney Bridge Upside Down* (1968), and the new novel, *The Talkback Man*. Eleven years is a long gap for a man who has mastered his art. I don't think it is out of bounds to guess that some of it may have been spent in the kind of near-alcoholic despair which is comically yet vividly rendered in the character of Phil Rhodes, the talk-back man of the new book who long ago published a now-forgotten novel called *Driven*. At least Phil Rhodes's heroic (and losing) battle with the bottle is convincing enough to seem written from the inside.

A couple of other remarks will complete this glum survey of responses to Ballantyne's books. E. H. McCormick in his *New Zealand Literature: a Survey* gives brief but honorable mention to *The Cunninghams,* as do G. A. Wilkes and J. C. Reid in their *The Literatures of Australia and New Zealand.* M. H. Holcroft discusses it well and sympathetically in *Islands of Innocence* (1964). And Ballantyne had one consistently friendly reviewer in David Hall on the *Listener.* As a story writer he is represented in two of the three Oxford anthologies of *New Zealand Short Stories* (1954 and 1966, edited by Davin and Stead respectively). Apart from one or two newspaper reviews and a review by Dennis McEldowney in the *Listener,* I have not been able to find a word anywhere on *Sydney Bridge Upside Down.*

Perhaps Blair's phone call found him in the right mood that morning. Or at the right time of life. For Blair's voice made the past reverberate. He afterwards marvelled that his reply had begun to shape itself so swiftly. Years since he and Blair had spoken at length. Never more than casual meetings since, things of chance, wry words quickly spoken. He should have been more surprised. It was Monday morning too. . . .

There was an old man who lived on the edge of the world, and he had a horse called Sydney Bridge Upside Down. He was a scar-faced old man and his horse was a slow-moving bag of bones, and I start with this man and his horse because they were there for all the terrible happenings up the coast that summer. . . .

I would like to be able to explain to myself my confidence that I could never mistake the first of those openings for Ballantyne, nor the second for Shadbolt. There is a portentousness about the Shadbolt passage, a pregnant, orotund tone, as of a man with his thumbs in his braces, speaking 'significantly'. Clearly drama will follow. It is deliberately casual ('Years since he and Blair had . . .') but the more-than-colloquial keeps breaking in ('. . . spoken at length'). The off-the-cuff tone is belied by the counter-signals of literary effort ('For Blair's voice made . . .' where natural speech would demand 'Because . . .'; or the literary inversion of 'He afterwards marvelled . . .'). And then there is that characteristic Shadbolt lyric tremolo ('. . . things of chance, wry words quickly spoken') seeking to cash an emotional cheque before anything has been deposited in the account. These are strivings for effects of style that will be matched in the plot by artificial crises, implausible dénouements, melodrama.

The passage quoted is the opening of *Danger Zone*. By comparison, Ballantyne's opening to *Sydney Bridge Upside Down* is impeccable—the prose economically tailored to the limits of the statement made. (That there will be 'terrible happenings' is simply announced.) But transcending the limits of 'social realism' (which is as far as Ballantyne's critics have looked) there is a suggestion of fairy tale—'an old man who lived at the edge of the world', and 'a horse called Sydney Bridge Upside Down'. And there is the voice of the story-teller ('I start with this man') who in the second paragraph goes on:

> I start with Sam Phelps and Sydney Bridge Upside Down, but now I go to a cliff-top on a January day, a sunny afternoon, mid-afternoon. I was there with Dibs Kelly.

On the top of a very high cliff there is a fight between two boys near a tree which they agree is shallowly rooted and might fall down the cliff if you climbed it. At the bottom of the second page the fight reaches its climax:

> 'I'll dong you, boy!' he shouted.
> As he came in, I caught him, my feet in his stomach. He went flying, smacked the dead tree pretty hard. The tree did not fall over the cliff. Dibs Kelly did.

Has Dibs Kelly really gone over the cliff? Has he been killed? We will have to wait to find out. The next paragraph begins: 'I go back now to the beginning of that day, my brother and myself in pyjamas. . . .'

This is Ronald Hugh Morrieson-style narrative, but under perfect control.

In his *Paris Review* interview John Berryman lamented the lack in America of a literary culture to match that of Britain:

> We couldn't put out a thing like the *Times Literary Supplement*. We just don't have

it. Education at the élite level is better in England, humanistic education. . . . Cambridge, Oxford, London, and now the red-brick universities provide a much higher percentage of intelligent readers in the population—the kind of people who listen to the Third Programme and read the *Times Literary Supplement.* They are rather compact and form a body of opinion from which the reviewers both good and mediocre don't have to stand out very far.[2]

No doubt Berryman was unduly sanguine about the benefits of an English education, but one recognizes what he means. And if an American should feel this, how much more is it the case in New Zealand! One feels there is no firm critical ground on which to take a stand, that reviewers are subject to every wind that blows, and that even the occupants of teaching posts in our university English Departments, confronted with something local and new, are, with a few obvious and honourable exceptions, mostly babes in the sacred wood. In this climate of uncertainty portentousness is easily mistaken for the real thing; while a subtle voice—as Ballantyne's at its best undoubtedly is—goes unheard or undervalued.

There was a revealing case of this in the *Listener*'s recent review of *The Talkback Man.* It seemed clear that the reviewer had enjoyed the novel and that it had left her disposed to recommend it. But could anything simply enjoyable be *good*? Like so many of our reviewers she was ill-equipped for the job and much too busy to do any background reading. (She admitted to having read nothing else of Ballantyne's.) So she hedged her bets. The novel was readable; but it was 'lightweight' (twice), 'superficial':

. . . which removes it from the Great Literature stakes. But it's also free of affectation, lively and sometimes funny. It gives a very convincing portrait of a man on the edge of an alcoholic slide and a devastatingly accurate depiction of a certain slice of New Zealand life.[3]

All that and *superficial*? Wasn't this reviewer really fumbling her way towards the recognition that the book wasn't boring, and that she was glad of it? She even complained that Ballantyne might have been 'overlooked' because he wasn't sufficiently 'literary'. But having half-rebelled against the 'literary' criterion, she proceeded to apply it. If there had been in the book any of that portentous Masculinity which is the mark of the Major (the man with the thumbs in his braces) she might not have liked it half so well, but she would no doubt have pinned a medal of honour on its chest.

It goes without saying that Ballantyne is *not* one of the novelists treated in *Critical Essays on the New Zealand Novel* edited by Cherry Hankin; and that there is no book planned on him in Oxford's New Zealand Writers and their Work series edited by James Bertram.

The Talkback Man, as several reviewers have pointed out, has a mystery element. It is also topical, and as a result of developments on the Auckland radio scene (chiefly the rise, and rumours of imminent fall, of Gordon Dryden's Radio Pacific) more topical than Ballantyne could have known it would be. Phil Rhodes, its central character, is a talk-back man for Radio Queen City's StirLine, but he is losing his appeal (as is talk-back itself), the accountant is breathing down the neck of the station manager who in turn is leaning on Rhodes. Rhodes has a drinking problem, a love of the little bit of fame and popularity his public role gives him, and a touching eagerness to achieve 'good talk-back'. The decline of his performance and thus of the show is being hastened by a mysterious caller ('the nark') who assumes a variety of voices but reveals himself somewhere in the course of each call by addressing the talk-back man as Pete.

Phil Rhodes's background overlaps fairly obviously with Ballantyne's, though there is no simple identification. Rhodes has been a journalist; he has had a number of years' OE (overseas experience) including some success in Fleet Street. More painfully, he has long ago published one novel, *Driven*, which had a brief vogue while he was abroad and has since been forgotten. Some of Rhodes's most anguishing (and to the reader, touching) moments occur in the course of separate encounters with two people both of whom have read and admired *Driven*. (After the first of these Rhodes has his first alcoholic blackout. Though he stays on his feet he simply 'loses' three hours of a day, as if a fuse in his memory box had blown.) The chief character of *Driven* is Pete Crapshott; but more than that, in his Fleet Street days, as editor of a magazine called *Astonishing Aspects*, Phil Rhodes has sometimes assumed the identity of his character. As Phil explains to one of his drinking cronies:

'I went through the type of identity crisis fashionable in that era. Who was I? Why must I wear the masks everybody expected me to wear? That sort of crap. Fact is, I *became* Pete C for a time. If they wanted masks, I'd give them a decent one. I gave them Pete C. A much more assertive character than Phil R. A bit of a madman, even. Terribly tough on nincompoopery, a savager of humbug, political or otherwise. . . . The thing for you to grasp . . . is that Pete C wasn't simply a character in a novel. For a time he was actually at large in London.'

So it makes a kind of sense that 'the nark' should address Phil as Pete. But what is his motive? The novel, *Driven*, is dangerous, prickly ground for the talk-back man—it unsettles him 'on air'. Then the nark begins to ask why 'Pete' came back to New Zealand; and what happened to Pet Walton . . .

All this is revealed slowly, and gradually explained. It works well as a plot element, building tension and arousing anticipation at the same time that it frees Ballantyne to work under its cover at what is basically his skill—the patient accumulation of authentic detail. This is an Auckland novel, as authentically Auckland as *The Cunninghams* is (I guess) Gisborne

and *Sydney Bridge Upside Down* is (another guess) Hicks Bay. Before I leave the plot element, however, I should add that there is in it a bonus for assiduous Ballantyne readers (if I can speak of us in the plural). Phil Rhodes appeared first in *A Friend of the Family,* an interesting and harrassed young executive, editor of *Astonishing Aspects,* with the novel *Driven* already behind him, and with the habit, in bars, of adopting the role of Pete Crapshott. His motto (taken from a novel called *Born in Exile*) is 'the routine of my life disgusts me, the hope of release is a mockery'.*
He is fiercely resisting the death of the spirit which the Phil Rhodes of the new novel has come much nearer to.

The Phil Rhodes of *The Talkback Man* is divorced (he finds it difficult to recall his wife, and refers to her as 'What's-her-name'). He lives in a Ponsonby boarding-house and 'unwinds' after his show each day at the Bull's Head Tavern in town with semi-alcoholic regulars like Bernie Cobb, an importer, and a retired headmaster known as Sir William or 'the old educator'. In the course of the novel Rhodes makes it to bed with former TV star Cathy Hope, with his Polynesian landlady Gwenda, with a solo mum called Evelyn met at a party, and even with his station manager's wife Janet. Each is very different from the others and only the last of the four is difficult to like; and Rhodes, at the same time that he pleases himself, radiates a somewhat unfocused but genuine affection for all of them. This is part of the novel's strength—that its tone matches what might be called the moral condition of the chief character; and that though he is under siege, sure to be defeated, trying and failing to hang onto sobriety, sanity, self-respect, he nevertheless remains courageous, buoyant on the whole, with a sense of humour and a generous acceptance of his fellows.

Rhodes's style, like that of the novel, is hard-boiled and understated (there is compression and skill in the understatement)—but though so little parade is made of feelings (no melodrama, none of those moments Rhodes talks about in *A Friend of the Family* 'when those telly puppets suddenly start screaming at one another and you wonder why the hell they're doing it, then you realise you've struck a dramatic peak'), still, feeling and compassion abound, and even a sense of community. The arc of the novel is across middle-Auckland from Ponsonby, where Rhodes lives, to the centre where he works and does most of his drinking, to Parnell and Cathy Hope's flat. It only ventures once further afield, and that is to a party in Remuera, alien territory, where Rhodes wishes he were back in Ponsonby.

The Ponsonby scenes, in which the Polynesian characters predominate (the night at the Glue Pot, for example, when Gwenda's picture is in the

---

* *Born in Exile* is a novel by George Gissing. No doubt the title, as well as the resonant despair of the quotation, suits Ballantyne's purposes at this point.

paper and Samisoni decides to stand for mayor) are among the best in the novel, and they present an aspect of life that hasn't appeared in our fiction before. If I miss anything it is some straight descriptive writing, which, even if it might be considered a little static and old hat in terms of the novel now, would have had the effect, I think, of giving a richer texture, a greater sense of fictional density. There is always a danger of thinness in too much dialogue; but it has to be added that Ballantyne's dialogue is stripped down and pointed, at once life-like and selective, never random, as economical as every other aspect of his writing. I have a strong sense of community in this novel, a richer sense of *place* in *Sydney Bridge Upside Down*. And though I miss that texture of place (is the harbour, for example, anywhere referred to?) I can see that this is a change of emphasis we are due for. Community is what has been conspicuously lacking from most of our fiction.

Ballantyne wrote one other novel imaginatively set in Auckland, though the place is not acknowledged. To anyone who knows Auckland there can be no doubt that Robby's morning walk in *A Friend of the Family* takes him from the Newmarket side of Grafton past the hospital and on into town. In fact everything in *A Friend of the Family* with the exception of a reference to newsreel theatres (p. 37) and one to squares and parks (p. 77) belongs to Auckland. But the novel was written in London, and no place is given a recognizable name. The setting is not positively identified as England or New Zealand. I remember finding this distracting when I read the novel in typescript in 1965. Re-reading it now I find it bothers me less—possibly because I see it even more clearly as Auckland, and so the confirmation of names isn't called for. But this confidence about the scene creates a minor problem. In *A Friend of the Family* Rhodes is editing *Astonishing Aspects* in a building that an Aucklander might feel sure he can locate close to Queen Street; but now, in the new novel, Rhodes's editorship of that magazine is twice referred to as being part of his Fleet Street experience. The later novel thus—by accident or design—designates the scene of the earlier one as London, which it patently is not.

Ballantyne is good at establishing and maintaining a cast of characters. In *The Talkback Man* the characters are varied, interesting, and convincing. Ballantyne's observation is sharp and his presentation deft and subtle. He doesn't intrude on the action nor cajole us in an attempt to make us feel what we have not felt or see what he has failed to show. He doesn't tell, he presents. There are no hectic 'dramatic peaks', no purple prose. The final and least measureable writing skill is the ability to judge correctly what can be left out. A novel that gives us as much to build on, and so little constricting interpretation, as this does should leave us with a sense of liberation, if we are willing to be liberated and not habituated to being told. Our imaginations are set free to complete what lies under, or behind, the surfaces sketched out in the telling of 'what they say and what they do'. Is Phil Rhodes deplorable or admirable? Is his life empty, shallow and worthless, or a brave battle worthy of respect? It is right that these questions should not be answered by the novelist; and that when we ask them ourselves, both the affirmative and negative answers should seem inadequate.

The Talkback Man is punctuated by numbered StirLine tapes in which we hear the voice of Phil Rhodes dispensing his 'on-air' wisdom. The extracts are revealing about the character, a gloomy reflection on modern urban society, and yet at the same time funny and inventive. They are characteristic of Ballantyne's realism at its best, being both accurate, negative, and buoyant. As an aspect of style the device is excellent, breaking up the forward momentum of the narrative, generalizing our society and the character of Rhodes by means of particular images. And then there are one or two gems which are like poems or short stories in their own right—in particular STIRLINE/Tape 122, with its reminiscence of Nice evoked by the sound of a rooster crowing in Auckland, and its reflection on the state of marriage.

In *The Cunninghams* the basic narrative pattern of Ballantyne's fiction was laid down. Under all the surface changes (and they are important) his vision remains the same. A threat is uttered or at least implied. Life goes on. Indeed, even under gloom and threat, Ballantyne's chief characters seldom lack bounce—they are whimsical losers; but the hairs on the back of the head creep and tingle, and in the end the blow falls. That is the pattern of *The Talkback Man*. But the last sentences are at once explicit and open. Phil Rhodes could, if Ballantyne wished it, reappear in a further novel.

JANET FRAME:
LANGUAGE IS THE HAWK

Living in the Maniototo is Janet Frame's first work of fiction since *Daughter Buffalo* in 1971. The jacket describes it as 'a Novel' and if it is that it is her tenth, though the description may arouse the wrong expectations. Perhaps it needs some classification like 'post-modernist fiction'—but that would suggest an exercise in theories Frame is probably indifferent to. She works by instinct, and what she offers is a mixed genre. She has a large, and deserved, reputation among the critics; and she receives attention in the most influential places (*Time* gave the present book its lead review). But I don't have the impression that she sells particularly well—not even in New Zealand where she has the great advantage of having been admired somewhere else. She is like the manifestly brilliant child in the classroom who is always disappointing the teacher's notion of how brilliant children ought to behave. The medical profession in New Zealand (a notably conformist country) dealt with her before she had published a word by locking her away for most of ten years and subjecting her to so many electric shock therapies a doctor at the Maudsley Hospital in London told me he considered the treatment she had received to be 'unbelievable, barbarous'. It was her short stories, first published in the 1950s, which won her release from that incarceration, and her novels—especially her first, *Owls Do Cry* (the only one available in paperback)—which earned her the honour and respect she is now treated with wherever she goes. Honour and respect, however, cannot deliver back to her those lost years, nor restore the social confidence destroyed during a crucial period of young adulthood. Janet Frame leads a reclusive life, emerging from time to time to travel outside New Zealand, but always avoiding public attention. At a recent writers'

A review of *Living in the Maniototo* written for *The Melbourne Age*, November 1979.

conference in Wellington she was an invited guest, but she vanished after her presence at one of the sessions had been noticed and welcomed by the chairman.

Frame's capacity to elicit both admiration (amounting almost to awe) and disappointment is well illustrated by an anecdote of Mark Goulden's who was for a time her London publisher. In his memoirs, *Mark My Words*, published in 1978, Goulden describes Frame as one of only three people he has met in his life to whom he would apply the description 'genius' (another was Dylan Thomas). Goulden admired Frame's talent but wanted to advise her on how to make the best of it in her novels. She was enticed out of hiding to his office, recommended to drop her off-beat fictional obsessions, and given four recently published successful novels with the idea that she might emulate them. She was also provided with a comfortable flat in London. Her task was evidently to bend her 'genius' to the requirements of the market and produce what her publisher (obviously percipient, but equally obviously, I think, naïve) would consider a good saleable product. Frame seems to have accepted the instruction meekly, though a day or so later she sent him a devastating analysis of the four novels he had offered her as models. The novel she then wrote, Goulden records, began beautifully—'a superb and imaginative effort . . . with every prospect of developing into a great book'. But before it was finished Frame had left the London flat and returned to New Zealand; and when the completed manuscript arrived it was not at all what he had hoped for: 'we were back in the old depressing atmosphere of mad people and doom and despair'. Goulden's reflection on this is weary but accepting—'Well, that sort of thing happens in publishing'. Clearly his interest in her was at an end.

The novel produced by way of this odd pact was Frame's fifth, *The Adaptable Man*, and it is at once a revelation of its author's brilliance (the flow of language and invention is extraordinary) and of her integrity. If it could be taken 'straight', as her publisher would have wanted, it would be almost totally bogus—a vast pastiche of 'the English novel', with a village, a duck pond, thatched cottages, a heavy overlay of Iris Murdochian symbolism, and written as if its author were an Englishwoman who had never set foot outside the British Isles. The willing, meek, 'adaptable' Frame—the Frame who must have wanted most terribly to please, *not* to offend, *not* to deserve her electric therapy—produced it. But the other Frame, that most authentic, firm, and *un*adaptable lady, planted landmines everywhere in those bogus English fields. The novel is a destructive device set to explode in the face of the man who had blandly suggested she should put aside the facts of her own life and write as if the world were other than she knew it to be. Its beautiful young student 'hero' murders an Italian immigrant (drowns him in that fictional duck pond) in order to prove to himself that he is an 'adaptable' twentieth-century man, and seduces his loving mother leaving her embarrassingly pregnant; and at the end of the novel the weight of a huge chandelier, installed in a picturesque olde cottage, pulls down the ceiling and falls on the chief characters, killing them. So much for Frame's interest in the market.

We are now at novel ten, and all ideas of compromise have long since been left behind. Frame writes her own books in her own way. They are not 'depressing' (Goulden's word); but they are true to life as she knows it—full of colour and beauty, but also of the sense of death, and worse than death, of fear, ugliness, and horror. If one could apportion these elements exactly I think it would be found that in *Living in the Maniototo* the positive elements—the humour, and the bright colours of the living world—easily predominate.

In addition to the positive and negative in Frame's representation of her world there is a third element—satire—that has something of each. It is always clever, often brilliantly so, and usually funny, but it can have the effect of undermining our belief in the basic fiction. The more successfully she uses a character to represent some quality or trait she dislikes, the less humanly complete the character becomes. An example of this in the present novel is the narrator's second late husband, Lance Halleton, French teacher turned debt-collector. As French teacher he is one of Frame's heroes—those who serve language:

I loved him because he had an abiding passion for the French language. The apparent purity and vastness of his feeling gave him, in my eyes, a kind of greatness, for I feel that language in its widest sense is the hawk suspended above eternity, feeding from it but not of its substance and not necessarily for its life and thus never able to be translated into it; only able by a wing movement, so to speak, a cry, a shadow, to hint at what lies beneath it on the untouched, undescribed almost unknown plain. (p. 43)

But Lance is stricken unaccountably in middle life with a national (and international) disease:

It was the *cost* of all things, including the cost of living which now worried Lance: the cost of living, the national debt, who would pay, what was being paid for and how could one know when it was finally paid? (p. 42)

In this state of 'financial patriotism' Lance takes employment as a debt-collector, wears a white bowling hat (adorned with a trout fly), gym shoes, 'walk' socks, shorts, and a striped blazer, becomes dedicated, even vindictive, in his pursuit of debtors, and dies of an 'inexplicable spasm in his throat' on the night he catches up with Yorkie Wynyard (himself disguised as a debt-collector), the most unscrupulous runner-up of unpaid debts on Auckland's North Shore.

A reader has to be flexible and open-minded to get the best out of Frame—to recognize that her fiction is not 'pure' because, as well as being the vehicle for ideas which another writer might segregate into separate essays, it challenges its own genre, questions its own 'reality', and finally collapses in upon itself, leaving us both with the sense that 'language' is 'the hawk suspended over eternity', and that it is a vast illusory palace erected over the chasm of death.

At the centre of *Living in the Maniototo* is the widow Mavis Furness/ Barwell/Halleton (her maiden name and those of her two husbands) who is also, at least in her own mind, Alice Thumb, a novelist, and Violet Pansy Proudlock, a ventriloquist. As Janet Frame herself has done in recent years, the narrator travels at intervals from New Zealand to the United States, and the novel has three principal locations—Auckland, Baltimore, and San Francisco. In each location a different atmosphere predominates, and even perhaps a different mode, or register, of Frame's fiction. Auckland (Glenfield on the North Shore, renamed 'Blenheim') is home territory and, not surprisingly, the object of satire. Baltimore is like a return to the New York scene of *Daughter Buffalo*: it is gloomy, ugly, the urban death, the deprivation of sense and of nature. (A New Zealand boy, visiting, refuses to go out of doors because there is no '*outside*'.) Finally San Francisco, specifically Berkeley, is the scene in which the narrator's character as artist is permitted to function.

One does not read Frame for a 'story', but a narrative summary will show the way this novel moves through a variety of levels of reality, rendering the real unreal and vice versa.

After the death of her first husband, Mavis (or Alice), the narrator, travels to Baltimore to stay with an old friend, Brian Wilford. She hears non-existent wolves howling in the snow-bound night and feels the ghost of Edgar Allen Poe, who died there, still walks the streets. (This makes a connexion between Baltimore and 'Blenheim', because a famous New Zealand poet died in the streets of 'Blenheim', in fact was taken in by the narrator and died in her house.) With Brian Wilford she visits Tommy, a maker of jewelry, who believes he is being attacked by the Blue Fury, a detergent advertised on TV. As she and Brian are leaving Tommy is attacked again and vanishes in a flash, leaving only 'a smell of laundry and the penetrating fumes of a powerful cleaner'.

Mavis/Alice returns to 'Blenheim' which, being 'over the bridge' from Auckland, is made sister city to Berkeley, 'over the Bridge' from San Francisco. She marries the French teacher who becomes a debt-collector and who dies as described. In Part Two she returns to Baltimore and while Brian is at work her days are taken up with Mrs Tyndall, the Negro cleaner who lives in hope of winning a trip to Florida on a lucky number phone call, or of earning a miracle by contributing money to God's Diamond Account Book kept by an evangelist, Brother Coleman. Mrs Tyndall suffers a stroke and dies in hospital clutching a shopping bag to her breast, while Brian and the narrator are calling up their New Zealand childhood (rather in the manner of Sandy Stone's Melbourne) by remembering and singing the favourite tunes of the Sunday 'wireless'—'Jerusalem', 'The Old Rugged Cross', and 'The Stranger of Galilee'. Brian's nephew Lonnie comes to stay, hates Baltimore, refuses to go out of doors, is sent to a family in the country, steals their collection of silver dollars, and is sent back to New Zealand.

Mavis/Alice now moves to Berkeley where an American couple, Irving and Trinity Garrett, who have read her two published books, and who are leaving for a holiday in Italy, have offered her their house as a place to work on a new book. The Garretts are soon killed in an Italian earthquake ('They were attending the opera and were buried with the rest of the audience among musical instruments and half-sung arias') and it is found they have left their home to their guest. They had previously invited two couples to stay and Mavis/Alice, now owner of the house, feels obliged to let the invitation stand. The novel she has planned to write, set in Menton, France, is to be about the Watercress family who have gone there to study New Zealand's most famous writer, Margaret Rose Hurndell, who once lived there. But the Garretts' four friends (all expatriate New Zealanders, or with New Zealand connexions) arrive and drive the Watercress family from her mind. She must write instead about them.

The remainder of the book (Parts 3, 4, and 5) develops the characters of these four guests and of the plan of one of them, Roger, to spend a few hours in the desert preparatory to a crossing he intends to make of one of the great deserts of the world. (He has yet to choose which.) What happens to Roger and the other three is observed and recorded by Alice Thumb, novelist, and might be described as the longest section of 'straight' fiction in the book—a novel within the novel. Frame keeps the narrative pace down, expanding and articulating her sense of the characters at the same time that the crucial events are slowly unfolding.

At this point we seem to have settled into something like a conventional fictional world—we are far enough inside it for the characters to seem 'real'. But now the four guests depart, and at once the Garretts arrive back from Italy. (Quite as much as killing her characters off, Frame enjoys bringing them back from the dead.) It becomes apparent that the four who have occupied a large section of the novel are Alice Thumb's creation, in place of her novel about the Watercress family. This is as disturbing to her as it is to the reader—more so, in fact, because it suggests to her that she herself may have only a fictional existence. She returns to Baltimore but her friend Brian has died. On the eve of her return to New Zealand she is left pondering the relationship between the 'original' and the 'replica', a problem which has occurred to her at various points in the novel.

For all its diversity, *Living in the Maniototo* is a coherent, single work, because in all its parts and through all its registers, there is consistently the quality of Frame's mind, a rare and beautiful intelligence. It is also unified, I think, by one governing idea or preoccupation.

It is the same idea found in various guises in Shakespeare's last plays —that the distinction between 'art' and 'life' is, if not false, at least less absolute than we usually suppose, because all of our life comes to order only as we ourselves imagine it and so bring it into a conceptual framework. To be a General I must first imagine a General, and then imagine myself a General. We grow into our imaginings. So to proceed as if there is life which is 'real', and imaginings which are not, is too simple. There are, rather, gradations of reality which are different for different people; and though you and I may be untroubled by the Blue Fury, to Tommy it may indeed be a powerful destructive agent. Language is the instrument of imagination. It is the hawk suspended above eternity.

That I think is Frame's premise. Yet against it there operates her knowledge of an intransigent area of experience which the imagination cannot entirely absorb or absolve. Her narrator, Mavis/Alice, has spent 'the years of [her] late teens . . . in a psychiatric hospital because at that time it was thought to be a crime, a sin, a sign of disease instead of dis-ease, to be suffering from unhappiness'. This fact is only referred to in passing, but one memory occurs more than once and becomes part of the structure of the book. Irving and Trinity Garrett have had only one child, Adelaide, who died at sixteen, having suffered from lycanthropy, and this is something the narrator has seen in her hospital years and is haunted by (those imaginary wolves howling in the Baltimore night are not unconnected):

I can't ever forget the thirteen-year-old twins I knew in hospital, the beautiful black-haired, blue-eyed children dressed in their dark blue and white striped hospital dresses made of the stiff material used for mattress covers; their bare feet swollen and blue, their arms and the upper part of their body bound in a canvas straitjacket; standing together on the stairs leading from the dayroom to the small exercise yard; and over the years I still hear in my mind the sound of their barking, yelping, whimpering as they made their bizarre canine gestures to each other and in their adolescent awakenings tried to mate each other, like dogs. And at night when the moon was full they would howl, above the turmoil of the screams and cries of the night. (pp. 122-3)

The language is spare, plain, and in its way beautiful. These are facts which cannot be played with, enlivened, enlarged upon, or altered. This is intractable, and must be simply recorded. Yet even in those spare sentences, language and imagination have made some kind of sad reconciliation with the brute fact. This is one pole of the broad range which Frame's skill as a fiction writer is able to encompass.

Footnote: *Living in the Maniototo* contains a number of in-jokes for literary New Zealanders. Margaret Rose Hurndell (apart from the Royal connexion for those old enough to remember Princess Margaret Rose) obviously suggests Katherine Mansfield, and the Watercress family who go to Menton to study her might be the Mansons (or even the Steads). The poet whose death in the streets of 'Blenheim' (i.e. Glenfield) Auckland is connected with the appearance of the black fantail can only be James K. Baxter. And Peter Wellstead, the novelist who became famous after his death mainly because it was found he had lived all his life in the Maniototo (the blood-soaked plain) and never wanted to leave it, suggests Ronald Hugh Morrieson and Hawera (though the Maniototo is of course a real plain in Otago).

PART II: POETRY

PRELIMINARY:
FROM WYSTAN TO CARLOS —
MODERN AND MODERNISM
IN RECENT NEW ZEALAND POETRY

... it would seem to be a truism that ... what *creates* the artist-writer is not the ideas (experiences, perceptions) he has nor the fact that he has them but the fact that he gives them a form in writing. ... The butcher, the baker, and the candlestick maker (after all) have ideas and experiences too.

Ian Wedde, 'Introduction', N.Z. Universities Arts Festival
Yearbook 1968.

In so far as the discussion of New Zealand poetry has had any critical structure over the past quarter of a century the structure has come from Allen Curnow's introductions to his two anthologies and from the counterstatements these elicited. What I propose to do in the present lecture is to enquire whether we can't discover another set of terms—not because there's anything wrong with the ones we have, but because a new point of observation is likely to alter the picture, and it is surely time for a change.

Before I depart from it, however, a word about Curnow's critical viewpoint. It was very much a product of the literary thinking of the 1930s. It placed great emphasis on 'truth' and on 'reality'; and Curnow added a regional element by implying that in our case the 'reality' laid bare by the poem might be expected to be recognizably 'New Zealand'. As a general expectation this was not unreasonable. But was it also, as some poets felt, prescriptive? Certainly Curnow himself could not have written some of the

An address to the Writers' Conference, Victoria University of Wellington, August 1979.

best of his recent work if he had stuck exclusively to what he called in his 1963 lecture on this subject 'the New Zealand referent'.[1]

It was something in the literature of the 1940s and fifties which called itself 'international' that Curnow particularly set himself against—a provincialism (as he saw it) which tried in effect to by-pass the limitations of the region by excluding regional reference and making the poem look as if it might have been written anywhere. I agree with Curnow that that kind of strategy—the attempt positively to evade the features of the region—is bound to be self-defeating. (And it was Allen Tate not Allen Curnow who called Internationalism 'The New Provincialism'.) But there is another kind of internationalism which is in no sense an evasion of those local responsibilities Ian Cross urged upon us in his opening address. Let's concede with Curnow that most good writing is likely to have regional features. Nevertheless the language we use—the English language—is in some degree international, and this is something to be thankful for. Imagine if we spoke Danish, or Dutch, or Swedish—how exclusively it would throw us in upon ourselves, and consequently outward upon the homeland for relief from our own provinciality. Or perhaps worse, if we spoke some language exclusively our own.

Let's propose then that we take the international fact of the English language as our basis and consider our poetry historically, as part of the broad development of poetry in English during this century—not in the provincial spirit that we must subserviently follow what's happening 'Overseas', but rather in the spirit of an affirmation, recognizing that we are part of the community of the English language and that this is something which gives us considerable freedom of action. Such an approach will inevitably direct our attention to technical questions, questions of poetic strategy and poetic form, rather than to (in Curnow's phrase again) 'the New Zealand referent'. It is, after all, about nine years since Murray Edmond suggested in *Freed* 3 that it was time 'to construct a poetic rather than to name them hills & define a national consciousness', but I don't see much sign that anyone has followed his suggestion.

I have to admit that I'm drawn to do this partly because I'm at present writing a book in which I consider the origins of poetry in English during the first fifty years of this century. In my previous book on that subject, I was interested in an historical umbrella—I called it 'the new poetic'—which would cover Yeats, Eliot, and Pound. Now I'm more interested in what separates Yeats on the one hand from Pound and early Eliot on the other. In particular I'm curious to answer for myself the question why Yeats, for all his greatness, should seem not to be a living force on the practice of poetry, while Pound, on the other hand, is still animating the writing of poetry and the development of poetic theory. One admires Yeats as one admires a great piece of statuary from a past century. His work is admirable, complete, imposing, and remote—a monument of its own magnificence. Pound's, by contrast, is like an artist's studio. It is all unfinished, uneven, fragmentary, but still alive—still active among us. We have neither assimilated nor dispensed with Pound.

I said a moment ago that Curnow's critical position with its emphasis on 'truth' or 'reality', was very much a product of the thinking of the 1930s. Let's look for a moment at this. If we go back to the period of the First World War we find English poetry divided between Georgians and Modernists—a conflict which it seemed by 1930 the Modernists had won, so that for a long time 'Georgian' became a term of abuse. But of course within the Georgian movement there were—as there are likely to be in any literary movement—a variety of talents. There were indeed literary sentimentalists who wanted to versify bluebells and cottages and country lanes; but there were also truth-tellers and realists who wanted to write of life as they found it, including poverty, ugliness, and suffering. These realists became the war poets we remember and honour. Most notable among them was Wilfred Owen, who declared 'the true poets must be truthful', and 'the poetry is in the pity'.

The poets of the 1930s inherited I think this strand of Georgianism—the realism, the truth-telling, the sense of public responsibility.[2] They gave it a political emphasis. Their poetry was committed to uncovering the ugly truths about society which conventional literary sentimentality had conspired to cover; and from this it was hoped might spring the seeds of political revolution or at least of social change. So poetry in the 1930s was harnessed to something beyond itself. It became an instrument for social change.

Since the term Georgian was out of favour, and since these young poets of the thirties—Auden, Spender, Day Lewis, MacNeice—admired Eliot and *The Waste Land,* it seemed at the time, and has seemed to literary historians since, that they were the inheritors of Modernism. In fact they were not—and I will try to show in a moment why they were not. In England Modernism had no inheritors. Eliot's *The Waste Land* and Pound's *Cantos*—the two great monuments of Modernism—have no significant direct offspring in Britain, except perhaps in the work of Basil Bunting. The line of development out of early Modernism occurs in America. In his 1960 anthology *The New American Poets* Donald M. Allen was able to trace four post-war poetic movements, the Beats, the Black Mountain Poets, the San Francisco Renaissance, and the New York Group, together with a fifth nameless and heterogeneous group, all back to a common point of origin in Pound and Carlos Williams. This is a very broad and variable stream, but the poets have enough fundamentally in common for it to be regarded as a single stream. Of course British poetry learned something from early Eliot, and even a little from Pound; but

Auden—the dominant figure of the 1930s and forties in Britain—is really the inheritor of what I called the Georgian realist tradition, not of Modernism.

Pound, and Eliot in *The Waste Land*, had made a breakthrough in poetic form parallel to that made in the same period by Schoenberg, Webern, Berg, Stravinsky in music, and by Picasso and Braque in painting. They created what can be called 'open form'—let's not try just for the moment to say what it is. Auden returned British poetry to closed forms. He acquired a certain surface liberation—he engaged in tricks and fireworks of various kinds—but in the very fundamentals of poetic form Auden was conservative. He took British poetry back more or less to what it had been before the American invasion; and there, for better or worse, it remains. The line of development that runs, for example from Thomas Hardy and Owen through Auden to Philip Larkin is far more real than anything one might trace in British poetry out of Pound and Eliot.

I state these as historical facts. They haven't been often or fully recognized; but I find them confirmed in one recent and somewhat surprising place. In his book *The Thirties and After* Stephen Spender writes:

To be modern meant in the thirties to interpret the poet's individual experiences of lived history in the light of some kind of Marxist analysis. In relation to the modernist movement in the arts which began at the end of the last century and continued in the work of Eliot and Pound, this was regressive. For the essence of the modern[ist] movement was that it created art which was centred on itself and not on anything outside it; neither on some ideology projected nor on the projection of the poet's feelings and personality. One might say that the moment the thirties writing became illustrative of Marxist texts or reaction to 'history'—and to the extent which it did these things—it ceased to be part of the modern movement.

A little further on Spender says, 'We were putting the subject back into poetry'. This is true and not true. Because 'putting the subject back into poetry' is much the same as taking the subject out of it. 'Subject' in either case has become something distinct from the poem, like the load put on the donkey's back. For the young writers of the thirties that load—that subject—was 'truth' or 'reality' (we are back with Curnow's terms) and the more of it you could get on to your donkey the better. It is arguable however that nothing is quite so 'true' or so 'real' as the donkey itself. (Ian Wedde, in the Introduction I have quoted in my epigraph, quotes Howard Nemerov asking, 'When you look at a cow, do you see the form or the content of the cow?') The Marxism of the thirties, in other words, combined with that Georgian realism of an earlier period, to reinforce a distinction between the poem and its subject, the language and its 'content', the donkey and its load, which Modernist theory had tried to dispense with. It is on that point that the British and American traditions have tended to split. And because New Zealand in those years tended to be much more Britain-oriented than it is now, our own poetry followed the British example. The young New Zealand poets of those years would have read everything of Eliot and probably something of Pound—just as their English contemporaries did. But the theoretical basis of the Modernist experiment was certainly not understood in those years, even perhaps by those who had made it. Eliot's criticism hardly explains the success of *The Waste Land*—how could it, when the final form of the poem was as much Pound's doing as Eliot's? And in any case, from 1926 to 1939 the Modernists were themselves confused by the economic and political *zeitgeist*. Pound went crazy on Social Credit theory, so that vast stretches of the middle *Cantos*—right up to the *Pisan Cantos*—are as loaded with ballast as any Marxist could wish. It just happens from the Marxist viewpoint to be the wrong ballast. Eliot went away into his own brand of right-wing religiopoliticking, which infected his later poetry and I think impaired it.[3] No one was exempt in those years; and we would hardly expect—or want—our own poets to have been unaffected by the pressures of the age.

I'm suggesting, then a distinction between poetry which is simply 'modern' in its time, and the poetry of the Modernist movement. Owen and Auden were distinctly modern poets in their time, but they were not Modernists. The Modernist experiment was initiated about sixty years ago—its great texts are *The Waste Land*, the best of the *Cantos*, perhaps Carlos Williams's *Paterson*—and it bore fruit in poetic developments that have followed in America. The distinction—again very broadly—is that for the Modernists a poem is not a vehicle; it is a work of art whose material is language—language in action—language at maximum energy, or resonance, or intensity. The realist tradition, by contrast, tends always towards using the poem as a vehicle. You may decorate the vehicle, but the critic who inspects it will want to know what's *in* it, and what value its 'content' has beyond the values of art. Does it promote the Revolution, or national consciousness, or God, or morals, or something called 'values'? Or does it (as someone called Needham complained of a book of poems he reviewed in a recent issue of *Comment*) contain 'untenable attitudes and beliefs'?

Does all this mean, then, that my distinction between moderns and Modernists is one between moralists and aesthetes, roundheads and cavaliers? It has, I suppose, or it has developed, something of that character, at least in its very broad outlines. As Spender said in my earlier quotation, the Modernist movement 'created art which was centred on itself', whereas the new young poets of the thirties saw themselves as engaged in 'putting the subject back into poetry'. But the Modernist would not concede that the pure poem, the poem as pure work of art, tells less truth than the poem as vehicle. In fact he would argue that the truth which can be lifted out of the poem is less true than the truth which is

indissoluble from it—because insofar as a statement can be removed from
its 'vehicle', precisely in that degree it fails to partake of the truth of imagination. And it is perfectly respectable to argue that the truth of imagination is less vulnerable, more durable, more comprehensive, subtler—in
fact *truer*—than the truth of politics, morals, philosophy, or whatever
removable, abstractable, restatable 'content' the poet as moralist, or as
realist, chooses to load into his vehicle. At this point there are a number of
resonant statements by Keats that might be called up in support; but I will
quote instead a short poem by William Carlos Williams which some of you
will know:

> so much depends
> upon
>
> a red wheel
> barrow
>
> glazed with rain
> water
>
> beside the white
> chickens.

Why so much depends upon a red wheel/barrow; *what* depends upon it,
the poet hasn't permitted himself to say. What he has ensured is that we've
seen the barrow—in fact that we've *imagined* it—noted its colour bright-
ened by the glaze of rain and set against the whiteness of the chickens, and
encouraged us to ask ourselves why such experience is important. It's important of course because it's not possible to abstract from it. It's what
might be called primary living as distinct from the compulsive interpreta-
tions of living which occupy so much of our waking life. It's not enough;
but it is the staple diet of consciousness beside which all intellectualization
is cake and cream. Imagination depends upon a red wheel/barrow; I would
say sanity depends upon it—and so does the truth of poetry.

If I'm making myself understood you will have noticed that I'm beginning to take sides, and that's something I really don't want to do. I have a
preference for Modernist poetics—or perhaps for my own poetics as I
derive and formulate these from Modernist texts. I acknowledge that preference. But it would be ridiculous to use it as any kind of measuring stick
for the worth of particular poems. Clearly very bad poems are written
every day according Modernist principles; and the whole history of
English poetry up to about the time of the First World War got along very
nicely without Modernist poetic theory. So I don't want to use this distinction in order to prove that some poems or poets are better than others. But
there is just this to be said. If one looks at developments in the arts from an

historical perspective it does seem there is a certain flow of the tide. You can choose to swim against it if you want to, and you may swim brilliantly. What you can't do is turn it back. It's conceivable, for example, that someone might have written polished satiric couplets in the manner of Pope after 1790, but it's not conceivable that by doing so he would have made any appreciable difference to the onset of the Romantic Movement. He would have been swimming against the tide of literary history. And my own feeling is that the broad tide of poetry in English during this century, the durable part of it, will be seen in retrospect to have moved towards open form, towards the poem as imaginative act rather than as vehicle, towards the maximizing of linguistic energy, towards the sense of language as the material of an art not the servant of an idea—towards all that is characteristic of Modernism at its best. And if that supposition is correct it answers an earlier question of mine: it explains why Yeats seems a splendid but remote monument, while Pound is still an imperfect but operative force on the production of new poetry. It also explains what I mean when I say—as I do now—that New Zealand poetry in the 1960s and seventies has moved forward. It's not a question of poetry getting better but rather of poets doing what is most appropriate, or most apposite, to the age in which we live.

Let me go back now to the 1930s. It was the decade in which politics bore in upon everything, including poetry. As Spender said, he and his contemporaries were putting the subject back into poetry. They were dedicated to 'truth'—the truth of urban squalor and economic repression, and the hope for political revolution or economic reform. Poetry became responsible and public, and the most influential new voice in Britain, and surely in New Zealand too, was W. H. Auden's. So in New Zealand we find poets as different as Fairburn, Curnow, and Glover in revolt against Georgian sentimentalism, influenced strongly by what I've called the Georgian realist tradition, believing (in Owen's phrase) that 'the true poets must be truthful', confronting economic, political, social, historical realities which had previously been evaded in New Zealand letters. Instead of God's own country, a land of milk and honey, South Seas Paradise, the land of kowhai gold and Christmas under the pohutukawas, we're presented with a land of mean cities and mortgaged farms, 'a land of settlers / With never a soul at home'. Glover's

> But all the beautiful crops soon went
> To the mortgage-man instead
> And *Quardle oodle ardle wardle doodle*
> The magpies said

or Curnow's

> The pilgrim dream pricked by a cold dawn died
> Among the chemical farmers, the fresh towns; among
> Miners, not husbandmen, who piercing the side
> Let the land's life . . .

or Fairburn's

> This is our paper city, built
> on the rock of debt, held fast
> against all winds by the paperweight of debt

—these are the true poets being truthful. Poetry has become a vehicle for the truths of history, politics, economics. The workers are celebrated; our economic and cultural subservience to Britain is deplored; the beginnings of a true national consciousness are discovered in the contemplation of our history and in our relation to the soil and the sea:

> Fair earth, we have broken our idols:
> and after the days of fire we shall come to you
> for the stones of a new temple.

All this must have been exciting while it was happening and it's still exciting to look back on. It was a happy conjunction of talent with the times. The public themes were not simply political as they tended to be in Britain; they were broadened to express a regional awareness and a national consciousness. Curnow in particular, but also Glover, wrote public poetry which had none of that hollow official flavour, none of the thumbs-in-braces bombast that characterized nineteenth-century poetry for public occasions. It was a fortunate moment for New Zealand literature.

But the very momentum of the times, here and in Britain, meant that technical problems were glossed over or brushed aside. There are times when external forces provide so much of the energy needed in the arts that all the artist has to do is hang on and steer. When that momentum of the thirties and forties died away, what was left? I would say an uncertainty about the fundamental techniques and purposes of poetry. There were bound to be new poets after the war, and surely no one ought to have expected them to want to go on repeating what Curnow, Glover, and Fairburn had done.

These new New Zealand poets seemed to gather around Louis Johnson in the early fifties, and one of the things they proposed to do was to 'people the landscape'. They were going to write urban poetry, where they felt the staple of their predecessors had been images of rural life and of untamed land- and sea-scape. But this, on the face of it, perfectly reasonable switch of attention only made more obvious the limitation of possibilities which the realist tradition imposed. It was all very well to want to deal in human material rather than in images of unpeopled landscape; but it seemed in practice to involve taking on the role of the fiction writer with totally inadequate means—summing up the neurosis of a suburban housewife, or the poverty of spirit of a wealthy merchant, or the craving for love under the exercise of political power, in a few glib verses—just as Auden wrapped up the life of characters, some fictional, some historical, in a single sonnet or a dozen four-line stanzas. Louis Johnson was an able and an amiable *entrepreneur*, and a man to whom I personally have reasons to be grateful. He was an open and encouraging editor. But it was going to take more than discontent with Curnow's anthologies, and cameraderie among the poets, if New Zealand poetry was to find a new direction. What was needed was a movement which would have fundamental theoretical implications.

In the 1960s, I think it can be argued, such a movement occurred. A new wave of young New Zealand poets discovered what I'm calling the Modernist tradition. They found it partly in Pound and Carlos Williams; they found it even more in the post-war American poets who, as I said earlier, constitute a broad development out of Modernism.* Ian Wedde was the first of these poets to make a strong impression. His poems began appearing in student publications in the middle sixties, and I'm sure his presence must have helped to trigger off the slightly more radical movement represented by the periodical *Freed* which ran through five issues from 1969 to 1972. I don't have the chronology exact but I'm conscious that in the space of just a few years Wedde, David Mitchell, Murray Edmond, Alan Brunton, and Jan Kemp—together with Russell Haley who was a good deal older—had all arrived on the Auckland scene. Five of the six I've named are graduates of the Auckland English Department (the sixth is currently enrolled), but I don't think they acquired their poetics from the Department. They acquired them from one another, from their reading, or just by a process of osmosis, out of the air.† All of them were published in *Freed*, together with Bob Orr, Bill Manhire, Rhys Pasley, Arthur Bates (who later became Arthur Baysting, and more recently Neville Purvis), and one or two others. Some of them were later to appear in Baysting's 1973 anthology *The Young New Zealand Poets*.

Freed was not the beginning of the new movement, but it was the strongest and clearest single assertion that the new poets of the decade were taking a differing path from their predecessors, and that they were inter-

---

* The various discriminations possible within the Modernist (or as one may choose to call it, post-Modernist) tradition, are very important, but there is no room for them in a discussion such as this which aspires to represent recent literary history only in very broad terms.

† This was perhaps unduly modest on behalf of at least one of my colleagues, Roger Horrocks, whose American Poetry classes were attended in the late 1960s-early 1970s by Wedde, Edmond, Brunton, Kemp, and Haley. Horrocks in fact contributed an article to *Freed*, 4. Some of these poets must also have attended Allen Curnow's M.A. course on Wallace Stevens.

ested in matters of poetic theory. We have all learned—and quite rightly—to be very reverent about the advent of *Phoenix* at Auckland University College in the early 1930s—the periodical in which a New Zealand poetry we can take entirely seriously had its beginnings. I wonder whether a proper perspective might not teach students of our literature to see the advent of *Freed* in the late sixties as an event of comparable symbolic significance.

It's time now to attempt to say what is meant by 'open form'. I will approach the question slowly, and inevitably my terms will be broad and will omit fine distinctions. To some here who know the subject well the exercise will seem unsatisfactory or unnecessary. But not to undertake it would leave me open to the accusation of evasiveness on a crucial point; and an attempt at definition—however unsatisfactory—could be useful if at least it had the effect of teaching some of our reviewers to avoid the kind of mistake Ida Baker made when she was living in France with Katherine Mansfield and she asked how much milk cost per metre.

Closed form might suggest formal measures, stanzas, and rhyme—and in the case of Yeats or Auden it most often does. 'Open form' might suggest free verse—and again, in the case of Pound or Carlos Williams, it does. But in fact the distinction is much more fundamental than that. It comes back to the question raised by the Spender quotation of whether you can distinguish a poem from its subject. It comes back to our conventional social and linguistic distinctions between one compartment of life and another —literature as distinct from politics, politics as distinct from philosophy, thought as distinct from feeling. Far from being an aesthete who wants to separate literature from life, the Modernist poet, the 'open form' poet, wants literature to invade, to absorb life, almost to become indistinguishable from it, to collapse conceptual distinctions. Life does *not* order itself into narrative, or into logical argument; so in the degree to which the poem organizes itself that way, it falsifies. Life does *not* explain itself or point a moral; so the poem which does these things is artificial. That is one aspect of open form—an openness to experience *as it occurs*, not a bringing of experience to be judged at the bar of previously formulated ideas or ideals; an attempt to get nearer to the true feel of experience; a preference for the possibly incoherent actual as against the organized abstraction.

As far back as the last century there was a movement against those organizational abstractions on which long poems had traditionally been constructed. Late in the century the idea got about that there could be no such thing as a long poem—a long poem was a contradiction in terms, because the structure which held it together was essentially non-poetic. In the 1890s poetry was effectively reduced to the lyric, because only the lyric was all poetry, free of the unpoetic superstructure on which longer poems were hung. Imagism around the time of the First World War was a further effort towards purification. Not only was the superstructure removed; the artificialities of rhyme and stanzas went too. But Imagism tended to be visual and static, and Pound moved quickly to Vorticism. The poetic moment became, not the static image, but the moment of maximum linguistic energy. Again, this was a moment which couldn't be sustained, so the long poem continued to seem an impossibility.

Yeats wrote a few narrative poems; but on the whole he never departed from the poetics of the 1890s which taught him that true poetry was the lyric—the short poem—and it was lyric poems he wrote all his life. Pound, on the other hand, had an epic ambition. He wanted to write a long poem—a poem (as he said) containing history. But how could you write a long poem if both narrative and logical structures were artificial, non-poetic? I'm not sure whether Pound ever articulated how he solved this problem, but he did it by a principle which I describe as accretion, or aggregation. Whether your basic poetic unit is the image, or the vortex, or both—insofar as the units are pure, and come from one man at one phase of his life, they will be found to cohere, to have natural unity, without artificial structural linking. The broad interests, the recurring emotional concerns, the individual tricks of speech and ways of looking at the world, all these, I think, constitute what recent American poetry has called the 'Field'—and it is the Field that gives such unity and coherence as the work requires.

Poetry, then, is not a form but a quality. Achieve the quality, one might almost say, and the form will look after itself. So the *Cantos*—the best of the *Cantos*—or equally a poem like *The Waste Land*, and many Modernist poems since—are built up of these radioactive fragments, without logical or narrative linking. In this way the long poem becomes possible again, while at the same time the purity of poetry is retained. And I repeat that by purity is meant, not the aesthete's detachment from life, but on the contrary immersion in life, likeness to life—life-likeness in the very absence of those mental structures which life as we live it moment by moment doesn't have. And to get even nearer to veracity, to that linguistic re-enactment of life as it feels moment by moment, there is an attempt to exploit, as the basic material of poetic music, the natural speech patterns, the runs and pauses, the interweaving of breathing and vocalizing, which is the poet's own individual manner of speaking. As Michael Harlow said in a recent review 'the poet is listening to the character of his own speech and scoring it on the page spatially and semantically'. The word 'scoring' is important because it reminds us of the underlying 'musical' structure of Modernist poetry. And this emphasis on spoken language can be seen indirectly to enforce a permanent local element wherever Modernist principles are applied. The poet may derive his theory from the French and the Americans but it requires him to use the language of the tribe.

'The true poets must be truthful', Owen said—and now perhaps we can all agree he was right, but with the proviso that you must choose your truth. And as I said earlier, it is quite as responsible and respectable to take the view that political, or economic, or national, or moral truths are themselves simplifications; and that the poet trying to get inside the very skin of experience is a greater truth-teller, a more profound realist, than a poet who sets out to improve the world. 'An artist', Keats wrote to Shelley, 'must have "self concentration", selfishness perhaps.' And he went on, 'You I am sure will forgive me for sincerely remarking that you might curb your magnanimity and be more of an artist'.

The staple book of poems of the 1950s contained thirty poems, each of a page or a page and a half. Look at the products of the Caxton Press for the twenty years from the end of the War and you'll see what I mean. Each poem has a subject and works its way towards a statement—usually a moral statement—which one often feels carries no great conviction but is really an artistic device for rounding the thing off. My own 'Night Watch in the Tararuas', which went into Curnow's Penguin anthology, is a pretty fair sample of the type—the scene set, the problem elaborated, the conclusion drawn:

> And know that though death breeds in love's strange bones,
> Its failing flesh lives warmer than the stones.

It was poetic strategy I had learned especially from the early Baxter. Of course plenty of good poems were written in that mode—a mode which I suppose goes back to Wordsworth's 'Tintern Abbey', and even to Gray's 'Elegy in a Country Churchyard'. But if you have no ambition to be a moralist, if in fact you believe that moral pronouncements tend as often to falsify as to illuminate, and if you don't want the concluding line to shut the gate on the experience which is the occasion of the poem, then you must look for some other structural principle. Modernism provides such a principle. Putting it technically (and over-simply), Modernism is a mimetic principle, an alternative to the didactic principle.

The thirty-poem book was the staple of the 1950s, but some of the older poets did try to expand into longer forms. Fairburn's *Dominion* had already provided an example of such an attempt—and one can see in it evidence of an awareness of Pound and Eliot. But *Dominion* (1937) is basically a heavy-handed piece of economic and political didacticism. And when Fairburn added two further long poems in the 1950s, 'To a Friend in the Wilderness' and 'The Voyage', they were both verse elaborations of very simple moral propositions—so simple that the elaboration comes to seem, not a case of art for art's sake, but morals for art's sake, which is worse. The moral is hardly more than a structure used because the poet is afraid to proceed without one. Even Glover's 'Arawata Bill' sequence of the same period, which ought to have been able to stand on its own feet as a piece of scene-setting and characterization, had to be rounded off with a bit of conventional moralizing, as if that was where we'd been heading all along:

> R.I.P. where no gold lies
> But in your own questing soul
> Rich in faith and a wild surmise.
>
> You should have been told
> Only in you was the gold.

And as for Charles Brasch in a long poem like 'The Estate'—re-reading it recently I was reminded of Matthew Arnold's complaint about the 'modern English habit (too much encouraged by Wordsworth) of using poetry as a channel for thinking aloud instead of making anything'.[4] Brasch does a great deal of 'thinking aloud' in *The Estate*. Fairburn was actually anxious about what he called 'aestheticism' and the spirit of John Keats creeping into our poetry in the 1950s. In fact he needn't have worried. It was Wordsworth not Keats who still presided.

James K. Baxter enunciated what was to be the predominant literary attitude of the 1950s when he said, in his celebrated address to the 1951 Writers' Conference in Christchurch, that a poet must be 'a cell of good living in a corrupt society'; and he concluded: 'I have dealt with the development of ideas rather than the development of verse-forms; mainly because to me verse-form seems a tool for sharpening ideas.' There you have that separation of form and content—'verse-form' on the one hand, 'ideas' on the other—which had been characteristic of the 1930s. In 1951 nothing had changed. There was still the donkey and his load—but agreement about what the load should be was going to become more and more difficult.

I thought of calling this lecture 'Recent Trends in New Zealand Poetry', which was Baxter's title, partly just to make more obvious the difference between what Baxter was able to see as new in 1951 and what I am able to see as new almost three decades later. I didn't call it that, partly because I don't like the word 'trends', and partly because I thought of a better one (which I will explain later). But clearly an important event in recent years, and one which the terms of Baxter's address in 1951 could not account for, was the development of his own poetry during the 1960s. By the late fifties his simple poetics of 'ideas' 'sharpened' by the 'tool' of 'verse-form' had run him into the turgidities of his 1959 collection, *In Fires of No Return*.

And he perhaps perceived—in the twilight way Baxter did perceive theoretical matters—that there wasn't a poetic vocation to be made of cheap fiction in verse. He needed a new start, and he made one by putting himself (or *a* self) squarely into the centre of the poems. This was a development which owed a great deal to recent American poetry (particularly to the work of Lowell, and perhaps Berryman) but not exclusively to what I've been describing as the Modernist tradition. The best of Baxter's later work is represented, I think, by the sonnet sequences, and there you can see him using something like the principle I've called accretion, or aggregation, to achieve a longer poem. The individual units—those radioactive fragments of which the longer poem must be put together if there's to be no narrative or logical structure—are in Baxter's case not as open as the units that make up a long poem in the direct Modernist tradition. In fact the continual shaping of experience to fourteen lines is a very considerable constriction, even though rhyme and five-stress lines have been dispensed with. There is also the linking device of the persona—the self at the centre adopting the speaking and acting role throughout. He continues to be a moralist too, or at least to engage in moral reflection. But the moralizing is absorbed into the persona—it becomes an aspect of character, a way of projecting the living body of the self, rather than the artificial imposition of structures on experience. The result is a considerable freeing up of Baxter's poetry, a shaking off of that formula the fifties inherited from the thirties and forties, where the final statement of the poem tended to have the effect of a gate clanging shut on the imagination. Baxter's late sequences are more open—and I think better—than anything he wrote previously. There is a more vivid sense of reality, a less structured approach to experience, a more free and flexible interaction between the language of the poem and the world beyond, and a richer sense of the life and presence of the persona:

> Yesterday I planted garlic,
> Today, sunflowers—'the non-essentials first'
>
> Is a good motto—but these I planted in honour of
> The Archangel Michael and my earthly friend
>
> Illingworth, Michael also, who gave me the seeds—
> And they will turn their wild pure golden discs
>
> Outside my bedroom, following Te Ra
> Who carries fire for us in His terrible wings
>
> (Heresy, man!)—and if He wanted only
> For me to live and die in this old cottage,
>
> It would be enough, for the angels who keep
> The very stars in place resemble most

These green brides of the sun, hopelessly in love
With their Master and Maker, drunkards of the sky

Baxter's talent—I think one should say Baxter's genius—finds its fullest expression in these late sequences. And there is another characteristic they have at least in common with Modernism, if not derived from it directly: that is that the forward movement, the sense of a momentum of expression, is more important than the '*mot juste*', or the polished phrase, or the brilliant image. That is where Baxter divides most clearly from Curnow. Curnow is all perfection of phrase; Baxter deals in beautifully judged approximations; and while one admires, in fact one can be left breathless and spellbound, by Curnow's lines and phrases—it's also true I think that it is the perfections which shut the reader out, rendering him spectator; it is the approximations (*if* they are beautifully judged) which draw him in, engage his imagination, leave him some active part in the completion of the poetic task.

So I have arrived by this comparison at another aspect of Modernism, and it is one that goes right back to Mallarmé and the French Symbolists. Perhaps the most fundamental sense in which the Modernist poem is 'open' is in never quite completing the statement, never closing the account, never letting that gate clang shut on the imagination of the reader. It is 'open' in reaching out and engaging the reader's imagination in the poetic act.

So (to recapitulate) we have now as elements in Modernist practice first the lack of logical or narrative structures, and in their place the aggregation of radioactive fragments within a 'Field'; second, the scoring of speech patterns to create a music which must predominate over any externally imposed form; and third, the use of suggestion, approximation, a carefully judged incompleteness as a way of engaging the reader in the action of poetry itself—all these combining ideally to increase the sense of an achieved reality.

Words are the poet's material, just as the sculptor's is clay, the painter's is pigment, the composer's is sound. And here I think a nice balance is called for to maintain on the one hand the independence of poetry against the realist, and on the other the seriousness of poetry against what I will call, for lack of a more precise term, the surrealist. The realist, as we've observed, often tries to make the words serve something beyond poetry—an idea, a programme. The surrealist, I think, tends to deplete the language by diminishing its reference to a verifiable world, and thus to turn poetry into verbal play. I come back to the red wheel/barrow: it is a fact (there is, in Curnow's phrase, 'a reality prior to the poem'), and the fact is *imagined*. The barrow is the meeting point of subjective and objective. The words 'red', 'wheel', and 'barrow' have sound values and associations. They have a texture of their own. But they also *mean*—they *refer*; and the art of poetry must exploit to the full every potential the words which are its material have. So I find the surrealist* strand in Modernism the least satisfactory, except perhaps as an occasional weapon for deflating pomposities. Even in the work of someone as brilliant as Alan Brunton (who illustrates the kind of thing I mean here by a surrealist) I feel there is a thinness in the language because the poet has let invention supersede perception. The language is showing us the mind of Brunton rather than the world as it appears to the mind of Brunton. To seek deliberately to detach the mind and the poem from its physical and social environment is I think a self-defeating game for a poet to play. So it's in this sense I currently feel poetry must be public: not in making political, or moral, or religious, or philosophical, or national pronouncements (though of course it may want to do any of these things). Primarily the poem must be public *in not being private*. It must be one man's vision, or one woman's vision, of a shared world.

When I chose my title—'From Wystan to Carlos'—I had in mind that Allen Curnow had called his first-born Wystan; and that Ian Wedde, about thirty-five years later, had called his first-born Carlos. And though I haven't enquired and don't know whether either of them was actually naming a child after a poet, Curnow in 1939 can't have been unaware that Auden's first name was Wystan, any more than Wedde can have forgotten that W. C. Williams's middle name was Carlos. (I might by the way have brought Pound into it because Bob Orr, one of the *Freed* poets, called his first child Ezra.) So I use the two names to signify the road New Zealand poetry has travelled during these decades. By a strange irony W. C. Williams was born a couple of decades before Auden; but Williams in this lecture has been one of the poets representing Modernism, and Auden something more conservative. And the change from Wystan to Carlos represents—as I've explained—not a case of poetry getting better, but of poetry moving with what I see as the tide of literary history.

It also represents, however, an expansion of possibilities, and it was something which had to come, I believe, if our poetry was not to grind almost to a halt, or settle down into a staple of polite middle-class writing which is what most of the poetry in Britain in the seventies has amounted to. Fleur Adcock is I think a case of a poet perfectly attuned to the British literary scene at the moment—enormously accomplished, no doubt of it, but so much of her skill directed towards that deadening effect which oc-

---

* There is in fact no surrealist tradition in the poetry of the English language. I hope my context—and the contrast with realism—will make clear what I mean here. My preference is for the point of balance between subjective and objective, where language consequently is used at maximum stretch. 'To orchestrate the real' is how I sometimes put it to myself.

curs when the absence of stylistic vices becomes more important than the presence of virtues. When poetry refuses to live dangerously it gives away a good deal of its reason for living at all.

You may think it's exaggerating to say that our poetry needed that infusion of energy which the new poets of the sixties gave it, but in that context it's relevant to consider the recent career of Allen Curnow. If I discussed these matters with Curnow himself I suspect he would say that if you have talent you don't need to worry about literary history and poetic movements, and if you don't have talent they won't help you. And with the confidence it must give him to have published three new books since 1972, two of them very good collections and one of those two, the latest, among the very best he has written, such a response wouldn't be surprising. But it doesn't seem to me irrelevant to ask what happened to Curnow's poetic career between 1957 and 1972, and to point out that in those fifteen years he published only one poem. A man's career can illustrate literary history without his being aware of it; and I should say Curnow as clearly as anyone else illustrates, in his silence at the end of the 1950s, that the movement in which he began had run its course. When he reappeared in 1972 his poetry had—I would say had of necessity—assumed at least some of the features I've suggested in this lecture are the features of Modernism.[5] And perhaps the most interesting point for my purposes is to recognize that of all the poems in his recent books, the longest, 'Moro Assassinato', is the freest, the most open in form, as if the pressure of the events which the poem relates, together with the knowledge that they had, built into them, a beginning, a middle, and an end, released Curnow from his usual anxieties about shaping, and so released the language of the poem to find its own form with greater flexibility than any of his other poems display. 'Moro Assassinato' is his most recent poem; and of all his poems it is the one that is nearest to the Modernist tradition in that it deals least in those finalities of phrasing which I suggested earlier can have the effect of rendering the reader a spectator rather than a participant in the poetic art.

Curnow's example is a reminder—Kendrick Smithyman is another—that it's important to avoid a sort of stylistic puritanism which says either you're a Modernist or you're old hat. There is a 'with-us-or-against-us' syndrome—a mild kind of paranoia—that goes with any *avant garde* development in the arts; and in that sense, of course, the Modernist tradition is *not* liberating—far from it. One can find young poets enclosed in a current mode, more aware of the mode than of what's going on outside the window. At that point it becomes a trap. The ampersand, the oblique stroke, the phonetic spelling yr for your, th for the, t for to, become substitutes for poetic perceptions and originality. We all know this. But the alternative folly is to use *this* folly as an excuse for refusing to look at a whole development—an excuse for shutting one's mind to it.

Kendrick Smithyman is probably the best case of a poet very much grounded in what I've called the realist tradition of the thirties, and with no inclination to alter the basic pattern of his poetry, who nevertheless has read very widely in the whole Modernist tradition, including the American poets of the 1950s and sixties, as a result of which I think his forms have become more flexible and his use of the vernacular freer and more inventive. Smithyman is like Baxter in having adapted the practice of American poets to purposes very much his own.

Of course there's no possibility of being anything like comprehensive; but other poets whose work could be discussed in these terms include people as diverse as Hone Tuwhare, Alistair Paterson, and Janet Frame—Tuwhare because of his adaptation of free form to the use of a very Kiwi and sometimes very Maori, vernacular; Paterson as an example of someone who began in what might be called the school of Johnson and has since sought consciously and deliberately for models and precedents that would liberate him from that mode; Frame for almost the opposite reason—because a combination of immense talent with a refusal to take herself quite seriously as a poet results in what seems almost a casual or accidental opening out into free form.

Of the group of poets who began to appear during the 1960s David Mitchell, Alan Loney, Murray Edmond, and Alan Brunton (despite my reservation of a moment ago), Bill Manhire (who owes least to the Modernist tradition),[6] and of course Ian Wedde, are the ones I'm most conscious of reading, not in the spirit of an indulgent senior, but as practising poet alert for sharpening plunder; and I'm going to conclude by saying just a brief word about Mitchell and Wedde.

David Mitchell has been silent since *Pipe Dreams in Ponsonby* came out in 1972, although I hear he has new work ready for publication; and of the group I've named I suppose he may be the one most vulnerable to a cold critical eye, the easiest to dismiss from your mind when you don't have the poems open in front of you. He's probably the most instinctive of the group, the least conscious in his practice, the one who has least theory to fall back on. But he's also the one I go back to with most pleasure, or at least with no less pleasure than I find in Wedde. I welcomed *Pipe Dreams in Ponsonby* when I reviewed it in 1972 and I don't feel there's any need either to take back or to repeat what I said then. Recently I re-discovered my copy of *Freed* 3 in which Mitchell's poem 'The Singing Bread' appeared, and I was struck again by the fact that he could write something stuffed with all the old claptrap of the sixties, full of echoes of Ginsberg and Miller, the totally predictable Paris poem, and yet to my ear a magical exercise, sustained with only minor subsidences for almost three hundred lines, carried forward on no recognizable framework except what I've suggested is the aggregation of fragments within a 'Field'. Only the tradition

of Modernism could account for such a poem, and before 1960 there was
no one in New Zealand could have done it.

When I reviewed Arthur Baysting's anthology, *The Young New Zealand
Poets,* in the *Listener* a few years back I tried to define one strange effect
Ian Wedde's poetry had on me by saying I found it agitating, like watching
someone trying to thread a needle. It still often affects me in that way, and
I think this must be something to do with the kind of high energy source
that animates Wedde's writing and is transmitted through it. Wedde's
temperament is affirmative—very different from the dourness of Loney or
the bleakness of Murray Edmond—nearer, I suppose, to Mitchell's
lyricism, but with a more obvious backbone. Wedde tends to be expansive,
rhapsodic, apostrophizing, ecstatic—even an exclamatory poet; and an unsympathetic view of him might illustrate that description by counting up
the number of occasions oh! and ah! occur in the *Sonnets for Carlos* and the
number of different ways he has of spelling them. Far from finding myself
unsympathetic to Wedde I want to say he too comes through to me as a
splendid and original poet, occupying that dangerous ground where the
celebratory may at any moment pitch over into the effusive and sentimental—the same area occupied by the best of Keats's poetry (and I've suggested already that poetry should live dangerously).

Yeats has a theory somewhere that nations throw up their anti-type in
the form of their best writers—the dissolute Burns affronting puritan
Scotland, the uncommitted Synge affronting political Ireland. By that
theory, I think, dour, undemonstrative New Zealand must be affronted by
Wedde's vitality, by his expansive energy, by (to use the phrase Arnold
used of Keats) 'that indescribable *gusto* in the voice'. Wedde has assimilated
the poetic developments I've spoken of in order to give fuller expression to
that forward rush of feeling which is native to himself. There is a momentum in his poetry which is fresh and exhilarating; and at the same time
there is density of reference—objects, scenes, talk, people—so that there is
never the sense that this is merely a mindscape. Even when he writes in a
tightly organized form, as he does in *Sonnets for Carlos,* he still manages to
keep the poem 'open' in most of the senses I've attached to the term; and in
particular, whereas Baxter tailors experience to fourteen-line rough-hewn
off-cuts, Wedde measures his lines, but keeps the poem moving, spilling
over from one sonnet into the next:

44

& what's better to do than celebrate
the fact? Look
                        the dark bloom's left your eyes
spring's ripe   the horizon the blue sky
the air pour towards you   the bean flower's sweet

again   that fucking ferryman grates
his rowlocks in mid-channel again   high
clouds are spinning like tops again & I
couldn't ever have enough of all that

& you again & again & again:
waking, quickening, travelling through one
world after another   through all the weird
stations of the earthly paradise named
for one impossible diamond-backed dream
or another, as though no one else cared

45

or could care
                    in all the wide
                                        world or worlds . . . !
Oh well.
                    I wanted to write poems about
spring, about you 'Primavera', about
the nagging dream of solitude
into which you break like a beanshoot curled
upon itself. But the shoot's put out

its sexy flower, you've got up, I'm late
again, Carlos is almost a year old . . .

can I ever catch up? do I want to?
turning for one last look back: that beacon,
that weird station, the lovely confusion
of the trip, your memory breaking through
to bless the present summer sojourn,
to soothe love's forever healing burn.

In tracing the development 'from Wystan to Carlos' I have not been trying to lay down prescriptions which poets should follow (any prescriptions
are for myself) and I have not offered a measure by which poets can be
judged better and worse. I have tried to describe a piece of our literary
history and to suggest that there has been in recent years an expansion of
poetic possibilities. In particular I suggest that the change in Baxter's
poetry during the last decade of his life, the continuing fluency of Kendrick Smithyman, and the re-emergence of Allen Curnow as a major voice,
together with the appearance of a group of younger poets of whom Ian
Wedde seems at present the most energetic and versatile, are all explicable
in a set of terms which must include a proper understanding of the
Modernist tradition as a variable but powerful force operating upon the
practice of poetry now. Without that tradition our poetry would be less

alive, less confident, with a narrower range of possibilities and an uncertain future.

POSTSCRIPT

To complete—or at least to extend—the picture I should add that my negative feelings about certain recent manifestations of 'post-Modernism' hinted at here in the remarks about 'surrealism' (see p. 154) were developed in a review of a number of books of poetry in *The London Review of Books*, 1 May 1980. Wondering why I admired many talents yet found John Tranter's anthology *The New Australian Poetry* boring, I wrote:

It is not that one necessarily demands 'Australianness', explicit regionalism, of Australian poets. It is rather that one requires of poetry —any poetry—the real, the concrete, the particular, not on any theoretical grounds but simply because without it the language will seem underemployed, lacking in texture. The aspect of Modernism that seems to predominate in Australia and New Zealand at the moment (probably in America too) is the one drawing ultimately from French Symbolism, specifically from Mallarmé. 'Poetry is not made with ideas, my dear Degas, it's made with words'. Mallarmé's put-down is perfect and right when directed against the notion of the poem as vehicle for an 'idea'. It is something English poets need to take to heart. It is the source of that magical quality Modernist poetry at its best possesses. But like all critical ideas it needs to stand against the background of its counterstatement to make safe sense. Removed, it becomes a doctrine of verbal abstraction.

. . . what the poems of Pound, early Eliot, and Williams at their Modernist best force upon us remorselessly is things, scenes, sounds, voices, particulars—a real teeming world. Mallarmé's 'Poetry is made with words' is complemented by Williams's 'No ideas but in things'. When modern poetry loses the sense of what John Crowe Ransom calls 'things in their thinginess', it slides away into verbal gesture. . . . In *The New Australian Poetry* I was impressed, sometimes dazzled, by the way so many of these poets could sustain fantasy, invention, surrealism, a sort of metadiscourse without meaning or reference, like the game children play of going round the room without touching the floor. But how long can you watch even the cleverest juggler before you begin saying 'So what?'

In that confrontation of Mallarmé and Degas there are, in fact, two abstractions proposed. There is the abstraction of Degas' 'ideas' ('I have some wonderful ideas for poems'). But there is also the abstraction of Mallarmé's 'words'. A mystique of language for its own sake is both the power source and the danger of Modernism.

A.R.D. FAIRBURN:
THE ARGUMENT AGAINST

It is good that A. R. D. Fairburn's *Collected Poems* should look like a book of poems and not like a text. But the order in which Fairburn's separate volumes are presented here seems to me arbitrary. There is nothing on the contents pages to indicate dates of publication, and the printing types used on these pages do not make sufficient distinction between titles of volumes and titles of sub-sections of volumes. *The Rakehelly Man* is listed as a title but not of a poem. There is nowhere an alphabetical list of poems or of first lines. A reader finding an interest in Fairburn awakened by this book would have to go outside it for elementary information. Mr Glover has got the poems into print; his foreword is brief and gritty; but as an editor he might have been more helpful to the uninitiated.

In Dunedin recently I found myself arguing (in accord with Dr E. H. McCormick's complaint in *Landfall* 77 about academic critics of New Zealand writing) that our universities were producing weed-killers instead of fertilizers. Now, as if to test my sincerity, I am confronted with Fairburn's collected poems, and with the doubts, irritations, and dislikes they arouse in me.

Writing after the death of T. S. Eliot, Allen Tate mourned that 'high civility' had 'almost disappeared from the republic of letters'. 'Its disappearance', he went on, 'means the reduction of the republic to a raw democracy of competition and aggression, or of "vanity and impudence".'[1] I believe I understand the complaint, and even in some degree share its

A review of Fairburn's *Collected Poems* (1966), *Landfall* 80, December 1966. That there is an argument *for* I have acknowledged in my Introduction. A vigorous counter-statement, or counter-blast, to my review can be found in Ian Hamilton's article in *Comment* 32, September 1967, 'Fairburn and Dr Stead'.

feeling. But did Tate reflect that it might have been written by Sir Henry Newbolt or Sir Edward Marsh (or equally by Senator Yeats) after reading some of T. S. Eliot's early reviews? Will it occur to those who echo it here that it might have been written by Alan Mulgan confronting Fairburn and his younger contemporaries in the 1930s?

Fairburn's reputation in New Zealand is considerable. He is more widely admired, I think, than any other of our poets. His work is read in schools. It is accessible, enjoyable, and the demands it puts on readers are not severe. The 'civility' which hedges it round is peculiarly Kiwi. Dr Allen Curnow, Mr R. A. K. Mason, Mr Antony Alpers, Mr Harold Innes, as well as Mr Glover himself—each in his different style has reminded us that Fairburn was swimmer, golfer, rugby player, yachtsman, that he had opinions and spoke out, that he was six-foot-three and good company in a pub—'a big man' (in Mr Mason's description), 'big in every way, in mind and body and spirit'. The literary reputation this image in part protects has not been questioned. It is not going to be snuffed out by an article. The poems are all here, in print; Fairburn has finished writing them; it is time to look at them at least without being required to keep in mind that their author (like anyone else) was capable of spending his energies profitably on other-than-literary pursuits.

What is the function of 'criticism'—and especially when the critic's responses prove to be largely negative? I cannot conceive of its function as that of 'maintaining literary standards', or, as Eliot once proposed, 'correcting taste'. 'Standards' are supported by concrete blocks, and 'taste' is largely a matter of decorative convention, social or literary. I am not sure what 'literary standards' are if they can be abstracted from feelings and taught in public institutions. 'Literature' is a confronting of personalities, occurring somewhere between the cold, immovable words on the page and the living eye which perceives them; and perhaps criticism is rightly only a form of biography not of the poet's life, nor of the critic's, but of the life generated in successive confrontations. It is no science. It proceeds from feelings before rational analysis has anything on which to work, returns to feelings for its final sanction, and though it may be 'better' or 'worse' it can never be 'right' or 'wrong'.

I do not, anyway, want to measure poems against any formal conception of what is a 'good' poem, but to measure a kind of life against those human qualities experience has taught me to respect.

'New Zealanders', Allen Curnow writes in his Penguin anthology,

do not trouble themselves much about the historical divide which separates their latest three or four decades from their first seven or eight. . . . Yet this divide is the most significant fact to be regarded in any realistic retrospect upon the country's literature, upon the qualities of mind and imagination it has nourished.

I would like to think it is 'common sense' that makes me doubt this 'fact'. It is comfortable to draw a line and place oneself and one's contemporaries on the right side of it. 'History' is then, not a mere record, but a Principle whose blessing, long withheld, has lighted on *us*. But if to believe in ourselves we have to belittle our forbears as a class, pretending they were all victims of delusions, we are not merely committing what seems to me an impiety, but inviting a future in which successive generations will draw the line again, nearer to themselves. What does this 'historical divide' signify if Katherine Mansfield, for example, stands on the far side of it, and Fairburn on the near? Either nothing; or that she had more to contend with and he less, which magnifies both her achievements and his failures.

If there are, as Mr Curnow believes, particular 'New Zealand' anxieties (about, for example, the precise relation between our actual and our literary experience) then they are anxieties we all share and will go on sharing. The writers we value will be those who surmount them and make use of them. If Fairburn was the poet Mr Curnow believes he was, he needs the historical no more than the personal myth to make this plain. If he was not such a poet, neither myth will protect him for long.

Can one talk about verse simply *as* verse—meaning the movement, the run of the lines, singly and together, the syntax and grammar, the conjunctions of vowels and consonants, but excluding reference and meaning almost entirely? If so, it is doubtful whether Fairburn ever surpassed the quality of the best verse in *He Shall Not Rise,* the 1930 volume which dismisses itself in its last poem ('Rhyme of the Dead Self'). The talent on display is aesthetic. The talent for living which in mature poetry gets worked into, becomes indistinguishable from, the others, is hardly yet present. But there are signs of its growth: even the sardonic Fairburn is now and then dimly revealed.

The aesthetic talent is what a poet is born with—like a talent for logic, or mathematics. It must be there or there is nothing to discuss; but it cannot alone (one might argue that Auden's *inherited* facility is greater than Yeats's) determine the stature of the poet. Fairburn's command in this first book is not merely of verse forms, but of a line that lengthens or shortens, rhymes or fails to rhyme, echoes, falters, runs on, with a perfect sense of how to keep itself attuned to a music without becoming merely predictable. It delights us, as the movement of water does, by echoing some knowledge within us of Chance and Choice, causation and indeterminacy.

The deficiencies of the poems are plain. Little of the man's life is in them. They lack his strength, his energy, the range of his passions, his intellect. Their referential (as distinct from their plastic) substance is literary. One must penetrate the conventional language if one is to discover any sense of actual experience behind them. It is probably more the lack of energy than the faded language that Fairburn rejected. At every stage in his career he resorted to that language (which Wordsworth called, in a withering phrase, 'the family language of poets').

In embryo the whole of Fairburn is in this book. It seems to promise a great deal.

In the second published volume, *Dominion*, a violence of the will is offered as a substitute for the manifest weaknesses of the first. It is as if we had moved from one aspect of the poetry of the 1890s to the other, from Dowson to Kipling (a Kipling of the Left), only to be reminded that both, the weakness and the violence, proceed from the same uncertainty. 'Dominion' is an ambitious national epic in which there is some confusion about whether the 'nation' resides in the people or the place. The poem surveys our history in broad inaccurate sweeps. It offers two largely unrelated visions of the present—one particular, rural, and idyllic; the other general, urban, and unpleasant. And it concludes with a vision of the future in which

> We shall arise at morning, and clothe ourselves,
> and walk in green fields.
> And we shall have dominion over the earth
> And the forms of matter.

This is, it seems, what awaits us on the far side of that rending struggle apocalyptically/abstractly/absurdly described in the final section of the poem, where a notion of dialectical Progress (Hegelian, not Marxist, Fairburn once assured me) is set forth in verse whose energy is breathtakingly 'trumped up'.

To the social and historical arguments of the poem M. H. Holcroft has patiently put the unavoidable objections:

> . . . it implies a strictly limited conception of humanity. There is the suggestion of a Calvinistic morality applied to the social background: the sheep are separated from the wolves, but there is no room for intermediate breeds, and no awareness of the immense haphazardness, the pathos of good intentions gone astray, the selfishness and the goodness, and the blind conflict . . . which seem to me to be nearer the confused reality of human experience. . . . It is true that New Zealanders struggle under a burden of debt and that the brave new world of the south is shadowed by the narrow doors of Threadneedle street; but it is also true that most of the debt has been shouldered with an easy optimism by politicians who imagined themselves to be free agents setting up the foundations of prosperity. There was no compact with financial oligarchs, no evil compounding with the sons of Mammon, no conscious spinning of a web that later generations could name The System. To visualize the deliberate exploitation of posterity, is to overlook the nature of history. . . .[2]
>
> *The Deepening Stream*)

Mr Holcroft also writes of 'a spontaneous lyrical impulse' in the poem, and of 'the efficacy of Mr Fairburn's lyric gifts, asserting itself against the thickening influence of the ideology'. He is right that what value the poem has exists in these lyric passages; but it is difficult to remove them from the flavour of the poem as a whole; and even if this can be done, objections remain. We are confronted once again with that faded 'literary' language, the old high tremulous emotive talk Fairburn all his life went on producing and running away from.

> O lovely time! when bliss was taken
> as the bee takes nectar from the flower.

This is the language of *He Shall Not Rise*, but it is now mounted in a pulpit bearing a great moral weight on its narrow shoulders.

> Fairest earth,
> fount of life, giver of bodies,
> deep well of our delight, breath of desire,
> let us come to you
> barefoot, as befits love,
> as the boy to the trembling girl,
> as the child to the mother. . . .

'Dominion' is full of violence, a violence, it is always assumed, which stemmed solely from the Depression. I suspect however that it had as much to do with literary as with social problems, and that it was something the poet was in part directing blindly against himself. He was in revolt against the pallid personality discovered in his early poems, a personality he could not accept as his own. Simultaneous with this discomfort, intensifying it, must have come Fairburn's full realization of the 'modern' movement in poetry, and the feeling that he was hopelessly 'out of date'. Only a New Zealander could have responded so precipitately to an alteration in Greenwich Mean Time.

'Dominion' is thus doubly ambitious—in design and in style—conceived as a sort of New Zealand 'Waste Land', and executed in a manner intended to reveal, among other things, a vigorous, tough-minded, modern poet. The maturing of a poet's personality will demand, and help to create, an alteration in his style. A style chosen because it has impressed him, rather than because it relates precisely to his own needs, will not make him a better poet. In a large part of 'Dominion' Fairburn is running ahead of himself; the 'lily-white lad' of 'Rhyme of the Dead Self' is still publicly strangling himself instead of getting on with the slow painful business of growing up.

The language of the early lyrics, for all their virtues, is a self-enclosed literary language, lacking in precise reference. A great deal of 'Dominion', in freeing itself from that 'poetic' language, fails to achieve poetry because it fabricates the 'reality' it pretends to reveal and denounce.

> The army of the unliving, the cells of the cancer:
> small sleek men rubbing their hands in vestibules,
> re-lighting cigar-butts, changing their religions;
> dabblers in expertise, licensed to experiment
> on the vile body of the State; promoters of companies;
> efficiency experts (unearned excrement
> of older lands, oranges sucked dry),
> scourges of a kindly and credulous race;
> economists, masters of dead language;
> sorners, bureausites, titled upstarts . . .
>
> and those who embrace their misery
> in small closed rooms,
> sucking carious teeth, sniffing
> the odour of themselves, gentlemen's relish:
> 'You must not confiscate our sufferings,
> they are private poetry.'

Fairburn in these sections of the poem ostentatiously cast aside 'private poetry'; what he offered in its place was public rant.

With the aid of Miss Olive Johnson's excellent bibliography a dozen of the poems published in *Poems 1929-41* can be certainly identified as having been written after *He Shall Not Rise* and before 'Dominion'. Of these, 'Winter Night' is a Georgian lyric, with all the cosiness of its convention.

> The candles gutter and burn out,
> and warm and snug we take our ease. . . .

'Empty House' is an experiment in freer form, introducing details like 'a plug for the vacuum-cleaner' which suggest the influence of the 'Pylon' poets. 'Landscape with Figures', 'Street Scene' and 'Deserted Farmyard' are satires of an English scene, none of them notable poems. 'The County', by contrast ('a mordant bucolic', as Mr Glover describes it), has been worked at and is pointed and witty.

Few of these poems mark any distinct advance over those of *He Shall Not Rise*. But there are two poems belonging to this period—'The Sea', and 'Disquisition on Death'—which stand alone. Fairburn seems to have been content with neither. He never published 'The Sea' in a collection; and he calls 'Disquisition on Death' 'an unfinished poem', and dates it 1929, as if to insist that it is not to be considered with his mature poetry. Both poems are in some degree obviously derivative, but what Fairburn has taken in each case he has made his own. They seem to me superior to anything else he wrote at that time; and of all his work the 'Disquisition' is, I think, the poem I read with most pleasure. Why was he dissatisfied with them when their shortcomings, to say the least, are no greater than those of the poems he chose to represent him? A possible explanation is that they were written in some degree spontaneously, and fell outside the categories of his poetic intentions at that time. It is more likely a poet will recognize whatever faults such poems have than that he will see the inadequacies of his own formulated strategy; and indeed, they may be judged wanting precisely by their failure to accord with poems which, however inadequate, are as he meant them to be. Yet if his intentions are in some way mistaken or misguided, the poem which causes discomfort may be the very one proceeding most naturally from himself, out of his full sensibility.

'Disquisition on Death' has philosophical pretensions; and some of its language has no reference, hardly even an existence, outside of literature. Yet everything in it is gathered up in an exhilarating forward momentum that is the poem itself.

> It is this body-death they fear indeed,
> this scavenger of flesh and all living substance,
> this is the very fountainhead of fear.
> How should so beautiful a thing as death
> be a stench in the nostrils, be clothed in such bitter finality?
> For death is but the digestive organ of God,
> by its prime metabolism giving
> fresh form and shape to the immortal spirit;
> so that the leaf, the fruit, bowel and gut of swine,
> the beggar's scabs, the flesh of emperors,
> the lips of Guinivere and the blood of Christ,
> dissolved and scattered, have worn a million shapes.

The poem contains statements as lofty and pretentious as Fairburn wrote anywhere ('But where is the tower that shall outlast all time/ . . . O it is builded in the heart of man')—yet it does not depend on them. They are not the pillars of a structure. The 'thought' is only another manifestation of *energy*, and the poem is 'unfinished'—which I suspect means that the impulse governing it was strong enough to resist Fairburn's efforts to pull it all together into an orderly conclusion. Instead, it ends with a high-pitched but convincing account of a love affair, in which the tone of voice is maintained unfalteringly, and all Fairburn's skills have free play.

> . . . the setting sun and the far
> golden hills like mice embalmed in honey. . . .
> There's no knowing how it happened, or how
> by the mere merging of body and perishable dust
> grace should have bloomed in us. . . .

It is unfashionable to talk of 'beauty', but that is what Fairburn achieves in the final section of this poem, and in a measure rare in our poetry.

Poems 1929-41, and the same collection published with additions in 1952 under the title *Strange Rendezvous,* seem to me to lack coherence, unity of purpose. Perhaps they seemed so to Fairburn. He prefaced the 1952 collection with, and derived its title from, five lines of Wordsworth's (which Mr Glover omits without explanation from the present volume):

> Strange rendezvous! My mind was at that time
> A parti-coloured show of grave and gay,
> Solid and light, short-sighted and profound;
> Of inconsiderate habits and sedate,
> Consorting in one mansion unreproved. . . .

The effect is of a poet's notebook rather than of a finished collection. There is no one governing personality, conviction or purpose, only a succession of attempts at 'poetry', and little development even of means. Fairburn is striking out in all directions and never quite finding himself. Even the best of these poems lack density or depth. There is the impression everywhere of surfaces, a dimension lacking, an inability to see, and consequently to say, more than one thing at a time, so that everything, despite the command of verse forms and the poetic dressing, is in the nature of prose. Fairburn's struggle is not with an intractable reality which has been seen and which resists arrest, but rather with the feeling that the observed reality ought to be more 'poetic', grander, more high-toned than it is. In poetry, as perhaps in life, Fairburn was constantly in search of the big experience, the explosive moment. Failing to find it, he alternately fabricated, scolded, or threw away the whole problem for a quick laugh.

> There should be the shapes of leaves and flowers
> printed on the rock, and a blackening of the walls
> from the flame on your mouth. . . .

There should have been, perhaps, but there were not. Is it too much to say that his disappointment, like his expectation, was naïve?

In a few short lyrics in the 1952 collection ('The Estuary', 'Sea-Wind and Setting Sun') and in the grave pastoral couplets of 'Wild Love', Fairburn achieved something like the completeness his early work might have led one to expect.

> So, like a leaf quitting a tree, I go
> and by your leave take leave
> of what we may never again
> not ever again in this dispensation
> hope, or dare, to achieve.

As he grew older Fairburn resorted more and more to the writing of comic verse. I say 'resorted' because, though his comic verse is always diverting and sometimes very funny indeed, his earlier work testifies everywhere to a literary ambition which was hardly to be fulfilled in trifles. If Fairburn could not satisfy himself he could at least satisfy his friends and his public. He had a lively sense of humour and was an agile rhymer. But it is a mark of the fragmentation of his personality that the solemn, high-toned poet and the funny man are so totally segregated in the poetry. In a few of the earlier poems one can see the whole personality merged in something that is serious without loss of a sense of the absurd, or comic without being weightless.

> Lying in the sun beside the sea
> the sky the huge hard bulging bum
> of a metal kettledrum, the sea
> hot parchment tightly stretched for the sticks. . . .
>
> I am neither sea nor rock but living flesh
> I can swim but not as a fish swims
> I have fear and the knowledge of opposites.   ('The Sea')
>
> Kant's dead, the gods be praised.
> That old man ruled me five years or more,
> wagging the finger of reproof under my nose,
> bloodless, lifeless, sexless he ruled me,
> he and his system, a two-and-elevenpenny clock
> with an alarm like the conscience of Calvin.
> He's dead, and I no more eat German haggis. . . .
>
> The Sphinx smiles, say some, I say she sneers.
>   ('Disquisition on Death')

These are varieties of 'wit', something richer and more complicated in its effect than Fairburn's characteristic humour. In his later work the solemn prophet and the clown, each of them half a man, part company almost entirely. Both are present in 'The Voyage', but they take turns to speak.

Reading the 'serious' poems in *Strange Rendezvous* I find myself wondering again and again how the author of the comic verse could have been so totally excluded that Fairburn could write, for example (in Epi-thalamium'), 'Strip quickly darling', and 'leap on the bed', without any consciousness of the potential absurdity of the visual image they evoke. We are required to enter these poems as one is supposed to enter a church, appropriately dressed, and in the right frame of mind (Fairburn's own when he wrote them). To bring our whole personality is to commit a sacrilege against Poetry. In 'Song for a Woman' Fairburn writes,

> His vision of my loins, I know,
> blooms like a rose as thrust on thrust

> he loves me, till his brow is wet,
>   and splits my womb and spills his lust.

Inevitably one prefers the comic variant of this unreal 'vision':

> He plucked her in the portico,
>   and not content with that
> the ruffian rumble-dumbled her
>   upon the back-door mat.

('The Rakehelly Man')

Much of Fairburn's comic verse seems, in fact, an unconscious parody of his own poems, as if the part of his personality excluded in the serious writing were protesting against that exclusion.

Several years ago in a long review of Allen Curnow's poetry I extracted from the Introduction to Mr Curnow's Penguin anthology, and applied to his own work, the principle that there must be a 'reality prior to the poem' if there is to be a poem at all. That principle seems to me as sound now as it did then—so long as it is understood that the *kind* of 'reality' can never be prescribed, and that it may as often direct our vision inward as to some outwardly experienced form. I was saying, or understanding Mr Curnow to say, that though a poet may derive from other poets his modes of dealing with experience, he must nevertheless deal with actual experiences, and not with fabricated ones. ('I hear the sleet upon the thatch' is fabricated.)

This is a general statement of a proper relationship between the poet and his world; and though it may seem simple or obvious anyone who has tried to write poetry will recognize the problems it points to. But the particular application of any truism will always cause disagreement; and looking again at Mr Curnow's Introduction I find him arguing that James K. Baxter lacks the sense of that reality, while Fairburn is in full possession of it. Every poet will lack it from time to time, and his writing will suffer accordingly. But if one poet is to be used in this way as the measure of another, it seems to me precisely a confidence about the reality of his subjects (one might as accurately say his 'feelings') that gives Mr Baxter's work, through all its variations, the doggedly personal voice, the resoluteness of tone, that Fairburn's lacks.

Fairburn was troubled in his later years by what he regarded as a prevailing 'aestheticism'. For this he partly blamed Keats:

In spite of his greatness, it is difficult to resist the thought that somewhere in Keats was the seed—or possibly the ground—of corruption; and that Wordsworth was really the more substantial poet. *(Landfall* 20, December 1951.)

He was troubled by the obscurity of much of the poetry being written, and by its lack of 'philosophical' substance; he saw the London publishing world as a fairy encampment; and he half conceived of himself as a modern New Zealand Wordsworth, somewhat isolated in maintaining the true function of the poet. Good poetry might have emerged from all this had Fairburn possessed the confidence to maintain it. But he was (or seemed to be) constantly tempted, troubled, irritated, and diverted from his own concerns by the poetry that was fashionable. He was perhaps always over-conscious of an external literary world, a world of fashion and success, and not conscious enough of that inner necessity which ought to govern each new step a poet takes; and he was so fluent, simply as a writer of verse, that it must have been more difficult for him than for most poets to be sure when he was writing poetry and when he was not.

Fairburn's claim to be taken seriously as a 'philosophical' poet must rest on the two long poems written in the late 1940s. 'The Voyage' is described in his own Notes as

a poem about faith, and works. In particular, it is about what Keats called 'Negative Capability, that is, when a man is capable of being in uncertainties, mysteries, doubts, without any irritable reaching after fact and reason'.

It is odd that Fairburn should have located a source, or a parallel, for this poem's 'philosophy' in the very poet in whom 'the seed—or possibly the ground' of aesthetic 'corruption' lay. But Keats meant, surely, that a poet's most valuable perceptions were discovered *in* the 'uncertainties, mysteries, doubts'. Fairburn makes of that idea a programme, in the course of which he evades rather than experiences the motions of uncertainty. He stands, like a swimming instructor, on the brink of life rather than *in* it, urging us on. No one could doubt his faith in the value of swimming; it is only that, preaching it, he has no time for the practice.

In the allegory of the poem Life is represented as a voyage to death, an unknowable destination. The captain is asked where the ship is going, but he cannot answer. (He bears a close relation to the poet. He weaves on a hand-loom in his cabin; and the poet addresses us through him.) He can only affirm the voyage itself. 'Who are we', he asks, 'to know the complete, the illimitable pattern?' We must get on with our work, take pleasure in it, and ask no questions. 'It is a sentiment', Denis Glover once observed, 'that would move tears of banality in a Hitler, a Holland or a constellation of Commissars' (*Landfall* 27, September 1953).

The 'faith' the poem requires of us is faith in the voyage, not in anything beyond it, not in a destination—and this could constitute a perfectly respectable point of view (though hardly a striking one) if Fairburn, rising to a romantic crescendo in the last lines, had not tossed it overboard:

> and dolphins gliding and breaking at our bows
> will lead us on, and the wind filling our sails
> gather us into glory.

Is it mere pedantry to ask, of a poem that has presumed to instruct us, what this 'glory' means; and to point out that if it means *anything*, it contradicts the whole of the preceding argument?

The weight of the poem's didactic argument is further called in doubt by the alterations of tone, and more, by the elaboration of the idea. The idea, as such, is very simple. It is, after all, capable of statement in the Notes. If the length of the poem were truly governed by the idea it might well be brief. But the metaphor of the voyage is extended, and for what other reason than to produce 'poetry'—more and more of it? The philosophical pretension is, in fact, only an excuse for the aesthetic exercise.

'The Voyage' is not so much a single poem as a small collection—some comic verse, some fine lyric passages, and a prophetic utterance—contained loosely within the one structural metaphor. 'To a Friend in the Wilderness' might seem to possess a more genuine unity. Fairburn's evocation in this poem of the rural pursuits he delighted in is as fine as anything of that kind he wrote—though its force, too, is diminished because it seems to lack a natural length, internally governed, and to stop only for want of breath. But again the poem asks to be considered as an argument, and again the argument ends on the brink where life (and poetry) might be expected to begin. How seriously is one to take a poet who asks himself, or pretends to ask, and at length, whether he should depart from human society and teach his children 'stone-age crafts, using/such simple gear as might be stored in a cave, or stowed in an ark'? That he decides against the idea is hardly the point. I simply question what made him think such an elementary decision might make dramatic substance for poetry.

A formidable intellectual lady once told me that 'To a Friend in the Wilderness' was 'the finest statement of the humanist position by a New Zealander'. Another, to whom I quoted the remark, said 'That, of course, is cant'. It is; and it is all the poem's pretensions deserve. To locate life's deficiencies outside oneself, and yet live with them solemnly out of a sense of moral responsibility, is at once to negate life and to take too much upon oneself. There is no evidence in this poem that Fairburn has imagined his way into the lives of those he calls (unconsciously echoing the comic opening of 'The Voyage') 'my people', and to whom he dedicates himself. They exist only as an assorted collection of grotesques. The gesture in their direction is *only* a gesture; and for all the evidence the poem offers, the reason for renouncing the ideal life described in it might as well be that it did not exist, or that the cave lacked hot water, as that the poet felt any genuine obligation. The poem's merits are wholly descriptive; but even the actual world described is breathlessly translated into an ideal, a Platonic, one:

> on that shore
> despair withers in the sun, in the salt air,

> love goes gloveless, faith is naked, the eye
> stares at the skeleton fact, the doomed lips
> smile at truth revealed, cry welcome
> to the flux, the fire, the fury,
> the dance of substance on the needle-point of mind. . .

It is sleight of hand which asks us to credit with a high sense of social responsibility the decision not to live in an ideal world. No man is offered the choice. Meeting the poem as an argument one can only reply that

> girl and boy,
> busy matron, sad-faced successful man,
> prim saint and puzzled sinner,
> grim loser and bad winner, pimp and peeping Tom,
> snotty-nosed cherub, anonymous letter writer,
> sleek parasite and host, master and slave,
> owl-eye, chew-cud, wolf-jaw, ferret-face. . . .

these—if they exist at all—would not be helped by a poet's renunciation on their behalf; but that he would be helped a good deal by seeing them as human beings.

Fairburn is sometimes represented as a man of many accomplishments, of which poetry was merely one—a man relatively indifferent to literary success. I don't believe this is true of him. Under all his self-protective changes of colour he remained an ambitious poet, anxious to get on. His *Collected Poems* is full of that anxiety. One hears a good deal about his bewildering variety. It is, rather, varieties of bewilderment. The personality that comes out of these pages, even on its funniest pages, is fragmented, frantic, and disappointed. He tries too much and too hard, and lacks certainty about all he does. The word 'immature' creeps up on me again and again, and I censure my own impertinence only to replace it with 'precocious'. Even the poems written in middle age seem precocious; and I find myself inclined to speak of the things I like not as 'poems' but as 'performances'. A talent is constantly on display, but where are the poems? They are there of course. But to measure them against the uses to which such energy might have been put, against their own apparent ambitions, is to find them wanting, and by a test they seem to invite.

I know Eliot meant it, and was right, when he said 'the poetry does not matter'. It was something Wordsworth, too, might have taught Fairburn, had Fairburn looked more than longingly and from a distance into his work. The human personality transmuted into poetry, or transmitted through it, is what matters—its magnitude, its strength, its capacity to suffer and affirm the common range of experience, and to lose itself there. I have in mind some lines by James K. Baxter.

Come now;
Poems are trash, the flesh I love will die
Desire is bafflement,
But one may say that father Noah kept
Watch while the wild beasts slept.[3]

Fairburn knew 'the flesh I love will die'. He proved, but hardly abstracted into a consistent understanding, that 'desire is bafflement'. But did he ever guess at the truth that, if poems are not trash, at least 'the poetry does not matter'? It is only within that understanding that poems which matter are written. To live one's life according to an ideal notion of what is appropriate to a 'Poet' is to live a dream, and to deprive oneself of the substance out of which poems are made. Am I saying—what might seem at first glance the reverse of the truth—that Fairburn gave poetry precedence over the quality of life, and as a punishment was defeated by both? The punishment seems outrageous.

R.A.K. MASON:
BRINGING DISORDER TO LIFE

R. A. K. Mason's poems exhibit a natural, urgent lyricism unlike anything else in our poetry. I suppose all his best poems to have been in outline (however later emended and polished) spontaneous expressions of feelings not always perfectly understood by the mind as it brought them forth. The supposition may seem presumptuous or naïve: it is the labour of every poet to make us feel just that. As Yeats has it—

> A line will take us hours maybe;
> Yet if it does not seem a moment's thought,
> Our stitching and unstitching has been naught.

Yet I retain my conviction; and a number of facts may be adduced in its support.

Mason's syntax, even in the earliest poems written while he was still at Auckland Grammar School, is strong, gaunt, spare, and almost clumsily swift:

> I am not stone not adamant not steel
> am no undutiful clod but all a man
> who in great battle . . .
>
> ('The Agnostic')

> Digged you out whence you were shrined
> I whom thing with scarce a mind
> all long lifetime you did grind.
>
> ('Lullaby')

I do not think that a very young poet could make such a compressed syntax

A review of Mason's *Collected Poems,* first published in *Comment* 16, July 1963.

by deliberating over it. Too conscious of an 'idea', an intention, a direction, and conscious at the same time of a style to be achieved, the young poet will most often write diffusely in the interests of his 'idea', or screw down his lines tightly, one by one, in the interests of the style, so that they break off one from another, failing to achieve fluid rhythmical and emotional connexions. Such a 'natural momentum' as Mason achieves very early can only be *made,* one feels, by a seasoned campaigner. Thus my immediate supposition that the urgency comes from a pressure not of Mason's own making may be reasonably supported. And one may add that a poet who learned young to make such a style at will—if such were conceivable—might be expected to maintain it, and not to cease writing lyrics as Mason did twenty years ago. In this sense Mason seems to me a poet without a craft, a poetic medium rather than a maker of poems, a man who has been the victim of poetic occasions and a poet who is victim of the failure of those occasions.

There is of course even in the 'purest' poetry some idea, some direction which it is intended the poem should follow. But how quickly Mason's lyricism subsumes the intention so that it becomes merely one part of the poem's completeness may be demonstrated again and again. In a very early poem, 'Old Memories of Earth', the initial intention seems to have been to make a statement asserting that earth is our only home, that there are no gods and no afterlife. But Mason's instinct is to embody dramatically what he sets out to deny. Thus the gods and the afterlife take on a reality equal with the earth-bound denial. A meaningful ambiguity is generated. The second stanza, for example, speaks of those who claim memories of some other world:

> Perhaps they have done, will again do what
>   they say they have, drunk as gods on godly drink,
>   but I have not communed with gods I think
>   and even though I live past death shall not

The gods are so strongly evoked that the 'I think' comes naturally to temper the denial; and the possibility of living 'past death', followed by the strong 'shall not', completes the ambiguity. (This is a process which occurs in a number of poems. 'In Perpetuum Vale', for example, *as statement* denies consciousness after death. Yet Mason's poetic instinct is to dramatize the voice—and the voice is that of the dead man. The poem is thus ambiguous, and richer than its intention.)

'Old Memories of Earth' recognizes, or creates, its own spiritual continuum, but one located in the sphere of earth—something which is history, and more than history, for the past is in us and with us in the present:

> And I recall I think I can recall
>   back even past the time I started school
>   or went a-crusoeing in the corner pool
>   that I was present at a city's fall.

The factual elements and the hesitancy of the statement might be called naïve, simple, almost simple-minded: by which the last line is rendered so much the more effective.

Now the figure which can hardly have been part of the initial intention, but towards which the imagination has been feeling its way, emerges:

> And I am positive that yesterday
>   walking past One Tree Hill and quite alone
>   to me there came a fellow I have known
>   in some old times, but when I cannot say:

> Though we must have been great friends, I and he,
>   otherwise I should not remember him
>   for everything of the old life seems dim
>   as last year's deeds recalled by friends to me.

One wonders why these lines, even in their inconsequential tailing off, are so powerful. The strength is partly in the voice painstakingly relating, humbly accounting for everything, puzzled and without disguise. ('And I am positive . . . but when I cannot say: Though we must have been . . . otherwise . . .') It is the human voice stripped of all learned accretions, all sophistications and disguises, reduced to simple honesty by the awful reality of the poetic occasion. The shadowy figure of the 'fellow' (both 'bloke' and brother) assimilates the poem's initial opposites—the gods and the spiritual denial. The 'fellow' is ghostly, timeless, yet of this time and place, of the earth. He is, I think, a foreshadowing of Mason's Christ, not the God who has assumed flesh, but the spiritual continuity of suffering earthbound man; so that Auckland's One Tree Hill is at once itself and, dimly realised, the present shadow of Calvary.

II

The preoccupations of Mason's poetry which might be called 'philosophical' are those of the intelligent child and adolescent—and by that I do not mean in the least to disparage them. There are certain fundamental perceptions the clarity and vividness of which shock when they come for the first time—perceptions of death, of infinity, of necessity, of size; and these have 'philosophical' extensions which the child pursues or is bewildered by. The running boy on the Bycroft's biscuit tin, who carries a biscuit tin picturing a running boy carrying a biscuit tin picturing a running boy . . . this is to the child a bewildering image of infinity. So is the consideration of his ancestry, forced back and back (and involving sometimes the question of where our 'freedom' lies) until it ceases to be human, ceases to be animal, ceases to be of the world as it is; or the attempt to imagine space, and then to limit it by drawing a boundary around it, which at once poses the problem that something must lie outside the boundary. Then there are those first realizations that we are conscious, and define our consciousness only by contrast, with the resulting perception that a 'perfect' state would be a state of negation—which either dissolves all notion of Heaven, or necessitates the possibility of vacations in Hell in order that the blessed may be sensible of their state.

If such considerations are abandoned as habits of thought it is not because they are foolish, or because as problems they are ever satisfactorily solved. Life imposes a necessary pragmatism. One does not 'get on' in the world by brooding over the fact that one's mind will lose in time its capacity to elicit from one's arm a co-ordinated movement.

A part of Mason's lyric gift is that it can reconstruct in poetic form these primitive perceptions, these primary acts of self-consciousnesness. His early poems in particular are, for the most part, large and simple images of the individual soul standing grimly between its two chaoses—that of the past and that of the future. 'Miracle of Life', for example, stares back into the flow of the life-stream and considers what a small event, in so long a chain of cause, might have terminated the possibility which has been miraculously preserved and delivered into the present. 'Sonnet of my Everlasting Hand' sees the atoms of the hand which writes as having lived through the whole history of the world—

> have swept up Africa in withering sand
> and smitten all the seething Spanish land
> or charged on China . . .

At last they have come

> to house the mutable spirit of this strange
> uncomprehended thing, at once their bier
> and womb: for even now they long to range
> again that midnight future which I fear.

The physical and intelligent identity of each man is drawn out of the vast Process, is seen struggling to hold itself whole, and at last dissolves back into its elements: in this vision of mutability Mason's tragic sense of human brotherhood is generated. It is a brotherhood not simply of the present, but of each man in his time and place with all men of all times and places. Our intelligence commands, even as it is victim of, the whole of time; and the young poet who was 'present at a city's fall' has also

> Burnt Dian's temple down at Otahuhu
> and slain Herostratus at Papatoe
> and here in Penrose brought Aeneas through
> to calm Ausonian lands from bloody Troy

Thus the 'Sonnet of Brotherhood' is not primarily concerned with a national brotherhood—though it is perfectly valid to make the point (as I think Mr Curnow has done) that in its detail the poem draws strength from a distinguishable New Zealand situation. Nor, however, is it primarily concerned with an international brotherhood, socially or politically conceived. The poem is a statement of the human identity besieged by its foreknown doom, and of the naturalness of charity in the conditions of that universal siege. Time is for Mason, as it must be for every traditional poet, his most pressing engagement.

The best of Mason's early poems are all of this primitive and general kind, reaching out from the present place and time, back beyond birth, forward beyond death. In their simplicity they rediscover, as the child discovers, the terrors and the joyful powers of human self-consciousness, where 'Each day brings on its common miracle'.

There is something of the quality of Blake's Songs in these early poems; and their assertions, at once humble and grand, have about them the glittering and clumsy innocence of the poetic state from which they have come unbidden:

> for there is nothing by man known or guessed
> that's not miraculous beyond belief.
>
> ('Miracle of Life' II)

III

The 1934 volume, *No New Thing*, though it contains Mason's best poems, gives evidence of an increased self-awareness in which the qualities distinguishing the earlier work could not be maintained; and in a few of these poems, Mason yields to the temptation to imitate himself, to take up consciously the courageous postures innocently assumed in poems like 'Wayfarers', 'The Lesser Stars', and 'After Death'.

> Son of sorrow sire of sods
>   still I gird back at the gods
>   boldly bear five feet eleven
>   despite hell and earth and heaven.
>
> ('Stoic Marching Song')

> For my bitter verses are
>   sponges steeped in vinegar

> useless to the happy-eyed
> but handy for the crucified.   ('If the drink . . .')

In declarations such as these Mason's spareness of line, his dramatic sense, his ability to create the vigorous speech of a man thinking and feeling —these save him from the mawkishness that would certainly result from any attempt by a lesser poet to speak so well of himself. But a literary self-consciousness has entered; and the poetic self, the adopted mask, is not always perfectly conceived to fit the reality behind it. Mason seems to have been persuaded that his best poems exhibited (as Fairburn described it) a 'smouldering pessimism'. But if one looks carefully at the early poems in which this 'pessimism' might be thought to lie, it will not be found in them. 'After Death', for example, would be ill-served by the description. It is a poem which affirms life by regretting that it must pass; and even its refrain ('but not for me') is part of the celebration, because the intensity with which the present reality is felt springs precisely from that recognition of its transience.

The best poems of *No New Thing* are concerned less with primitive glances into the vastness of past and future than with the particularities of human action and human suffering, here and now. On the whole they are better poems than those of the earlier collections, more maturely rounded out to fulfil all the potentialities of their conception. The style is muscular, direct and efficient, the images bold and simple. Our acts of charity ('On the Swag') are weighed against our acts of betrayal ('Judas Iscariot'). Human aspiration even at the expense of those we love ('Footnote to John II, 4') is weighed against the ironic horror of its fulfilment ('Ecce Homunculus'). The poems on sexual themes range over a wide scale of experience and attitude: utter rejection of the life process in 'The Young Man Thinks of Sons'; varieties of frustrated aspiration in 'Lugete O Veneres', 'Flattering unction', and 'Thigh to thigh . . .'; the urging of a possibility in 'Nox Perpetua Dormienda'; cold success in 'She Who Steals'; and affirmation, defiant in 'If it be not God's law . . .', triumphant in 'Since flesh is soon . . .'

A false critical distinction—one frequently made, and made recently by Mr Baxter in the *Poetry Yearbook*—will do damage to these poems, will indeed appear to dismiss some of them easily. I refer to the unreal separation of 'form' and 'content', where 'form' is conceived of as something larger than prosody. One can imagine a critic fond of this distinction arguing of some of these poems that they are formally sound, 'well written', but that their 'content' is naïve, untruthful, or even dangerous. But such a distinction, if it can be made at all, can only be made in speaking of discursive poems, poems which are, or imply, directives to the will of the reader, imperatives towards action. The best poems in *No New Thing*, whether or not they adopt the first person, are purely dramatic. Each adopts some traditional human posture, and without urging that posture as 'good', 'right' or wholesome, holds it firmly against all others. The achievement of the poems considered singly will be found in the purity of their enactment, in their vigorous exclusion of discursive extension. Their achievement as a group is in their variety of mood and attitude. For such a small collection of short poems they represent, within their uniform syntactical muscularity, a surprisingly wide range of moods and occasions from the primitive drama that goes on beneath the customs and restraints of our day to day lives.

IV

Most readers are likely to find somewhere near the centre of Mason's poetry an obscurity surprising at first sight because one thinks of him as the most accessible of our poets. Perhaps a distinction is needed here between poems which are 'difficult' and poems which are 'obscure'. Mr Curnow or Mr Smithyman can be difficult, as a poet like Donne is difficult. Some of their poems present an intimidating prospect. But the difficulty is there to be overcome; as we acquaint ourselves further with the poem, it will gradually resolve itself. Mason's poetry, on the other hand, seems on first reading simple, easily comprehended, because Mason works always in familiar poetic materials. Yet a poem like 'Be Swift O Sun' is like 'Kubla Khan' in becoming less amenable to literal comprehension the closer and longer our acquantance with it. It is a strange echoing chasm, and we move further into it only to discover a deepening obscurity. It is, I am convinced, a pure and spontaneous expression of feelings proceeding direct from levels below those of consciousness, and passing into their verbal form almost entirely without rational inhibition or control. For that reason it is perhaps best understood—if indeed 'understanding' is in question—best *experienced*, immediately and without thought. Very quickly I find myself relinquishing the notion that it is in any primary sense a love poem. Like most 'inspired' poems it is, if it can be said to be 'about' anything, about inspiration. But such a description will not serve. The poem is not discursive. It has, strictly speaking, no subject and no meaning. It *is*. It manifests a unified state, an 'undissociated sensibility'. It is not a statement of anything other than itself. It declares itself, as anything else declares itself, simply by being.

By describing the poem in these terms I am of course, avoiding an 'evaluation' of it. I do not, however, intend to deny the possibility of criticism entirely. One may speak of the elements of which the poem is composed; one may dismantle it. But the poem will be met only in reading it or hearing it read, not in speaking or writing of it. And if this is true of all poems, it is true of only a few in a degree so close to absolute.

The poem, the state of being it manifests, encompasses a number of opposites which incidentally define Mason's New Zealand *locus* more precisely than might be expected. The voice is 'placed' as it declares its antipodes, 'the dark fields of France'. There day is about to break; here, the sun is declining; here the poem's persona has it, yet urges the sun to depart—

> lest she be in need
> of light in those far alien ways.

Between these opposites run the ships, and the sun itself—but they do nothing to close the gap between the persona and its distant concern.

The woman herself encompasses opposites. She is the source of love and death ('those breasts where I found death'). She is associated with arrival and departure, and described in images which conjoin evening and morning. Her eyes commingle 'all innocence with all things wise'.

It would be very difficult to find precise objections to a criticism which read 'Be swift O Sun' as a love poem in which the poet desires the return of his mistress, knows she will not return, yet remains concerned for her welfare. I simply record that though such a meaning may be derived from the words on the page, I do not find it in the feeling they evoke. The poem as a whole is a resolution of its own opposites: male and female, nearness and distance, North and South, arrival and departure, light and dark, sunrise and sunset, sun and rain, innocence and wisdom—the dramatic voice holds them all in exact balance. If the woman must be characterized at all I can accommodate her to my view of the poem only as the Spirit of Beauty, the Muse. She is the objective, distant, opposite principle, a product of the subjective mind, but thrust out from it, given independence and equality; and the poem where it speaks most fluently and naturally exults rather than laments, because the subjective consciousness discovers itself, experiences its own reality, precisely in the degree to which it succeeds in distancing, dramatizing, and casting light upon its objective complement.

However remote such a poem may be from fiction, there is nevertheless a lesson in its triumph over subjectivity which I believe most of our active fiction writers have yet to learn. Its charity may begin at home, but it does not end there.

V

Mason's silence since about 1940 is, if I have understood his poetry correctly, the failure of a gift for which the will could provide no substitute. In some of the later poems, particularly in the three political poems 'Youth at a Dance', 'Prelude' (from *This Dark Will Lighten*), and the recent 'Sonnet to MacArthur's Eyes', one can see Mason attempting to substitute good intentions for poetic occasions. The attempts lamentably fail. It is scarcely overstating the case to say that in 'Prelude' ('Here are the children. . . .') he sells his own poetry short, blames the age for its deficiencies, and hails the dawn of a new age when, presumably, poetry will be easier. 'Sonnet to MacArthur's Eyes' adopts the tone of an indignant letter to the editor, and is rendered superfluous by MacArthur's remark quoted as its epigraph, the brutality of which declares itself more forcibly than anything the poem can do. 'Milton would have recognized the impulse', Mr Curnow says. So he would: but scarcely the execution!

That such poems were published, that they are republished here, confirms I think how much instinct and how little critical consciousness went into the making of Mason's best poems. I shall risk presumption at this point, and say that surveying the course of Mason's short poetic career I am led to the conclusion that if it is dangerous for a poet to be wiser than his gift, he is nevertheless unlikely to make a lifetime's use of it unless he is at least its equal.

VI

The inconsiderable bulk of Mason's poems, their dramatic intensity, their refusal to abstract and generalize, their predominant lack of interest in large social conceptions, their general regularity of metre and rhyme scheme, and their curious mixture of conventional and conversational diction—these characteristics place his work in an area not yet accurately charted by the historians of English literature. Mason is the foremost New Zealand poet, the only one of stature, among those who may be seen to belong stylistically with English poets such as Hardy, Housman, and the best of the Georgians*—poets whose work I conceive of as standing loosely together, the second wave of a revolution (preceded by the Pre-Raphaelites and Aesthetes, followed by the Imagists) against the large, expansive, optimistic, thought-controlled poetry of the great Victorians and their imperialist heirs. The fact that the Imagist movement, dissolving and

---

* A year after this was published Alistair Campbell wrote in the same journal (*Comment* 21, Oct. 1964, p.24) 'R.A.K. Mason . . . is undoubtedly a Georgian poet, but none of his critics has admitted as much in print.'

crystallizing into the mature work of Pound and Eliot, succeeded in enforcing a revolution in poetic taste, has tended to obscure the fact that such poets as I have mentioned (and I would include a number of Edward Marsh's Georgians) were not hindrances to that revolution, but its precursors.

Thus where the elements of literary self-awareness enter Mason's poetry, his poems reveal that over-deliberate reaction against Victorian 'optimism' current among his stylistic mentors. Like most poets Mason reflects a fashion in his weaker moments, and at his best declares himself *through* the fashion, transcending it. But lacking Fairburn's facility, being, as I have argued, a medium rather than a maker, Mason was never the victim of succeeding fashions. He could not, as Fairburn unhappily could, make the semblance of a poem appear on his page when there was none to be made. All his poems, even those that fail, are marked by the pressure of an occasion larger than the mere egotistical desire to manifest his personality in poetical form. It is this dependence on something larger than himself, something he could not properly control, which seems to me to constitute Mason's strength and his limitation. It makes him a poet less complete than Allen Curnow; but one whose work may well prove more durable than Fairburn's.

I should, however, admit here what may be apparent already: that I am not entirely confident in my own mind about where to place Mason's poetry other than historically, how to 'evaluate' it. It is I think a tribute to the poems that they leave one feeling critically disarmed, not unconscious of their limitations and deficiencies, but simply aware of them as formidable living organisims, seldom graceful in movement, but always strong and swift. It would be easy to separate critically the old, slightly shop-soiled diction from the realistic detail and say that no poet can accommodate such heterogeneous material; to ask, for example, how one is to accept in the same poem ('Lugete O veneres') the vivid reality of the boy's 'fat arse' and 'arm . . . mottled like a bar of blue soap', with the literary unreality of 'steeds' and 'manger'. But such a criticism would not meet truly the experience of reading the poems, which constantly defies expectation. The grating and uncompromising reality of the dramatic voice does not so much impose order upon disorder, as bring the disorder to life. If one values Mason's poems it is not, I think, for their distinct perceptions, for any sense of their having set down some valuable and permanent footnote upon universal experience, but simply for the feeling they impart of life itself going stalwartly and painfully on.

CHARLES BRASCH:
A LACK OF UMBRELLAS

Charles Brasch's new volume is divided into two parts—shorter poems, and a long poem, 'The Estate'. I shall review these separately; the latter first.

I

'The Estate' is divided into thirty-four sections. It is a series of meditations, mainly on themes of personal relationships and the problems of identity and difference produced by them, the whole work addressed to a single person. The difference between this and the shorter poems is that 'The Estate' contains perhaps the raw material that in the other work is translated into public poetry. After a number of readings my reaction is one of disappointment that so much fine writing should have been spent on a poem which must, with certain exceptions, remain a private communication. This is not an objection to Mr Brasch's subject as such (an objection which would invalidate Shakespeare's sonnets), but to his refusal at times to consider the obscurity that results in poetry which is more concerned with being faithful to an experience than with getting itself over the fence into the world where it must live. 'The Estate' only manages to do

A review of Charles Brasch's *The Estate* (1957) in *Landfall* 43, September 1957. At the age of twenty-four I did not find it easy reviewing *Landfall*'s editor's book in *Landfall*, especially when, having accepted the commission, I found I couldn't warm to the poems. Tact was among the gifts the gods chose not to bestow on me, though the ability to recognize the need for it was not denied, and the recognition did no good at all to my prose. I still think there are things here worth saying; I have added nothing but have allowed myself to delete a few insincere or clumsy sentences and phrases. It should be added that Brasch offered me his next book for review and I declined.

both these things in a few sections. The two sections included in Chapman's Oxford anthology (iii and xiv), and ii, xviii, xix, xxx, and xxxiv attain a satisfying impersonality. The remainder seem to me more or less equally divided between poems that half emerge into a world beyond their origin, and poems which remain shadows in a private world. (How for example are we to be sure whether the 'Puck' of section xv is a domestic pet, a man—or Puck? And when one has decided that he is a man, one simply regrets that such a well-written poem should remain obscure in its reference.)

Reading 'The Estate' through I had at times an image of a man standing on a narrow ledge facing into the storm of his own emotions. He does not fall, or get agitated, or shout, but stands resolutely assessing, questioning, attempting to come to terms with his situation, refusing to run from it. He is admirable. I respect his honesty, his calm, his perceptiveness, his grace of manner and voice. But the poem is a view of life, and for myself I find it too narrow, too passionately stoical at the expense of irony and variety. I cannot suppress the wish that an umbrella or a kerosene tin would blow down the wind and give us both a rest from such intensity and singleness.

> You are the limitless dark defining the circle
> Of fireside, lamplight; you the inconceivable
> Guest out of nowhere suddenly fiery and singing
> Before me, midnight word of transfiguration.

Here a private fantasy, intense perhaps to those involved, remains to the reader only an eccentric mystery.

Yet even some of the most personal sections of the poem do avoid self-indulgence by their artistry, their insight, and their sincerity. Through the rhetorical questions (a device Mr Brasch overworks in this poem) comes a convincing desire to understand; and by this means the poem touches and loses universality. There is a continuing struggle to realize situations and to include every element of their complexity. One is surprised by the areas of experience, often expressed abstractly, that are made real by the poet's control over word and rhythm. At its best, determination to be faithful to an actual moment and its particular insight becomes almost as powerful a discipline as the more purely aesthetic (Yeatsian) impulse to hold a fine gesture in the face of *all* moments. A tense, contemplative stillness is wrung out of the flux of things—

> Clear through dusk the waters
> Fall in the forest; now the first dews come
> With the first star: stillness: and unextinguished
> The peaks float, dark in the transparent west.
> Can we preserve till morning, for many a morning,

Making it ours through day and night and year,
This strength, this ripeness of heart by all earth's powers
Confirmed, by crystal air, transfiguring snow,
All that we know, all that we are, unfading?

But the successes occur despite the overall direction of the poem, not because of it. The poem as a total work of art seems to me a failure. Its successes nevertheless rank with the best of the shorter poems.

II

The trend of Mr Brasch's work has been towards the generalization of a myth, but the generalization as statement is perhaps not so important as the emotion which hangs on it—a universal emotion of regret for lost purity and peace. He has perfected the prophetic voice until, for the sake of the poem, we come to accept the specifically local myth as if it were true.

The tendency of his earlier work is continued in this new volume, but a great deal more is added. His technical skill has developed, and in consequence he is able to include a wider range of experience. The stoic grace and reverent cadence remain, and the subject is still not landscape but an inner struggle which finds its symbols in landscape. But the landscape is brought into clearer focus than before. Here is the first stanza in the book—

Ngaio and broadleaf people the grassy coast
Of green hills bent to the water
That stirs, hardly stirs in the wide arms of the bay,
Fingering the rocks lightly, for a season of calm
Laid asleep in its iron bed
Under the circling air, the dome of light.

These lines are not exceptional in the book's first section—they represent the standard Mr Brasch has set himself and consistently attained. For that reason perhaps, the myth carries greater force and conviction than it does say, in 'The Land and the People', a sequence of four poems in his first volume, where neither land nor people are clearly realized.

The myth is that of painful adaptation on a soil which is a living force hostile to our intrusion, and of our collective guilt at the violence with which we alter what was here 'before our headlong time broke on these waters'. Our arrival on these islands becomes a local Original Sin, the destruction of a Paradise of calm.

In many of these new poems, what probably begins as private awareness of inadequacy and frustration finds public acknowledgement in this form. The normal pains of existence that belong to the man, transcend themselves into an impersonal structure. In one poem a vision of ruins which may in the future inhabit now empty spaces, is seen with nostalgia because it is a sign of a reconciliation that must come between man and nature. Whether one sees this psychologically (a death-wish), theoretically (unacknowledged desire to be at peace with God), or in the local terms it offers, the poem is a good example of the Romantic poet finding in one aspect of his own situation a valid general symbol.

But there is also in this book an attempt to find the beginnings of reconciliation in the present. In 'Letter from Thurlby Domain' a house which has crumbled is seen as the payment of a debt, a sacrifice to the landscape. By its decay, the product of man's intrusion proves itself also 'natural'. And there are poems looking outward to specific people, particularly to men who have learned better than most 'the trick of standing upright here'—the Rabbiter for example, or Willi Fels.

> Shaping in a garden for fifty seasons
> The strong slow lives of plants, the rare and homely,
> Into an order sought by the imagination,
>   A precinct green and calm

Even if one is suspicious of the Pathetic Fallacy, it is only when landscape or seascape becomes an anxious mother instead of an alien god that one's disbelief breaks the rope of rhetoric on which it is willingly suspended.

> For everyone who sails away
> The waves are sighing night and day,
> And tides hold their breath at turning
> To listen, listen for that morning
> That brings the exile home at last

Here the personality attributed to the sea is inappropriate. Much better (and more typical of the volume as a whole) is

> that fathomless ocean breaking about us
> In sleep, and all things borne to dissolution.

Mr Brasch's poems are written with great care. They have not the dazzling intellectual quality of Allen Curnow's, nor the toughness of Denis Glover's. His precision is of a different kind, and exhibits itself (as Eliot's does in the *Quartets*) more often in the selection of an exact word than in the making of exciting images. His lines seem to fall naturally into an elegiac cadence, and perhaps the hesitancy of style in some of his earliest published poems followed the realization that this cadence was not poetry in itself. For some poets certain rhythms may exist that correspond to states of mind in which poetry is written. On occasions the poet may be aware of these rhythms simply as patterns of sound. His problem is to fill them with words, all of them meaningful, none of them superfluous. In the determination to attain verbal accuracy the natural cadence is lost for time, and this seems to have happened in some of the poems of *The Land and the People*: Mr Brasch is refusing to take the easy way. (Hence perhaps, Mr Curnow's complaint about 'the diffident, cautious pace of the verse'.) In this new book the two elements are fused more perfectly than ever before—neither surrenders anything to the other. The tension necessary to poetry develops in a balance between the precision of the single word and beauty of cadence—

> They are that memory
> Where each event finds place, where all that's acted,
> Suffered, thought, enters, being strained through time;
> Which they receive whether they sleep or wake,
> Which they must harbour in safest ignorance.

In these eighteen shorter poems the achievement is of a very high order, and critical objections it seems to me could only take the form of personal expressions of preference for another kind of poetry.

ALLEN CURNOW:
POET OF THE REAL

A Small Room with Large Windows contains (together with one newly published poem) fifty of Allen Curnow's best poems selected from four previous volumes, *Island and Time* (1941), *Sailing or Drowning* (1943), *At Dead Low Water* (1949), and *Poems, 1949-57.* It omits (appropriately in such a volume) the development towards a style; but it represents fully the mature style in its various stages. The volume declares plainly what might have been apparent anyway—that Mr Curnow's poetry has already achieved the fullness and coherence of a major work. Each new poem has been, not merely an addition to, but a extension and enrichment of what preceded it: the early poems are enlarged by their successors; the later gain in significance as their connexions with the earlier are established. The growth is organic. The achievement is greater qualitatively for having been disciplined in quantity. And if Mr Curnow is not in this distinction entirely alone among our poets, he is certainly supreme among the very few for whom it may be claimed.

To have said so much is at once to have established a curious gap in our criticism, such as it is. Mr Curnow's introductions to his two anthologies of New Zealand verse stand together as the most substantial critical account of our poetry so far written; yet that account, omitting as it must his own work, is incomplete. Among our other critics none, so far as I know, has written well or at length of Mr Curnow's poetry. This new volume, then, the most impressive single collection yet published by a New Zealander, calls for detailed critical examination. What is offered in this article can only be at best a sketch for such criticism.

A review of *A Small Room with Large Windows* (1963) in *Landfall* 65, March 1963.

I

To forget self and all, forget foremost
This whimpering second unlicked self my country. . . .
                    Allen Curnow, *'To Forget Self and All'*

Mr Curnow's critical method (it is a method, not a prescription) has been to look for the common experience of which the poems he values are the visible record. In this he is, I think, insisting upon the priority of the experience over the poetry it initiates. Life comes before Art. I recall a review contributed some years ago to *Here & Now* in which Mr Curnow described a poem as 'what a poet makes when he is passionately interested in something else'. I recall too an impromptu speech delivered at an Auckland Festival of Arts cocktail party, in which Mr Curnow remarked 'You can't write literature and you can't paint art'. These are not empty paradoxes. A failure of confidence, an inability to believe in the value of our own experience, a fear that the truth, if we discovered it in words, might not match the grandeur of our designs upon the world—it is lapses such as these which lead us to substitute 'literature', the *idea* of what a poem should be, for the 'passionate interest in something else' which ought to initiate, govern, and limit the writing. If we look for 'poetic' subjects, 'universal' subjects, (as distinct from discovering, or being discovered by, subjects for poems) we will—as surely as if we look for a 'poetic' diction and syntax—fail to write poems. For a poem is made, not of its subject, but in the honest meeting of language and experience.

A Small Room with Large Windows is a work of literature because it is the public record of a number of private occasions when a man was willing to face the reality of experience, and had the ability to embody its complexity in words. That 'reality' must be, as Mr Curnow remarks in the introduction to his Penguin anthology, 'local and special at the point where we pick up the traces'. If it is 'real' enough it will speak to all men, irrespective of place: it will be 'universal'. Mr Curnow's poems are an illustration of that simple principle, which stands at the centre of his criticism.

'Poets here' Mr Robert Chapman writes in his Oxford *Anthology of New Zealand Verse,* 'feel so at ease in their environment that they can simply assume it and find themselves freed to deal directly with the concerns of poetry everywhere.' One might find in the *Poetry Yearbook* more extravagant statements of this view, which I am content to call a heresy in our criticism; but I take Mr Chapman's as the most coherent. Our environment is our country and landscapes; it is our suburb, our house, the chair in which we sit, the newspaper we read, the radio we turn off; it is our family, our friends and our enemies. It is, in fact, what we experience. To 'simply assume it' is to make a very large assumption! And one may question whether any poem of consequence was ever written out of such an assumption—whether indeed, 'the concerns of poetry everywhere' are not always in some sense an attempt to resolve, or at least to meet, an imbalance, an unease between the mind and its environment.*

Against this invitation to abstract oneself, this wishful dissolution of pressing realities, Mr Curnow has stood firm, knowing that to be 'freed' from one's environment is to be freed from the necessity to live.

> *Why that'd be freedom heyday, hey*
> *For freedom that'd be the day*
> *And as good a dream as any to be damned for.*

II

What happens if you make the entire world into one vast region? . . . In our time we have been the victims of a geographical metaphor, or a figure of space: we have tried to compensate for the limitations of the little community by envisaging the big community, which is not necessarily bigger spiritually or culturally than the little community.
Allen Tate, 'The New Provincialism' (1945)

> *Compare, compare, now horrible untruth*
> *Rings true in our obliterating season:*
> *Our islands lost again, all earth one island,*
> *And all our travel circumnavigation.*
Allen Curnow, 'Discovery' (1943)

The themes of Mr Curnow's poetry may perhaps be best contracted and generalized (in terms which do not pretend to be the terms of a scientific psychology) as a preoccupation with a conflict between Imagination, which comprehends, encompasses, and reconciles, and the Rational Will which creates or destroys blindly, and which understands only by exclusion and simplification. The theme is familiar enough in modern literature. The attempt to realize something better, more inclusive, than a 'rational' order has expressed itself, for example, in T. S. Eliot's idea of a modern 'dissociation of sensibility', and in Yeats's concern at our loss of 'Unity of Being'. This has been a central preoccupation of the finest English poetry since Blake, Coleridge, and Keats. And if modern criticism has been prone to postulate a Golden Age when no such separation of the human faculties

---

* In *Landfall* 66 Professor Chapman protested that I had placed a 'misconstruction' on his sentence, but he did not explain how it had been misconstrued and I replied impenitently in *Landfall* 67. Even allowing that Chapman probably meant 'nation' when he wrote 'environment', it is difficult to acknowledge that writers here feel markedly 'at ease' or that it would be a good thing if they did.

existed, we may simply observe that precisely such a separation is expressed in *Antony and Cleopatra*, in the antithesis between rational Rome and instinctive Alexandria.

By assigning a local poet his place on so broad a canvas, I mean principally to affirm that Mr Curnow is a traditional poet; and that he has earned his place in the tradition in the only way it can be earned—by studying that which is central, and therefore permanent and unchanging, in human life as it is experienced here and now. I have no difficulty in seeing a certain kinship between, on the one hand, Shakespeare's juxtaposition of 'Rome' and 'Alexandria', and on the other, Mr Curnow's juxtaposition of 'reason's range' and 'green innocence of nerves'. The kinship exists, not primarily as a literary quality, but as a condition of life. It is achieved because Mr Curnow puts first things first; because when he writes a poem like 'Discovery' he is totally absorbed, not in the 'poetry' but in the imagined details of a voyage of discovery, and the known condition of a society which that discovery initiated.

In 'Sailing or Drowning' there is the same juxtaposition: it is the 'green myth' which bridges past and present, reconciling man to his fate, making 'the evening and the morning one'; and it is 'ambition', the rational aspiration of the explorers, 'has anulled that constitution'. In 'The Navigators' the word 'ambition' is not used; but it is implied in the half-concealed *Macbeth* image, in the 'rational successful hands that swept / Sea treasures up . . . hands that will not come clean'. These hands are 'successful', and their destructive acts are 'kept / In suavest history, gloved . . .' But theirs is the pride which goes before our fall. In 'Discovery', 'the mad bar-beating bird of the mind', dissatisfied with its European limits, bursts out to find, not freedom, but simply 'a vaster cage'—much as, in the later poem 'To Forget Self and All', the Caliban-Kiwi singing 'freedom heyday, hey' at the prospect of escape from the limits of his island, is only hailing a dream which will damn him if he acts upon it. For the extension of limit is to be found, if at all, not in space but in time—and time is the province of the Imagination.

Pride, ambition, a 'rational violence' proceeding from the belief that

> Simply by sailing in a new direction
> You could enlarge the world

—these have set us down at 'the world's end where wonders cease' ('Landfall in Unknown Seas'). Now the 'pilgrim dream' is 'pricked by a cold dawn' and dies ('The Unhistoric Story'). The Fall has been re-enacted for us in local terms. As in every such enactment the Fall is in one sense fortunate: unfallen we could not be saved, would have no world to re-make. Here and now (as everywhere always) we must

atone
> *To our earth's Lord for the pride of all our voyages.*

> ('Elegy on my Father')

III

Tradition . . . involves, in the first place, the historical sense, which we may call nearly indispensable to anyone who would continue to be a poet beyond his twenty-fifth year; and the historical sense involves a perception, not only of the pastness of the past, but of its presence.

> T. S. Eliot, 'Tradition and the Individual Talent' (1919)

I have mentioned some of Mr Curnow's most public and impersonal poems. In these the man is recognized only in the style, and in the phantasmagoria of island and time which is, though it has such wide-ranging implications, always distinctly the expression of one imagination. In later poems that general resonance is not lost; but the experience of the man is woven visibly into the texture, enriching and strengthening it. As an example of the increasing particularity of Mr Curnow's poetry, and of its increasing range, one may compare 'House and Land' (1941), perhaps his most popular, certainly his best-known poem, with the brilliant sonnet 'In Memoriam, R.L.M.G.' (1949).

'House and Land' is a miniature drama in which three kinds of understanding, each of them inadequate, are sharply portrayed. On the one hand there is Miss Wilson, custodian of faded English pictures, a silver tea-pot, and various family memories, the relics of a colonial past which preserve her against the intrusions of the present. On the other hand are the workmen—cowmen and rabbiter—who live entirely in the present, who, finding one place 'too bloody quiet', will move on to another. Between them wanders the painstaking historian; but the latter does not, as many readers suppose he does, comprehend the scene better than those who are in it. He no more than they possesses the 'historical sense' (as Eliot defines it above), and his attempts to formulate a phrase which will describe the society are rendered nonsensical by the literal preoccupations of his subjects:

> The spirit of exile, wrote the historian,
> Is strong in the people still.

> He reminds me rather, said Miss Wilson,
> Of Harriet's youngest, Will.

> The cowman, home from the shed, went drinking
> With the rabbiter home from the hill.

These contrasts are simple, and might seem to work mechanically if it

were not for the subtlety with which the scene as a whole is evoked. (It is
probably one of those unconscious balancing feats of the poetic imagination that the dog, for example, which might have been no more than a
scenic prop, trails his chain

> From the privy as far as the fowlhouse
> And back to the privy again,

in a delightful parody of the historian's attempt to bridge the gap between
Miss Wilson and her workmen.) Yet the poem, for all its merits, is caught
in its moment in time, a point in our history which can hardly repeat itself
in quite that way, and is in that sense a more limited poem than 'In
Memoriam, R.L.M.G.'

In this sonnet the old woman whose death is celebrated may be seen
(whatever the poet may have had in mind) as another view of the English
colonial gentlewoman of whom Miss Wilson is the prototype—a more
sympathetic and a richer view, which is able to support the idea of her life
and death as a sacrifice necessary to our being 'at home' where we are.

The opening phrases suggest the reaction of children old enough to comprehend the significance of the funeral:

> The oldest of us burst into tears and cried
> Let me go home . . . .

But the phrase which follows—'but she stayed, watching . . .'—sends us
back to read the lines again. Now, without losing our initial reading, we
see 'the oldest of us' as the first settlers, dissatisfied with their lot; and
'home' as England.

> but she stayed, watching
> At her staircase window ship after ship ride
> Like birds her grieving sunsets. . . .

The ships, reminders of her exile, have kept the local present at odds with
a past distant in space as well as time. But while the woman's mind was
elsewhere, her hands were preparing for the future:

> there sat stitching
>
> Grandchildren's things.

Now the densely-packed style concentrates (as in the opening phrases)
the present event and its history, so that the same words seem to contain
'not only the pastness of the past, but its presence':

> She died by the same sea.
> High over it she led us in the steepening heat

To the yellow grave; her clay
Chose that way home.

In its primary sense this describes the funeral procession making its way
'high over' (above) the sea into the hills where the burial is to take place.
But it suggests also the woman's symbolic role as first settler, leading 'us',
New Zealanders, over the sea from England to a place which was for her a
'yellow grave', a place of 'grieving sunsets'. So 'her clay' is the body of the
dead woman; but it is also her descendants who have found, in following
her, a 'way home'. The painful climb, at once a particular climb to a particular hill grave, and a period of our history, is now complete. The feet of
the mourners are

. . . seen to have stopped and turned again down hill.

Subtly the scene is changed: the ships, no longer symbols of exile, bask in
the heat; the land which was 'her oblivion' has become 'our broad day'. In
its final lines the poem turns again expansively to the dead woman:

Heaped over

So lightly, she stretched like time behind us, or
Graven in cloud, our farthest ancestor.

Our 'farthest ancestor' is newly buried: she is both the briefness of our
history and the whole of it, back even to our 'farthest ancestor', Adam.

IV

He, too, has resigned his part
In the casual comedy;
He, too, has been changed in his turn,
Transformed utterly:
A terrible beauty is born.

W.B. Yeats, 'Easter 1916'

There is a passage in Mr Curnow's introduction to his first anthology
which I underlined and surrounded with question marks when, at the age
of eighteen or nineteen, I first encountered it. Mr Curnow had suggested
that New Zealanders lacked the capacity for tragic emotions. Capacities
might rest unused; but I could not see that we lacked the capacity for
anything. Nor can I now—because it seems to me an error to believe poets
capable of emotions denied to all who are not poets. If that were the case,
to whom would poets speak but to one another? We must assume the true
poet's distinction to exist in what he makes of his emotions, not in his
capacity to experience them. We have no tragic play of any significance.

But if Mr Curnow could find among R. A. K. Mason's poems, if I can find among his own, some which exhibit the qualities of tragedy; and if there are people to read these poems; then there can be no thought of an inherent indigenous lack.

Most of us would take our notion of 'tragic' emotion from our experience of Shakespeare. And the old Aristotelian signposts 'pity and terror' (which Mr Curnow used) point towards it. The pity is a kind of detachment; the terror, involvement—and yet the two are simultaneous, a unified experience. The quality in literature which evokes that emotion in reader or audience, is an extension of the poetic imagination to a point where it can encompass in a single image the extremities of human consciousness, sharpening our sense of reality by the manipulation of opposites, eliciting our most intense affirmation, simply of the existence of things, or of life itself, by the contemplation of mutability and death. Such an image is felt, I think, in Mr Curnow's poetry considered as a whole; but it is strongly felt in a few poems, in 'At Dead Low Water' for example, and most notably perhaps in 'Spectacular Blossom' from *Poems 1949-57*.

If 'Spectacular Blossom' is a poem which exhibits, as I think it does, a difficult structural hiatus between its second and third stanzas, it is nevertheless so rich and exacting in its particulars, and so successful in implying their extension, that one is reminded of Keats's odes, and of certain poems of Yeats's middle phase.

> Mock up again, summer, the sooty altars
> Between the sweltering tides and the tin gardens,
> All the colours of the stained bow windows.
> Quick, she'll be dead on time, the single
> Actress shuffling red petals to this music,
> Percussive light!

The scene (here, and as the poem develops) is recognizably a suburb on the inner Waitemata, with its tin fences, its bow windows, its bright paint ('stained glass', and 'all the colours of the rainbow' implied), and its 'sooty altars' for the incineration of garden rubbish. The disorder, the scrappiness of the scene is suggested; and at the same time there is, cast over it, that peculiar transforming glare and heat of summer on a northern inlet:

> All over the dead hot calm impure
> Blood noon tide of the breathless bay.

But the scene is, from the opening line of the poem, a 'scene' in a more formal sense. Here Time (summer) is preparing its sooty altars for the perennial sacrifice of Beauty, who comes, 'the single/Actress', to take her ritual bathe before death. 'Quick, she'll be dead on time' stands in its colloquial sense, and literally as a reminder that the 'actress', alive ('quick') will meet her death at the appointed moment. Yet the central perception from which the poem evolves already associates the victim with her destroyer: they are the particular and the general of the same process. So the 'actress' (who is also clearly a real woman, just as her 'scene' is a real scene) is scarcely separable from summer which prepares the altar of her death. As central figure in the scene she controls it, shuffles petals to the light which moves like music on the water, 'harbours' the waters' reflected suns, is 'plucked at' (in stanza 2), eagerly enticed, by the pearly light striking off underwater shells, and in a final gesture of abandonment to her fate, tosses flowers to her attendants as she goes 'for ever and astray'. (Here 'for ever and a day' is implied, while 'astray' invokes the Fall.) Between stanzas one and two the question which the poem is to answer, or render irrelevant, hangs suspended:

> *Are the victims always so beautiful?*

Now the perfect accord between the victim and her fate is emphasized:

> I see her feet
> Slip into the perfect fit the shallows make her
> Purposefully, sure as she is the sea
> Levels its lucent ruins underfoot
> That were sharp dead white shells, that will be sands.
> The shallows kiss like knives.

In meeting her death (not a final death but simply the recognition of mutability and the necessary corruption of innocence) she is fulfilling herself, finding her place in the enduring processes of the natural world which are signified by the 'lucent ruins' and the transformation of shells to sands.

Here the question asked at the end of stanza one is answered:

> *Always for this*
> *They are chosen for their beauty.*

The victims of time are always beautiful, and not by chance. Those who are 'chosen' (fortunate) in being beautiful, are also 'chosen *for* their beauty', marked out to be destroyed. This is not the arbitrary concept it might seem. We are all, of course, the victims of time; but it is in the decay of exceptional beauty that the work of time most patently declares itself.

Once again, however, the rich texture of the poem has already run ahead of its rational structure. For if the meeting of the girl and her fate is so 'perfect', 'purposeful', and 'sure', how is her beauty to be distinguished from its destruction? How is 'beauty' to be recognized as a separate quality in the total natural process of time and change? If this final paradox is to be met, it cannot be done simply in the ritual death of the youthful 'actress', 'chosen for her beauty'. For this would be to isolate beauty from the process, and render the occasion at once more exceptional and less significant than it is.

It is a measure of the extraordinary range of Mr Curnow's talent, and the cause of the poem's one major difficulty, that the poet takes the bold stride he does into the final stanza. There has been, in the first two stanzas, enough to indicate the poem's genesis in a personal occasion. An unidentified persona has spoken throughout ('I see her feet / Slip into the perfect fit . . .'). Now, while the girl remains present, that persona comes into view—an ageing man. It is (and here the difficult transition) his death we witness in the final stanza—though it is also the girl's.

> Wristiest slaughterman December smooths
> The temple bones and parts the grey-brown brows
> With humid fingers. It is an ageless wind
> That loves with knives, it knows our need, it flows
> Justly, simply as water greets the blood,
> And woody tumours burst in scarlet spray.
> An old man's blood spills bright as a girl's
> On beaches where the knees of light crash down.
> These dying ejaculate their bloom.

Just as the girl has been made a single personification of Youthful Beauty, and is at the same time inseparable from the various manifestations of summer in the natural world, so the old man is generalized Age, while his particular lineaments identify him specifically with the pohutukawa tree. The knotted tree can produce its 'spectacular blossom' no less than the summer flowers. Its 'grey-blown brows' are prepared for the knife—'and woody tumours burst in scarlet spray'. The scarlet pohutukawa stamens float out on the water: that element 'greets the blood' of the 'old man', just as it greets the girl's. Now both Youthful Beauty and gnarled Age exist together as victims—of one another, of love, of their own need, but principally of the 'ageless wind', Time, that 'loves with knives' and 'knows our need'. The sexual undertone, present throughout, is brought out sharply in this stanza—appropriately, since it is in sexual experience that we are most undividedly participants in the natural process, and thus most completely its victims. The poem has touched one of those cruxes of human experience ('beyond reason's range') of which only the imagination can properly speak. One is reminded of Elizabethan uses of the verb 'to die' as an expression of sexual completion; of Keats's compression of sexual aspiration and the death wish; of Yeats's

> the young
> In one another's arms, birds in the trees
> —Those dying generations—at their song.

'Spectacular Blossom' invites such comparisons and is not diminished by them; and its conclusion astonishingly compresses and recapitulates the whole experience—

> These dying ejaculate their bloom.

Now the logical questions which have been interposed between the stanzas are easily met. The beauty of the girl is only set apart from the scene at a level the poem has transcended; all things, as they participate in the world, are changing and dying, and it is in this that *tragic* beauty exists.

> An old man's blood spills bright as a girl's

—he too is victim, participant, and celebrant of the perennial ritual. Between him and the girl there is, at this level, no distinction to be made:

> *Can anyone choose*
> *And call it beauty?—The victims*
> *Are always beautiful.* *

V

Positivism offers us a single field of discourse . . . and it pretends that this is the sole field of discourse, all the others being illusion, priestcraft, superstition, or even Nazism.
                    Allen Tate, 'The Hovering Fly' (1943)

> *What it would look like if really there were only*
> *One point of the compass not known illusory*
> *All other quarters proving nothing but quaint*
> *Obsolete expressions of true north (would it be?) . . . .*
>   Allen Curnow, 'A Small Room with Large Windows'

There is a quality of imagination, a uniqely comprehensive order of experience, which exhibits itself so rarely even within those areas we define vaguely as 'literature', that one can easily understand the Romantic poets' wish to place a definition upon it that would distinguish it from all other human faculties. Yet of the poets talented enough to recreate that order of experience in words, none is likely to wish for a world in which it predominated over all others. By its very range and comprehensiveness, by the degree to which it assimilates and (ultimately) accepts all, that experience is passive. It is a perfect contemplation from which no action can ensue; a 'negative capability', supreme among all others, but of little use when crops fail or armies invade.

---

*Postscript 1980: Re-reading this I wonder whether I gave sufficient attention to the fact that the poem is at one level simply descriptive. In the Penguin *A Book of New Zealand Verse* (1960) it is subtitled 'Pohutukawa Trees, Auckland'.

If our 'ambition' is destroyer of the 'green myth', it is also the source of our control over the natural world, from which stem comforts and certainties none but the most naïve would relinquish without a struggle. Facing this fact, W.H. Auden personifies man in his rational mode as the scientist and the lawgiver, and asks whimsically 'Where would we be without them?' The answer:

> Feral still, un-housetrained, still
>
> wandering through forests without
> a consonant to our names,
>
> slaves of Dame Kind, lacking
> all notion of a city
>
> and, at this noon, for this death,
> there would be no agents.

The 'death' here is the crucifixion, an act of 'rational violence', an event, as Auden sees it, occurring at every moment of our lives, both a sin and a necessity, destructive to ourselves only if it is not absolved by the imagination.

The greatest poets since the Romantics have conducted their campaign against rationality and science, not in order that the irrational might triumph or that material progress might come to a halt, but that there might be a place left for the only faculty which keeps due proportion, teaches humility, and casts a tragic dignity over all human aspiration. The campaign has seemed necessary, because in an age as successful as ours has been in learning to control its environment ('rational successful hands / That swept sea-treasures up . . .') the exclusiveness of method necessary to that success is prone to isolate the imagination, making it seem untruthful or even dangerous. Unbridled, reason and science will pretend (in Tate's words) that theirs is 'the sole field of discourse, all others being illusion, priestcraft, superstition, or even Nazism'.

'A Small Room with Large Windows' (of which the opening lines are quoted at the head of this section) ironically postulates a world of perfect reason and perfect conformity in which there would be, not 360 degrees to the compass, but only one, a direction from birth to death pursued by all things alike in perfect harmony:

> And seeds, birds, children, loves and thoughts bore down
> The unwinding abiding beam from birth
> To death! What a plan!

> Or parabola.

Each life would be launched like a firework into the same arc, would reach the same height, burn out, and fall into darkness—

You describe yours, I mine, simple as that,
With a pop and a puff of nonchalant stars up top,
Then down, dutiful dead stick, down
(True north all the way nevertheless).

There would be a kind of poetry in this. Simply to 'describe' (move through) one's arc would be to 'describe' it as if in words—and 'yours' and 'mine' would be indistinguishable, equally perfect.

A word on arrival, a word on departure.
A passage of proud verse, rightly construed.

Here the rocket's 'departure' might stand as the image of birth; its 'arrival' at the end of its trajectory as the image of death. The normal associations of the words are reversed or confused; for in this ideal world birth and death are occasions equal in their unimportance. For each there would be a 'word'; and the flight between them would be 'rightly construed' as 'a passage of proud verse'. (In a sense the verse would 'construe' itself; just as to 'describe' the fixed arc would be to describe it!) And for the rest?—

An unerring pen to edit the ensuing silences.

A 'perfect' world, a world without the contraries which only the imagination can wholly accommodate, has been ironically sketched.

In section ii the poem turns from the ideal to the real, from the 'plan' of a world to the world as it is, here and now, outside the 'small room with large windows'. The scene is a recognizable one; but its elements are deftly woven into an allegory of the contradictions which render the 'plan' ridiculous. Here 'what you call a view' is in fact '(if it is)' a composition of the traditional warring elements,* 'half earth, half heaven / Half land, half water,' where the human faculties (themselves warring) must find or make their place. Once again, but perhaps more richly and subtly than in the early poems, there is the old dichotomy: the pines suggest man in his aspiring, rational role; the mangroves, instinctive, primitive man. Yet they are of the same order and the same environment. The pines, though they 'hide their heads in the air', are subject to time and the elements, and knowing this, 'on bare knees, / Supplicate wind and tide'. The 'bad bitching squall' has them 'twitching root and branch', predicting the world's end, because

Foreknowledge infects them to the heart

The pines are individuals. (There are seven of them and they are 'ageing'.) As individuals they know their destiny is to die. The mangroves, on the other hand, which the pines (in both senses) look down on, are dis-

---

* Fire is apparently absent. But it, too, is discovered in section iv.

tinguishable neither one from another, nor from the total life process. They are 'the mangrove race', and as a race they persist in their 'muddy truckling / With time and tide'.

This is not, of course, a crude sketch in which some men are seen as rational 'pines' and some as instinctive 'mangroves'. The elements in this 'view' are disposed to present what is already there in the eye and the mind of the beholder. A correspondence is found between what is inside and what is outside the 'small room'. The delicate allegory of pines and mangroves has in fact touched at once the opposite poles of every human consciousness: man as an individual, and as a social being ('comfortable to creak in tune'); and man as part of an unending physical process. This is the real view in which the ideal cannot survive.

Now, by one of those bland and breath-taking gear-changes which characterize Mr Curnow's recent poetry, section iii becomes a generalized description of our society earnestly organizing itself as if only the right decisions need be taken and we would be launched at last into the perfect plan or parabola described in section i. But there is no agreement about where 'true north' in fact lies. Educational questions such as 'the Bible, or no Bible, free swimming tuition, / Art, sex, no sex and so on' are 'much *debated*': even in these abstract realms the contraries continue to manifest themselves. And while in society the 'decision' is still 'pending', the whole debate is rendered artificial by another assumption about our ultimate destiny:

> It is understood there is a judgement preparing
> Which finds the compass totally without bearing
> And the present course correct beyond a doubt,
> There being two points precisely, one in, one out.

The poem is not concerned to argue that such debates should cease; it simply absorbs them into a larger human context, delicately mocking the solemnity, the narrowness of 'view' which forbids recognition of the full circle of our experience.

The final section turns again briefly to the phenomenal world seen from the 'small room'. Sharp impressions succeed one another, first among them

> A kingfisher's naked arc alight
> Upon a dead stick in the mud

—in which life and death, without losing their distinctions as they do in section i, are brought together in one image, a single comprehension. The 'naked arc alight' contains both the swift curving flight of the bird, and its arrival, which seem to happen simultaneously. The bright blue wings catch the light, are 'alight' as they move. Yet at the same moment the bird 'alights' on the stick. (Anyone who has watched the quick, short flights of the kingfisher will have observed that there seems to be no decrease in velocity before the flight abruptly stops.) The rocket's burning parabola in section i, and the 'dead stick' it leaves, are now indivisible—for the imagination has recognized (as in 'In Memoriam, R.L.M.G.') not the artificial instant in time, but the living continuum.

So the impressions continue, unifying earth, air, fire and water, and concluding with the brilliant plunge of the gannet, an occasion at once beautiful and predatory, asserting the life of the bird and the death of its victim, a falling from the air and an ascent from the waters. Implying so much, that occasion can be left, in the context of so rich a poem, to speak for itself, to be itself and to evoke according to the capacity of the reader. Like all the impressions of this final section it is set down simply and cleanly, so that the words are like a clear glass (a 'large window'!) through which we observe the event itself:

> a gannet impacting.

These are the gifts of the phenomenal world, and they

> Explode a dozen diverse dullnesses
> Like a burst of accurate fire.

(*Note*: Having once seen those 'dozen diverse dullnesses' as the twelve Apostles, I find it difficult to think of them less particularly. There is nothing in the poem to justify such a reading. But I should like to think that it is in keeping with the mood and thought of the poem, and not entirely an arbitrary association.)

VI

> *Shape of a leaf, shine of a leaf,*
> *Shade of a leaf yellow among yellow leaves of*
> *The prophet Micah with a slip of perished silk*
> *Marks nothing, still is a character, a syllable*
> *Made flesh before the word . . .*
>
> Allen Curnow, 'A Leaf'

I have emphasized that Mr Curnow's poetry is broad in its range of implications partly because it is particular in detail, recognizing always the limits of its world. We are all in the habit of saying that poetry must be 'concrete'. Few of us look for reasons why this should be so; we simply observe again and again that 'abstraction', appropriate to large areas of science and philosophy, is destructive to poetry. What do we require of a poem when we say that it should be 'concrete', that its 'texture', its 'imagery', should be rich and full? In effect we are asking for an assurance that there is (to employ a phrase from the introduction to Mr Curnow's Penguin anthology) 'a reality prior to the poem'. To come honestly to grips with experience here and now (by which I do *not* mean writing descriptive or 'scenic' verse) is to submit oneself to the most rigorous of all disciplines; it is not to negate the constructive intelligence, but to subordinate it to the recognition of 'things as they are', in all their complexity, and thus to insist that our poetry should be a truthful report upon experience.

In the poem 'A Leaf' (the second stanza of which is quoted above) the leaf discovered in a Bible serves no purpose, marks no place in the text, but

> still is a character, a syllable
> Made flesh before the word.

It is a reminder that words are not autonomous; they are imperfect indicators and we must use them humbly.

Yet if our experience is to be real in memory and contemplation, if it is to be communicated and shared, it must be conceptualized in words. As men or as poets we must find some way (as another of the later poems has it) 'to introduce the landscape to the language / Here on the spot'. If Mr Curnow's 'landscapes' were only physical landscapes (as Mr Johnson, Mr Baxter, and Mr Doyle, in their *Yearbook* musings have so crudely supposed) the matter might be solved as it is by that race in *Gulliver's Travels* who never speak in words but simply present the object they have in mind. To speak of 'a leaf' we might take one from the load of objects carried about on our backs. There would be no problem. But the 'landscape' like the 'view' in 'A Small Room with Large Windows', is also a moral, an intellectual, an emotional 'landscape'. The word is made to stand for a present and total reality larger than ourselves, from which the mind isolates itself only to become nothing. It is this reality we must 'introduce . . . to the language', and from which, if a true proportion is to be kept, nothing may be abstracted.

The mind which reaches after such wholeness must concern itself with minute particulars. We will find our universe, not in the thought of a universe, but in the grain of sand. I recall shortly after 'A Small Room with Large Windows' first appeared in the *New Zealand Listener* a reader wrote to the editor complaining that a geranium would not grow 'wild on a wet bank'. Immediately a reply came back from the poet insisting that, irrespective of the customary behaviour of those plants in Wellington, there was, observable from the window of his house, 'a scarlet geranium wild on a wet bank'. Mr Curnow is not in the habit of replying to his critics. He has ignored the most flagrant misrepresentations of his position as anthologist. And it would not have been an occasion for a reply had the

New Zealand Listener's correspondent suggested that the poem failed *as a poem*. But a letter suggesting an error of detail, an untruth, was a matter for earnest concern. How could the geranium represent more than itself if it were only a geranium of the mind—if it were not first, potentially or actually, an experience.

This poetic honesty is no doubt the source of Mr Curnow's confidence of tone; it ensures a firm centre from which all his poems' further resonances extend outward. It is because the 'small room with large windows' is a fact before it is conceptualized that it can be made to suggest so much else—a head, from which the human consciousness peers out; or (in its function as title to the selected poems) New Zealand, the 'small room' from which we view our world. It is similarly, because the poem 'The Eye is More or Less Satisfied with Seeing' testifies at every point its genesis in actual experience, that its Janus figure is not a mere literary device, but stands at one level for the New Zealander, at another for everyman, caught between his opposing selves, rendered immobile by conflicting views of reality, and yet finding in that immobility his only moments of illumination, his only 'Unity of Being'.

To refuse to meet the 'landscape' of experience because we fear the cost; to put in its place an ideal, a 'dream', a 'plan'—this is to deny life. That is what Mr Curnow's latest poems imply again and again. Supremely those poems, for all the anguish which lies somewhere behind their achieved irony, are engaged in affirming life and a world which is real. The anguish is in the imaginative struggle to meet and encompass the contraries of which our 'landscape' is composed. What emerges from the struggle is a kind of affirmation Yeats called 'tragic joy'—a quality achieved only by those few poets who have on the one hand the talent, and on the other the will or the need, to discover the full extension of human consciousness in the recognition of human limit.

VII

That's

> *Exactly how it is now. It is. It is*
> *Summer all over the striped humming-top of the morning*
> *And what lovely balloons, prayer-filled (going up!) to fluke*
> *For once and for all the right time, the correct distance.*
> Allen Curnow, 'Keep in a Cool Place'

Considering the stages of Mr Curnow's mature style one is left wondering where he will go from here. Poems can hardly say more or say better than the best of his recent work; but they can say more simply, with fewer of the evidences of human effort. One has in mind, of course, a rare and inhuman strain—but when so much uncalled for has been given, it is pardonable to hope for more.

Mr Curnow, one feels, was never chosen by the Muse. He chose her, and thus can never be her victim. She speaks as he directs: at every point his poems are made. In this he is like Yeats; and unlike Eliot who was deserted by his Muse after 'Ash Wednesday', and had to begin late—too late perhaps—to remake his style. For Mr Curnow one further stage would seem (to the mind!) a logical progression.

Looking for signs to the future, thinking that I find them (in a poem like 'Keep in a Cool Place', for example) I foresee, if occasions demand poems from him, the possibility of a perfect, bland, and lucid surface, an ultimate simplicity which relinquishes none of the complexities, the *making* of what is given to some fitfully and imperfectly in youth, as Yeats made, and made better in the poems of his late middle-age, what was given to Keats in the Odes. Mr Curnow's poems deserve such a consummation. If he writes no more we shall have had from him more than we deserve.

DENIS GLOVER:
THE COLONY LIVES ON

I

A maker of clocks and watches in a country famous for its clocks and watches held an exhibition of his work. Most of those who attended were in the game, they knew something about making clocks and watches, and they were full of admiration. There wasn't one among them who couldn't learn something from the exhibition, which included a great variety of ways of putting together cogs and springs, ratchets, winders, backs and fronts, hands, numerals, pendulums, bells, chains, almost anything associated with time-pieces, including even a beautifully-carved minute hand three feet long, for a public clock. The workmanship was whole-heartedly approved. People wandered about saying look at this and how about that and could anyone else have done the other thing, until a younger watchmaker from the north who was certainly envious and probably malicious walked up to the master-craftsman and said audibly: 'this is all very fine Denis. But supposing I wanted to know the time.'

Everyone looked at the tables and now it became apparent that there wasn't anywhere a complete timepiece.

'Time,' roared the craftsman. 'My boy, when you're devoted to your craft as I am, you're not concerned with the time.'

Late in 1964 Charles Brasch sent me Glover's *Enter Without Knocking* to review for *Landfall.* I struggled to get it done before going overseas at the end of that year, but gave up and returned the book because the review insisted on taking a negative turn. On reflection these fragments from it seem worth putting into print.

II

Demosthenes says that in life luck is the greatest good and that it cannot exist without something else not inferior to it—namely prudent conduct. Following him we might say that in the case of style *nature* takes the place of good luck; and *art* of prudent conduct.   (Longinus)

Whatever success Glover achieves in 'Arawata Bill' derives from a conjunction of this kind; from the exact correspondence between Bill's search for a vein of gold and Glover's for a vein of speech. I am not claiming to know whether Glover was aware of the correspondence: I would guess not. If he is consciously writing allegory it is an allegory of human ambition in general, not of the poet's in particular. I mean only that Glover understands Bill's experience because it is his own in another sphere of action; that in Bill he found a subject that matched his talent because (in Demosthenes' terms) the proportion of 'prudent conduct' to 'luck' is about the same. Denis has clambered over the mountains of his craft and come home with a few grains of genuine dust.

III

You need to hear the speaking voice all the time you are reading Denis Glover's poetry: it is often gruff, sometimes harsh, but very seldom unmusical, and at times almost sweetly lyrical. Sometimes the poems force the question 'What distinguishes this as poetry?' The question isn't easy to answer unless you cling to the consistency of voice through what is now a fairly large body of verse.

> Some people shave in the mountains
> But not so
> Arawata Bill who let his whiskers grow.

IV

Denis Glover's poems call forth exclamations rather than the apparatus of criticism. He is like the duckling in the nursery story: when he's good he's very very good; when he's bad he's awful. *Enter Without Knocking* suggests most of the good Glover is already in the anthologies.

What is one to say first of the 'good' Glover?—of short lyrics, acknowledged successes like 'Once the days were clear . . .' or 'These songs will not stand . . .' It is not that they defy analysis, but that analysis seems superfluous when the success is manifest to all.

Glover has the ability to use with great variety and inventiveness the fundamental 'nursery' elements of poetry—simple rhyme, simple metre, simple metaphor; and he can use these lyrically or satirically. These are talents held in common with Fairburn. But added to them Glover has something more difficult to define—it might be called a sense of poetry in literalness, in facts, poetry in the plain prosiness of things:

> *Arawata Bill led his horse up the slow hill*
> *And his shovel was lashed to his pack.*

The transference of slowness to the hill is the only contribution Glover makes apart from the selection of fact. But how immensely purposeful 'And his shovel was lashed to his pack' sounds! Nonetheless it is a precarious method because success or failure with each reader is going to depend so much on whether he/she shares Glover's feeling for the 'poetry' of the chosen facts. There is 'a reality prior to the poem', but to many it will seem to remain 'prior', the poem left unmade.

It is the 'literary' Glover wants to avoid (as Wordsworth did, as all good poets do); but that's not to say the book doesn't lead us through some oozy (or boozy) patches of sentiment, whimsy, banality. On the other hand we are rewarded in our passage with some of the sharpest scenes and some of the purest songs in our poetry.

V

Glover's poetry doesn't really develop; it moves only as he finds or fails to find new subjects. The subjects exist mainly outside himself, particularly in two areas: man in action distinguishing himself from his fellows, becoming larger, more colourful, a 'character'; and the local scene, sometimes as backdrop for the actions of men, sometimes as an opposing force, sometimes just valued for itself. Into the 'character' category fall 'Harry', that bruised and jaded romantic, and the more sharply individualized 'Arawata Bill'. Among the 'Harry' poems are Glover's best; 'Arawata Bill' is a mixed blessing. Elsewhere, however, positive responses to his characters are going to depend to quite a large extent on sharing his particular brand of sentiment. Lacking it, I find his 'Old Soldier' a bore, and 'Young Roberts' a banal story banally told. And what is any reader likely to make of 'The Sportsmen' unless he happens to know something more than the poem tells him about 'Spider Porter', 'Stalky Adamson' and the rest (it all sounds frightfully Boys' Own Annual-ish), and

> Solomon that massive master lump
> Pitting himself against the First Eleven.

'Towards Banks Peninsula' is a more substantial piece, carefully written and full of sharp observation. But does Glover really believe in the myth he tries to make out of Mick Stimson, and if he does, why does his poem drain away in such a shallow imitation of itself?

> You are salty dust where you lie.
> But quickened is the anonymous sea,
> And the hours lick endlessly
> At the stone of the sky.

VI

Subjects outside himself, because Glover distrusts his emotion, his experience, himself. It is typical that to the title of the poem 'To her Eyes' should be added in parenthesis 'written for a bet', as if any other motive would have been an embarrassment. The refusal to commit oneself to feeling, and then the sneaking wish to let it be seen obliquely, self-protectively—it all seems part of that bristling public school and naval manner, ridiculously imported, needlessly sustained, and preserved with less than full confidence because there is a sense hovering somewhere in the background that our very best attempt to do the English thing, to keep the stiff upper lip, can be no better than second best. Glover may not dream of 'quaint old England's quaint old towns', but in him the colony lives on.

JAMES K. BAXTER:
(1) A LOSS OF DIRECTION

If it is worth making a general distinction in the literature of this century between discursive poets, and poets who have attempted to achieve the poem as total Image, James K. Baxter belongs with the former group. Whatever else is left unsaid, one can include Allen Curnow without violence in a thought which takes in Wallace Stevens and T. S. Eliot: they are, all three, poets who mould the language in their own ways, make it work as it has not worked before. On the other hand one has come to think of Mr Baxter together with Thomas Hardy and Robert Frost: poets who take the language as it is and who work with it at one level of meaning; but who can tell a story, describe an event, think coherently and convincingly, or combine all these activities, in a verse which is sparely and strongly constructed.

The verse letter is a form well suited to these skills, and *In Fires of No Return* (a selection from the whole range of Mr Baxter's work) opens appropriately with the well-known 'To My Father'. To praise the strong construction of this poem—the way, for example, a thought is unravelled through a demanding rhyme scheme and brought to its conclusion in a firm couplet—is not simply to praise technical competence.

> Your country childhood helped to make you strong,
> Ploughing at twelve. I only know the man.
> While I grew up more sheltered and too long
> In love with my disease; though illness can
> Impart by dint of pain a different kind
> Of toughness to the predatory mind.

A review of *In Fires of No Return* (1958) in *Landfall* 49, March 1959. This was the copy I sent Charles Brasch, to which I added at his suggestion an irrelevant paragraph, now deleted, about the fact that Baxter's book had been published in London.

The qualities of the poet's mind at its best find their counterparts here in the syntactical toughness and lucidity of the verse.

Similarly, when the technique is at fault it mirrors a personal fault, a false position. In the same poem sentimentality—of hero-worship, or perhaps of protesting too much—begins to soften edges in the sixth stanza:

> Almost you are at times a second self;
> Almost at times I feel your heart beating
> In my own breast as if there were no gulf
> To sever us.

There is a personal unsureness here, and hence elaboration to fill out the stanza form. The lines come to grief among conventions: one cannot separate the 'breast' from the kind of poetry in which hearts are always beating. And in this conclusion the simpler imprecision of 'sever' enters: a 'gulf' is the result of severing, not the instrument which severs.

Mr Baxter's early poems were especially notable at their best for the ease with which they assimilated the essential features of New Zealand landscape and settlement; and in 'To My Father', typically, it is the externalization of feeling in terms of locality that saves the poem where its more directly personal motivations falter. In stanza 9, for example (after the preceding stanza's incantation of memories in which each line is prefaced untidily by 'You') the poem comes marvellously to life in two fine lines:

> These I remember, with the wind that blows
> Forever pure down from the tussock ranges.

These are first, and most importantly, real ranges, a real wind. But the line is resonant within its own firm location: it carries echoes of a source, of purity, of loss—feelings traditionally associated with childhood.

This strength of self-expression achieved through the medium of landscape is most fully exemplified in the two poems which conclude Section I of *In Fires of No Return*: 'Poem in the Matukituki Valley', and 'The Fallen House'. The latter in particular moves with strength and certainty, from the economy of its first two lines—

> I took the clay track leading
> From Black Bridge to Duffy's farm

to the final pitch of

> O Time, Time takes in a gin
> The quick of being!

where a quite ordinary perception, supported by the full weight of the poem, attains momentarily the quality of revelation.

In what might be called (to date) Mr Baxter's 'middle period' he seems to have concentrated on the writing of narrative verse; and on poems about single figures against a New Zealand background—in this collection, for example, 'Returned Soldier', 'Farmhand', 'Elegy for an Unknown Soldier', 'Mill Girl', 'The Hermit', 'Venetian Blinds' and 'The Homecoming'. These poems are more obviously technical exercises—that is, the writing is more deliberate, less urgent as a personal concern—than the poems written before or since; and one is led to speculate on a possible 'motive' in the writing. They may have been written in part as an attempt to objectify the poetry, to remove it from the difficulties in a poem like 'To My Father'; and in part as a conscious attempt to 'people the landscape'. About some of these single figure poems there is something arbitrary, inconsequential. 'Returned Soldier' is undistinguished; the 'Elegy' is a long and ordinary preliminary to a fine (early-Curnowesque) last stanza. And 'Farmhand' is plainly sentimental.

'Mill Girl' and 'The Hermit' are poems of a finer quality. Here the arbitrariness is only in Baxter's vision of the world—a world in which it is predictable that young girls will dream of 'a table at the Grand', but lose their virginity 'On wet park leaves, or on a mattress in a back/Room at the party. . . .' and where old hermits in shacks go down on sacking to pray, their hearts 'like wax in God's meridian blaze'. The problem set by poems of this kind is that their subjects tend to become morality figures, to assume an aura of archetype. Each in its own way is a generalization, an abstraction. They have their existence in an uncertain area which is neither fiction exactly, nor social comment. They attempt what perhaps can only adequately be done in prose.

In Mr Baxter's case one feels that his single figures are distorted by an inclination to melodrama; that they are lit up, like a row of coloured lights, with the charge of a particular emotion which belongs to the poet rather than to something he has observed in the world beyond himself. The failure is difficult to locate, but possibly the mill girl and the hermit are unconscious projections of an element of self-pity in Mr Baxter, disguised as general social realities. One is the virgin poetic mind, certain to be ravished by society; the other is the outcast poet, feeding on scraps but in tune with God.

But in all the poems of this group—and especially 'The Homecoming' —there is again an evocation of locality, which is the more impressive because it enters only obliquely:

> She will cook his meals; complain of the south weather
> That wrings her joints. And he—rebels; and yields
> To the old covenant—calms the bleating

> Ewe in birth travail. The smell of saddle leather
> His sacrament; or the sale day drink; yet hears beyond
>   sparse fields
> On reef and cave the sea's hexameter beating.

This quality is present too in poems written in the ballad metres which Mr Baxter uses with such ease. Few poets have pinned down, casually, without obtrusive intention, so much of what the particular New Zealand scene feels like. And in poems like 'The Walk' and 'The Book of the Dead', life in this exact context is heightened by the presence of the unsatisfied ghosts of those who established it.

Section III of this book shows the most recent developments in Mr Baxter's poetry. He has returned to the writing of poems more directly concerned with personal problems. Concretion is less frequently sought in terms of locality; and for this he has regrettably substituted an assortment of conventional literary trappings—pickings off the scrapheap of poetry. Too often it is a poetry (to select from 'To God the Son') of 'cries', 'blood', and 'dirt'; of the 'blind', 'weeping', 'deformed', and 'maimed'; of 'pride', 'danger', 'lust', 'poison', 'scorn', 'guilt', 'anger', 'love', 'loss', 'skulls', 'death', 'dreams', 'fury', 'flesh', 'pain', and 'agonies'. In such poems the language is diffuse and irresponsibly used; the pitch is hysterical; the self-posing is melodramatic.

One can best illustrate the new verbose style in its failure by a single example. In 'Letter to the World' Mr Baxter builds the stage on which he is to act out an unpleasant piece of self-dramatization and asks his reader to accept it as an image of the world. The world is addressed as a woman. Too long (he tells her) he has ignored her face of 'blood', 'dirt', and 'tears'; and earlier he has written of this face as beautiful (given it 'the kiss of a kind mirror'). Now, bleeding 'from love's scar', he presents her with the facts about herself, his 'salt wife', whose Original Sin he appears to have engendered personally:

> Salt wife, when you were pregnant with your death
> You asked me for the kiss of a kind mirror
> And newly married then, I knew no better.
> I praised you for the paint upon your scabs
> And left out evil from each loving letter.
>   Now as the serpent stabs
> Of grief in my guts, among the wounds and swabs
> Of love's rough hospital to your proud flesh I come
> And the soul sweating in its iron lung.

In stanza 3 the soul as T.B. patient is discarded in favour of the soul as a bird ('Hopping and moping in a bone cage') which must 'wet his beak with blood' so that it will understand evil. Despite the bird's moulting from 'lust and rage', the poet leaves it in favour of the world, his 'blood bought bride' (who is also 'groaning in God's arms', and whose nails, for no very clear reason, are 'bright from the pounding abattoir'). Claiming thus to recognize her for what she is, he gives her the 'wordy ring' of the poem—

> With diamonds cut from my heart's stone,
>   Tears for your agony fallen.

Confusion of imagery proceeds from a confusion of mind and imagination; verbal imprecision from imprecision of observation and thought. One does not object to the poem simply because the false counters of thought are tiresome, or the diction unfashionable. The aesthetic objection is ultimately a moral one. The skin of feigned toughness provided by images designed to disgust fails to conceal the weakness within. The poet has offered a distorted image of the world and of his relation to it. He has acquired the mantle of the suffering prophet, second-hand.

One cannot presume to prescribe the course Mr Baxter's development as a poet should take. But an attempt to define the areas in which his poetry has succeeded, and those in which it has failed, ought to be a legitimate activity of criticism. There are some successes in the new style, notably in the firm short lines of 'Homage to Lost Friends'. But one cannot avoid the feeling that he will not again be seen at his best until he regains some of the qualities of the finest poems in *The Fallen House*—spareness, directness, and a firm consciousness of particular time and place.

(2) TOWARDS JERUSALEM

I hadn't intended to write any kind of a 'survey' of James K. Baxter's poetry—only something about his *Jerusalem Sonnets,* because I admired them as much as or more than anything else of his, and I didn't seem able to find more than one or two whose opinion I could take seriously who took *them* seriously. Now Baxter is dead and already a posthumous book, *Autumn Testament,* in proof before his death, offers (together with some prose pieces) his most recent poems. I write in London, in a hurry, with a number of Baxter books at hand but not all I would like. I have, too, a copy of my last article on Baxter, written thirteen years ago, also in London—a

A survey of Baxter's later poetry, in *Islands* 3, Autumn 1973.

review of his Oxford book, *In Fires of No Return* (1958). It has weighed on
me since (though I don't think I have re-read it until now) because of a certain sourness of tone. I took to task what were then Baxter's most recent
poems, and took them apart. I found the worst of them 'diffuse',
'hysterical', 'melodramatic', full of 'pickings off the scrapheap of
poetry'—and I offered ample evidence. My word-counting wasn't forgotten (I had used the same method earlier on the poetry of Alistair Campbell)
and Baxter cited it with as much bitterness as he could muster (which
wasn't much) in several radio talks.

His next book, *Howrah Bridge* (1961), somehow passed me by. Then
came *Pig Island Letters* (1966). It won me over so completely I felt my 1959
review must have been wrong—that my motives must have been mixed and
impure. Some poems in *London Magazine* round about 1967, and then the
Jerusalem Sonnets completed the process. It seemed to me there were no
New Zealand poems I wanted so much to read and re-read. That remains
true today.

Of course I had always admired Baxter. (That, perhaps, is what was
wrong with my 1959 review—that I neglected to say so.) In the early fifties
when I was a student poems like 'Rocket Show', 'Wild Bees', 'Letter to
Noel Ginn II', and one I don't have a copy of now but was called, I think,
'Venetian Blinds'—these and others were as important a part of my intellectual landscape as the poems of Donne and Eliot, Curnow and Fairburn.
They had in common a personal, informal, verse-letter tone, a formal,
well-managed stanzaic pattern, and a more or less contrived movement
through varieties of sensuous experience towards moral statements. These
poems of Baxter's more than any others probably lie behind my own
'Night Watch in the Tararuas'; and I suppose my present discontent with
that poem comes precisely from its forced march to a moral conclusion.
Those orotund Baxterian roundings-off—

> But loss is a precious stone to me, a nectar
> Distilled in time, preaching the truth of winter
> To the fallen heart that does not cease to fall.
>
> ('Wild Bees')

or

> I thought of our strange lives, the grinding cycle
> Of death and renewal come to full circle;
> And of man's heart, that blind Rosetta stone,
> Mad as the polar moon, decipherable by none.
>
> ('Rocket Show')

—they came naturally enough to him; but if I accepted them it can only
have been as a concluding seal at the bottom of the parchment, a stylistic

habit like the ending of a Beethoven symphony, not as statements of particular value in themselves. What brought me back to the poems was not their quality as statements but their creation of a personality in balance against its surroundings—people, places, scenes, events—in which everything quivered with a symbolic resonance, a heightened sense of life. They were poems of the twentieth century in the romantic tradition as it passes through late Yeats to early Auden; but they were distinctly our own experience. No poetry moved me in quite the same way, at so profound a level, as our own, not just because the sensuous world it recreated was the one I knew from day to day, but because the Eden we are all cast out from is that of the world fresh to our awakening senses. For me one of the most important functions of poetry was to take us back there, and Baxter was one of the magicians who knew the way.

I think I need not have felt too badly about that 1959 review. It was more brutal in finding fault than I would ever wish to be now; but it praised where praise was due, and it looked forward accurately enough to what Baxter's future development might be. No doubt I have become more open-minded; but for me the present discovery is that I do not (as I supposed I would) need to conclude either that I was emphatically wrong in my judgement of the earlier book, or that I have since grown soft in the head. Baxter's poetry improved dramatically during the last twelve years of his life. All the enormous promise apparent in those first two boyish books of the forties, a promise which seemed perhaps not quite to be fulfilling itself in the fifties, blazes forth in the best poems of the sixties. I doubt whether this is widely recognized. A haze of undiscriminating feeling surrounds Baxter, which his death may only serve to thicken. To many older writers he is the marvellous boy they welcomed on to the scene who gracelessly turned his back on them, first to play out the melodrama of the doomed, boozing, fornicating Calvinist, and latterly the farce of the Catholic hippie. To the young, on the other hand, he has become a culture hero, and if his poems were much less remarkable than they are I suspect his youthful disciples would not know it and would admire them quite as much.

If you have to write about poetry or lecture on it two things may make the task easier; if the poems are bad, or if they are good but obscure. In the first instance you can show where and why they fail; in the second you can show what they mean. But what is there to be said of successful poems whose meaning is plain except 'Behold!'? That seems to me the case with *Jerusalem Sonnets*—either you see their merits or you don't—and I knew when I resolved to write about them I would have difficulties. Why are they good? How do I demonstrate to someone who hasn't felt it the

superiority I believe they have? Why do they seem to me, taken together as
a single long poem, perhaps the most impressive yet written by a New
Zealander?

There is no easy answer to these questions. But now that I have sat down
and read all the Baxter I could get my hands on, in sequence, I feel a little
nearer to an answer—because I can see the qualities slowly emerging that
are given their fullest expression in the sonnets.

Towards the end of *Howrah Bridge* (1961) a new voice begins to be heard
which for lack of another word I will call that of the mature Baxter. It is a
relaxed, matter-of-fact note, sometimes, in its first appearances, juxtaposed
with more conventional, high-toned lines.

> Eagles have bathed their wings at the ocean streams.
> In a cold taxi coming from the mass
> With Bertha in her blue silk dress
> I think of money.
>
> ('This Indian Morning')

There is something expansive in those lines. In their connected-
disconnected way they have the 'feel' of actual experience. A younger Baxter might have written one poem about the eagles and another about Ber-
tha; he could hardly have succeeded in casually yoking them together in a
stanza whose ostensible subject was his own return from mass. Here, as in
'Election 1960', 'A Dentist's Window', 'The Sixties', and others, Baxter is
coming down off his high romantic stilts—not a stylistic event, not the
result of a decision to write differently, but a development in the man's
confidence, in his belief that he can be seen to exist without trappings.

Yet at the same time that this is occurring (if, as I suppose, all the poems
of part II of *Howrah Bridge* belong to one period) Baxter also returns to
those stilts for the last time and performs more remarkably on them than
ever before. 'A Clapper to Keep off Crows', the last stanza of 'Night in
Delhi', and three love poems, 'The Apple Tree', 'She who is like the
moon', and 'On the death of her body', in their romantic virtuosity remind
me of Fairburn at his most fluent.

> Beauty you possess, time's daughter,
> Lamp of my life, O hidden one,
> You who are the song you sing,
>
> Silently, silently,
> From faithful pillows on a night of love
> Pouring in my heart's gulf
>
> Your light, your song, your cataract of beauty.
>
> ('She who is like the moon')

With *Pig Island Letters* (1966) the informal tone predominates. The

voice becomes rougher, more natural, though the poems are quite as well
made. They are mostly in the first person, often without rhyme and
sometimes without a formal stanza pattern. The physical background, the
scene, is strongly evoked. But at the centre is the rough, grating, resonant
voice and personality of Jim the Catholic family man chafing with wry self-
knowledge against work and suburbia.

> but smoking one small cigar
> confess Christ, as the bones creak
>
> this excellent Friday, not
> expecting martyrdom—thus
> I hang my balls and car-coat
> at the church door, and go up
> to swap saliva on those
> metal feet that touch the lip . . .
>
> ('Easter Testament')

> 'Pity all things'—Do the tough
> kids need pity who wrestle
> under the bathing shed wall?
> or the girls whose broad muscles
> slide in bermuda shorts, all
> intent on a thunder-proof
>
> world of knowledge? I cannot
> pity what is; but look up
> at the karaka tree . . .
>
> ('A Wish for Berries')

The development I am describing is not dramatic or sudden but it is
distinct enough and occurs in a matter of a few years. Already those lines
are a long way from those last beautiful flings of romanticism in *Howrah
Bridge*. Compare them, for example, with

> I saw where in a wilderness did lie
> The royal spirits of our burdened age.
> Some slept; some roared, and shook the walls in rage;
> Crowned beasts in cages open to the sky . . .
>
> ('Night in Delhi')

and so on—lines which wouldn't look out of place, or out of countenance,
anywhere in the works of Shelley.

The full effect of the change can't be felt in one or two poems because it
is partly an effect of personality—the strong, uncompromising personality
whose vision of himself and of all men is dour as it always was but not
sour, dark, but not without flashes of humour. The poems are not all

equally successful. In 'Ballad of One Tree Hill' feeling runs away with the writing, inflating it, and some of the old, bad, self-pitying melodrama slips in. The sequence which gives the book its title has weaker moments too. But for most of the book the tone is level, confident, moving easily from present scene to reminiscence to moral observation and back to the present with a total effect richer than anything Baxter had achieved before.

> About twilight we came to the whitewashed pub
> On a knuckle of land above the bay
>
> Where a log was riding and the slow
> Bird-winged breakers cast up spray.
>
> ('East Coast Journey')

The skill in lines like these is in how little is needed to call up a whole scene: twilight, the whitewashed pub standing out above the bay, and then that detail of the log and its movement in breakers—so particular you feel it as something experienced. You cannot 'see' that log without seeing more than is literally in the words of the poem. The same is true of the lines which follow:

> One of the drinkers round packing cases had
> The worn face of a kumara god,
>
> Or so it struck me. . . .

We are directed to look at one man but those casual 'packing cases' bring with them the whole scene. And don't the 'bird-winged breakers' seem now to join with the face of the kumara god to suggest something hidden below the casual surface? Some revelation is at hand.

> . . . Later on
> Lying awake in the verandah bedroom
>
> In great dryness of mind I heard the voice of the sea
> Reverberating. . . .

That image of the log still rolls in the mind, like a body in the surf. The poet is seeking intensity of life in the knowledge of death:

> . . . As a man
>
> Grows older he does not want beer, bread, or the prancing flesh,
> But the arms of the eater of life, Hine-nui-te-po. . . .

Out of such hard-gained evocations of particular places, events, people, Baxter is continually wringing something which I think can properly be called wisdom—a wisdom richer than any available to him in conversation or in prose where, for all his colour and horse sense, he was also rambling and partial. In the best of these poems, in fact in all but a few which are weak, that prose Baxter yields precedence to the deep implacable will of the artist to discover the real and the true. I suspect it was the prose Baxter who had followers, the Baxter of 'Elegy for Boyle Crescent', for example (*Islands* 1), which has been recommended to me more than once as a moving document but which seems to me a shabby exercise in rhetoric, a giving in to the sentimental self that rises most readily when we believe we have a just cause. Then policemen are 'the fuzz' and 'the pigs', our culture is a 'death-ship' with 'burnt-out eyes and broken ear-drums', while 'junkies' become heroes and martyrs ('I never met a junkie who was incapable of love.').

Against that prose Baxter I set what I call the wisdom of the poet:

> . . . Shall Marx and Christ
> Share beds this side of Jordan? I set now
> Unwillingly these words down:
>
> *Political action in its source is pure,*
> *Human, direct, but in its civil function*
> *Becomes the jail it laboured to destroy.*
>
> ('Pig Island Letters 8')

Or this, which contains all that is true in 'Elegy for Boyle Crescent' quite as memorably and with none of the falseness and overstatement:

> This love that heals like a crooked limb
> In each of us, source of our grief,
> Could tell us if we cared to listen, why
> Sons by mayhem, daughters by harlotry
> Pluck down the sky's rage on settled houses. . . .
>
> ('Pig Island Letters 7')

The Rock Woman, published in 1969, is a selection (not a good one) from the whole range of Baxter's poetry. It includes only a few poems written after the publication of *Pig Island Letters*, but at about this time the transformation was occurring in which Jim the Catholic family man became Hemi the prophet. I can now see *Jerusalem Sonnets* (1970) as a development out of all that had gone before; but it is probably true that it needed the personal upheaval of his leaving home and of his wandering between the Jerusalem commune and the 'junkie' houses of Auckland, to shake the new poems out of him. The freshness of seeing that poetry requires doesn't come readily out of a settled suburban life. Nor did it come best to Baxter out of living in cities, which encouraged him in his darkest, broadest, and least convincing generalizations. If there were periods of boredom and irritation in Jerusalem it's clear there was much more, in the pace of life there and in the proximity of living things, to help than to hinder his writing. In his own way Baxter did what Fairburn (in 'To a Friend in the Wilderness') only talked about.

Jerusalem Sonnets may be read as thirty-nine sonnets or as a single poem in thirty-nine stanzas. It has one setting, one voice, one theme (stated on the title page). The sonnet form chosen has fourteen lines, spaced out in pairs but not 'paired' in any sense other than that, with no rhyming pattern. It is loose, but not as loose as it looks. The lack of a rhyme scheme means that no aura of appropriateness will be lent to any word by the form: only the statement being made will justify the words chosen. That statement must be (as in any sonnet) single, unified, the expression of one idea, not because the rule book says so but because that is all fourteen lines will carry. The difficulty is always that if you write economically fourteen lines is rather a lot for one idea, and too little for more than one. With the conventional sonnet, however, you have some leeway. For example you may complete your statement in twelve lines and simply recapitulate in a final couplet. In Baxter's sonnet every line must carry its weight of relevant meaning or look empty and irrelevant. To have said all you have to say in thirteen and a half lines is fatal. You have not filled the form, yet any additional words will seem weightless; they will clutter and obscure the effect. To put this point in a less technical way: I find it impossible to believe that anyone who had not Baxter's skill in handling rhymed stanzas could manage the 'freedom' of this sonnet form as well as he does.

But of course the achievement is not primarily formal; or the formal qualities are not distinct from the achievement as a whole, which I still find very difficult to pin down. Let me approach it obliquely in the following way: when I write letters I write them usually as fast as I can make pen or typewriter move across the page. When I write a piece of criticism (such as this present one) the writing inches along painfully with probably a third of the manuscript scored out and written over. Yet if I read my letter over before posting it it doesn't seem a worse piece of writing than the critical article. Why, then (I sometimes ask myself) shouldn't I be able to dash down critical articles as fast as letters? I suppose the answer is that in critical writing I am trying to say more difficult things—I am labouring to achieve clarity. In letters you don't normally try to define anything but simply to be yourself, and whatever a letter lacks in clarity of definition will usually be made up in that way. It's not easy to 'be yourself' even in letters, but you don't overcome the difficulty by 'trying hard'—whereas with expository prose you do: by trying hard you can achieve greater clarity. Poetry of any kind, but especially poetry of the kind Baxter wrote, is much nearer to a letter than to expository prose. The great aim is to give the fullest possible expression to all that the sensibility is capable of. More often than not poets fail—or rather their success is limited; that is why the sin of being more interested in the poet than in the poems is pardonable—because most poets, even those whose work endures, are more brilliantly charged with promise than with achievement. Would we admire Keats quite as much as we do if he hadn't also written those extraordinary letters? Weren't even the best of the early Baxter poems rather pale by comparison with the drunk in the gaberdine raincoat and galoshes who wrote them? Wasn't it possible to feel, because Fairburn was so much weightier than his funny poems and so much less solemn than his serious ones, that only half the man had gone into each?

What Baxter has managed in *Jerusalem Sonnets* (as in the best of *Pig Island Letters*) is to get something like the whole range of the personality into the poetry—but (this being poetry) it is a personality heightened and simplified. Here is the opening poem:

> The small grey cloudy louse that nests in my beard
> Is not, as some have called it, 'a pearl of God'—
>
> No, it is a fiery tormentor
> Waking me at two a.m.
>
> Or thereabouts, when the lights are still on
> In the houses in the pa, to go across thick grass
>
> Wet with rain, feet cold, to kneel
> For an hour or two in front of the red flickering
>
> Tabernacle light—what He sees inside
> My meandering mind I can only guess—
>
> A madman, a nobody, a raconteur
> Whom He can joke with—'Lord', I ask Him,
>
> 'Do You or don't You expect me to put up with lice?'
> His silent laugh still shakes the hills at dawn.

The beauty of these poems is subtle; even, for all the rough candour of the voice, delicate. I suppose 'the small grey cloudy louse' is accurate description but it is more than that, almost affectionate. The word 'cloudy' seems in its context beautiful enough to render the louse inoffensive, 'a pearl of God' despite the denial; and if we are invited in line three to see it as a 'fiery tormentor', in that role too it seems God's instrument, driving the poet out (and here we begin to experience the physical setting, as in all these poems) across the marae to the church and the 'red flickering/Tabernacle light'. A whole tradition of Christian asceticism has been tactfully evoked. Has Baxter the right to place himself in that tradition? He doesn't know. He knows himself as 'a madman, a nobody, a raconteur'—and we are left with the question he puts to God: is he or isn't he to put up with lice?—and with God's answer, a 'silent laugh' that 'still shakes the hills at dawn'. The humour is quiet, rich, an extension of the sense of life the poem imparts, not a belittling of it.

Depending on such qualities, the sonnets lend weight to one another and need to be read in sequence if their full effect is to be felt. Here is the second:

> The bees that have been hiving above the church porch
> Are some of them killed by the rain—
>
> I see their dark bodies on the step
> As I go in—but later on I hear
>
> Plenty of them singing with what seems a virile joy
> In the apple tree whose reddish blossoms fall
>
> At the centre of the paddock—there's an old springcart,
> Or at least two wheels and the shafts, upended
>
> Below the tree—Elijah's chariot it could be, Colin,
> Because my mind takes fire a little there
>
> Thinking of the woman who is like a tree
> Whom I need not name—clumsily gripping my beads,
>
> While the bees drum overhead and the bouncing calves look at
> A leather-jacketed madman set on fire by the wind.

This is again a case of revealing enough to set the mind of the reader unconsciously at work so that it 'sees' more than it is shown—a derelict church, insufficiently secure against the elements to protect from rain the bees that hive in its porch; a field in which an old springcart has been left to fall to pieces under an apple tree. . . . Yet the mood is not of decay but of regeneration. This is a spring poem. The surviving bees sing with a 'virile joy'; the apple tree sheds blossom; the calves are bouncing; and the poet, thinking of a woman 'who is like a tree', becomes for a moment 'a leather-jacketed madman set on fire by the wind' (again that subtle rhetorical force gathered up in the last line). The man and the world about him are brought into harmony. It is a moment of affirmation rare in a poet whose vision has been consistently dark.

But to go on dealing particularly with poems of this kind may be an evasion of a more general question which I now put to myself: 'Doesn't a set of doctrines and beliefs which you yourself find at least false and possibly repugnant lie behind these poems? In your enjoyment of the poems aren't you ignoring an essential part of their meaning?'

My answer to this is that I'm not concerned with what lies behind the poems but with what is *in* them. I ignore nothing that is there and I find nothing untrue or repugnant. They are not poems of doctrine but poems of experience. Our experiences as human beings differ very little. What differs is the interpretation we put on them. These poems present rather than interpret—and where there are elements of interpretation they come usually in the form of the poet's dialogue with himself in which there is conflict and contradiction rather than settled doctrine:

> If Ngati-Hiruharama turns out to be no more than
> A child's dream in the night—well then,
>
> I have a garden, a bed to lie on,
> And various company—some clattering pigeons roost
>
> At my back door, and when I meditate in the paddock
> Under the apple tree two healthy dung-smeared pigs
>
> Strike up a conversation, imagining, I think,
> I am their benefactor—that should be quite enough
>
> To keep the bowels moving and the mind thankful;
> Yet when the sun rises my delusion hears him shout
>
> Above the river fog—'This is the hill fort
> Of our God; it is called Hiruharama!
>
> The goat and the opossum will find a home
> Among the rocks, and the river of joy will flow from it.'
>
> (Sonnet 30)

Is his faith that he is achieving Hiruharama (Jerusalem) a delusion? The poem says so but the faith is given the last word. There is contradiction and no final answer. These poems are deeply grounded in the natural world; if they aspire beyond it that too is 'natural'.

I have not had *Autumn Testament* long enough, nor is there time now, to write about it. It consists of a long poem, 'He Waiata Mo Te Kare', addressed to Baxter's wife, to which six pages of notes are attached; then 'Autumn Testament', forty-eight sonnets in the Jerusalem Sonnet form; a further eight pages of prose, 'Letter to Colin'; and a final seven sonnets, 'Te Whiori o Te Kuri'. The poetry seems all to be drawing off the same vein as the earlier sonnet sequence and with undiminished power and richness. In particular the Maori elements seem here to have become a deep and genuine part of Baxter's intellectual and emotional life— something new in pakeha writing. The prose sections leave me unsatisfied. The 'brief tribute' by Frank McKay seems to me unfortunate and something of an obstacle at the front of the book.

On Frank Sargeson's wall, up above the fireplace, there used to be (perhaps there still is) a wooden cross. I think he told me it was the start of what a friend had intended to be a wooden doll or puppet and Sargeson had hung it up as a sign of respectability to catch the eye of any policeman who might call on him. One day I found among cards and pictures on the shelf above the fireplace a photograph of the young Baxter in his alcoholic raincoat. I climbed up and pinned the photograph on the cross where it remained for years curling at the edges and gathering dust.

When someone dies there are always things left unsaid which we regret. They are usually kind things, but in Baxter's case I find myself troubled by the fact that on the few occasions when we talked at length I listened so patiently to his monologues and didn't interrupt and question and contradict. I'm not sure why I was so obliging. It seems a kind of insincerity for which I am now punished by being stuck with it. We have, however, our conversations with the dead, and in mine I now interrupt him, usually with the statement 'Jim, you know as well as I do that there's no God.'

When I think of Baxter the man and the poet my first thought is always of the strengths he had which I lack. He would never have sat through a monologue half of which he didn't agree with, simply to be agreeable. Keats's idea of the poet—that he has no character because he is forever becoming, or at least adjusting to, the object of his contemplation—is true only of some poets (Keats, for example). It doesn't fit Baxter, who had a Wordsworthian ruggedness and certainty, never cared much about money or status or what the neighbours might think, and went resolutely his own way.

But there is another part of my dialogue with the dead Baxter. In it I interrupt him not to tell him there is no God but to ask him why he talks so much. He replies (and I can hear it in exactly his voice): 'The walls are caving in, brother. When I stop shovelling I'll be buried.' Or he says, 'Why does a man cling to his coat? Because he feels the cold.'

I think Baxter knew perfectly well what it meant to say 'There is no God.' But our needs are more powerful than our sense of probabilities and Baxter could not live without postulating an Authority, against which he then threw himself with all his force in order to be sure of his own existence. He became a Catholic in order to be a better rebel; and on the rare occasions when he tried to be a 'good' Catholic, as in some of the essays in *The Man on the Horse*, he sounded false and insincere.

It seems to me he died at the height of his powers and with a great deal yet to say. I think he was a major poet, and if I believed in his God I would say in my prayers: 'If You had looked on us with half an eye, Lord, You would have seen that our need of him was greater than Yours.'

HUBERT WITHEFORD:
RHETORIC AND WIT

In London in 1965 I was asked to organize readings of New Zealand and Australian poetry at the Royal Court Theatre during the Commonwealth Festival of the Arts. Hubert Witheford was among the expatriate New Zealanders who agreed to take part. He sent me a sheaf of typescripts of recent poems and I read them with delight and surprise. I had been conscious of him as author of 'Elegy in the Orongorongo Valley' (which Allen Curnow anthologized) and one or two other poems. I had long ago bought his first book and perhaps borrowed his second from a library, but I had remembered little of either. Whatever impression I had gained of this poet was inaccurate in that it had not prepared me for wit—and it was wit that distinguished the poems he had sent me.

The poems contained in that sheaf of typescripts have gone (with others) into *A Native, Perhaps Beautiful,* Mr Witheford's fourth book. Is the delight of my first encounter with them sustained? The element of surprise and of discovery is gone. But these are poems I continue to admire. They have encouraged me to look back into Mr Witheford's past.

From the start his talent has been real and his own. The style has developed but at each stage he has written well. He has been an 'intellectual' poet, or so it has seemed. Whether reviewers of his first two books, *Shadow of the Flame* (1950), and *The Falcon Mask* (1951), praised or blamed the 'abstract' quality of his poetry they were alike in finding the word appropriate. In *Arachne,* the Wellington periodical of the early 1950s with which Mr Witheford was closely associated, he was praised as 'a superior intellect' and as 'the first New Zealand poet able to express his deepest experience through hard abstract thought'.

A review of *A Native, Perhaps Beautiful, Landfall* 88, December 1968.

Some part of the literary theory which lay behind his early practice can be discerned in an article on James K. Baxter's poetry he wrote for the 1953 *Poetry Yearbook*. His view of English literary history derived from what was common to Eliot, Pound, and Leavis. It might have been called without unfairness a simplification of a simplification. The 'intellectual and emotional tautness' of Shakespeare, Donne, and Jonson had been lost in the Civil War period and regained only, in the twentieth century, in Pound and Eliot (with the help of certain French poets of the late nineteenth century). In New Zealand the high regard for James K. Baxter's poetry indicated that the old rhetoric still prevailed. Mr Witheford was out to wring its neck. We may assume that he hoped his own poetry would represent the 'new' precision and wit.

We can hardly blame him for the literary history. He was young, and he had the pronouncements of many academics of the time as well as of his poet heroes to confirm it. Further, however sweeping the general statements, Mr Witheford brought to bear on individual poems a practitioner's intelligence. Quoting, for example, from James K. Baxter's 'To My Wife' the lines

> Though your own self before the world I cherish
> Yet Him before the world and you I prize;

Mr Witheford continues

which, if not written by a saint—and it has an assertiveness that makes this seem unlikely—is the poetic equivalent of a bad cheque. In saying this one does not mean to suggest insincerity, or at least, one means to recall what a difficult thing sincerity is. It is all too easy to mistake what other people say for what we feel. It is as hard for a poet as for anyone else to become more than a relaying station for the noise around him.

Neither was the intelligence merely literary in application. As his prose contributions to *Arachne* demonstrate, it could be exercised in pungent comments on New Zealand, and more broadly Western, society:

The struggle of well-fed pressure groups for larger shares in the national booty is not a battle which engages the highest faculties of the human heart or mind. . . .

Humanitarianism flourishes where life is most easy, that is for the 19th and 20th century west, where the fiery core of religion is most nearly extinct. This new sense for the sufferings of others is an extension of the human consciousness that we cannot repudiate, but I do not think it can survive long in its present form. It defeats itself by looking too closely and exclusively at the material conditions of life. . . . Moreover, there is about the humanitarian ethic a dreariness that tempts to evil or what, by its standards, is evil. One cannot regard the trim state housing settlements without thinking that they imply the atomic bomb.[1]

I prefer not to guess where such reasoning might have led in terms of political theory—though it may be noted that Yeats, Pound, Lawrence, and Eliot had all been over similar ground. But the attractiveness or otherwise of the ideas is not relevant. My point is only that one might have expected the quality of (for example) that final sentence to find its equivalent, in poetry, in forms of wit.

But it is not wit—nor is it the 'ideas', nor the 'symbolism' (the former often unintelligible, the latter largely borrowed)—that distinguishes the first two volumes. On the contrary, to a reader looking back from this distance it is rhetoric (that same swan whose neck Mr Witheford was supposed to have wrung)—even the rhetoric alone—which certifies that this is the work of a poet and not of a charlatan:

> O giant powers that in the green leaves stir
> Under the iron skies of wintertime,
> O ancient strengths unheeded in the earth
> Waiting the wild and city-shattering spring,
> O friends long lost, O fierce deliverers
> Fearfully and with love I summon you.
>
> Your patience bears the ruin of the world,
> A grain of salt upon a sea-gull's wing.
> In subterranean tides your joy anoints
> The roots of love and death and prophecy.
> In need now known, from sterile shores I cry
> 'My life, my words decay. O save them by your gift.'
>
> (from *Shadow of the Flame*)

It had distinct merit, but Mr Witheford could hardly liberate us from 'sonorousness' until he had liberated himself. In the meantime, after the appearance of his second book, he had gone to England—an experience which profoundly influenced his life and hence his development as a poet. He returned to New Zealand in 1956 but his homeland now seemed intolerably barbarian, a colourless backwater of no consequence. The intellectual Kiwi is always a romantic at heart. We put Gauguin's pilgrimage into reverse, seeking a clearer definition of ourselves and renewed confidence by placing ourselves against the background that is both alien and 'significant'. After only a year back in Wellington our poet returned to London.

By now, however, Mr Witheford had reached that point when the first poetic impulse, begun usually in adolescence and sustained through the poet's twenties, runs out. This seems to have had little to do with change of place. His silence began in England, continued during his year back in New Zealand, and survived his return to London. After five unproductive years he began to write again.

I tell the story as if I had it from the poet or some other authoritative source. In fact it is part guesswork, patched together from notes and dates on dust covers and from the poems themselves—especially those in his third book, *The Lightning Makes a Difference* (1962). It is in the first two sections of this book that Mr Witheford's goose, or swan, sings its last fine songs:

> From far beneath the full moon a cold wind blows,
> The olive sea grows dark, the wet sands shine.
> Some dregs of saffron, in the west sky, drown
> And with them sinks the human occupation
> Of eagerness and shame. One day of it goes down.
> It is as if a sun of darkness healed me . . .
>
> ('Sun of Darkness')

When his talent is renewed five years later it has broken free of iambic regularity. The lines are mainly shorter, or at least more varied in length and less regular; statements are more direct, the cadences closer to those of speech. The wit that seemed to be promised in the prose ten years before is realized. These developments are sustained in *A Native, Perhaps Beautiful.*

> I know without opening my eyes
> It is ugly,
> It is mine.   ('The Displacement')

> As if the fountain
> Over Triton, his nymphs and dolphins,
> Could cease.
> Then through the withered air
> Unmagical, concrete,
> You would see them
> Cavorting, or puffed: or their gaze
> For ever
> On their sun-dried dream.
>
> ('Let the Dead Keep What is Dead')

> I take a drink from an undeniable
> Sportsman in a white polo-neck jersey. . . .
>
> ('Towards a Completely Flat Surface')

In the 'new' Witheford a great deal of his former subjective abstraction is gone—or it has been properly forced outward to meet and fraternize with an objective world which absorbs it and which is itself modified in the process. This meeting provides the necessary 'dramatic' element that distinguishes poetry from science on the one hand and subjectivity on the other. The world and the man confronting it come to life when the writing accords them equal status—and in the trick of achieving that equality is most of the art of poetry:

> On the close shore the colours reek
> Of lichen: they are drenched with sulphur,
> All that tends to green
> But halts or swerves.
> Perhaps the mud-flats give them their rich tone.
> There is such splendour in the shades, my soul,
> As you draw near . . .
>
> ('Looking Across Chichester Harbour')

> I look in the direction I think a poem may come
> Around the corner, up river, past Chelsea.
> Beneath, laden with garbage, glide the barges against the stream,
> To my right the agreeable towers of a failing democracy.
>
> ('Upon Westminster Bridge')

The 'drama' in Mr Witheford's case is minor. That is the nature of his talent. But the scale of his poetry is further limited by his having chosen to live in England. He lacks the 'public' voice that comes from confidence that one speaks for something, and to someone, other than oneself. This forces a kind of 'purity' on his poetry. There is little to tempt him into posturing or falseness. But with the public 'impurities' that are automatically excluded go most of the larger possibilities for poetry.

Mr Witheford writes out of a narrow circle of personal experience. He does not spend much time looking back, but reminds himself, rather, that there is

> About the autobiographical, always
> The smell of Lazarus

and promises instead of 'reminiscence'

> The salt explosion and the ambush moment
> Of creation.
>
> ('Let the Dead Keep What is Dead')

The warning is salutary. There is something negative and unappealing about the poet who, living away from home, draws nostalgically or bitterly on a dwindling store of reminiscence, some of which (like Mr Witheford's 6 o'clock drunks on trams in 'Evening in a Distant Suburb') will have taken revenge on him by going out of date. Nonetheless, the poem I enjoy most in this book is a reminiscence—or rather, a recreation—of an experience from childhood:

> *Barbarossa*
> Addiction to the exceptional event—

That flaw
In something like *My Childhood Days in X,*
And fault-line—as from the Aleutians
Down the Pacific to where I was when
It opened wide one day when I was ten.

The town-hall whistle blows. It's five
To twelve. Now homewards, slow,
Turning a legend like a stone, sea-worn,
Red-streaked. The bearded Emperor in the German cave
Sits in his armour; when will he wake and go
Clanking into the light to lead his hordes?

The gutters heave.
                    Upon the rumbling ground
I balance. I sit down.
A stop to stories of the death of kings.
I watch the telegraph
Poles. A great hand plucks the strings.

Upon the other coast Napier, too, sways
Most irrecoverably: flames. Looters are shot
By landing-parties near the gutted shops.
Half a hill
Spilt on the coast-road; squashed in their ancient Fords
The burghers sit there still.

I have quoted the whole poem. It will be seen that it begins by mocking
its own subject—the 'exceptional event' as recounted in 'something like
My Childhood Days in X'. The 'flaw' in the man (addiction to the exceptional event) and the 'fault-line' which produces the event (the earthquake
of 1931) meet and complement one another. So at line 7 we are back in 'X',
the child making his way home turning over in his mind the legend of Barbarossa. I now know—because I took the trouble to find out—what the
legend is. But I found (as so often happens) that the poem had in fact given
me all the information I needed. The legendary Barbarossa is not dead but
sleeps in his cave until the day when he will wake and lead his people back
to their former greatness.

The earth shakes. The child sits down. In lines 15 and 16 I pick up an
echo of Shakespeare's *Richard II*—

> For God's sake, let us sit upon the ground
> And tell sad stories of the death of kings:

—but that, I think, is incidental. One's attention is held in this section by
the convincing 'reality' (the behaviour of the telegraph poles) and by what
it is made to suggest. Does the earthquake signify that the emperor is stir-

ring under the earth? Was Barbarossa's the 'great hand that plucked the strings'? Was it the hand of god whose music will waken the emperor? The questions are legitimate but no answers are possible. Strictly the poem is telling only what happened.

The concluding lines are impressive:

> . . . Looters are shot
> By landing-parties near the gutted shops.
> Half a hill
> Spilt on the coast-road; squashed in their ancient Fords
> The burghers sit there still.

It is a pungent and witty image of disaster. Is it more than that? I noticed when I first read the poem that it seemed as if the burghers were not dead; and now—reading not to enjoy but to explain to myself my own enjoyment—I notice that they 'sit' encased in iron (their ancient Fords) as Barbarossa 'sits in his armour'. There is even a rhyme (Fords and hordes) to link the two separated passages. Perhaps the burghers are merely sleeping. Perhaps they will one day wake and come forth 'clanking into the light' in their Fords like Barbarossa in his armour.

How much of this is deliberate? It is important to ask this question in order to insist that it cannot be answered. And though, presumably, a 'full' reading of the poem will notice these parallels, one cannot insist that a 'correct' reading will make just so much, or so little, of them. The strength of the poem is in the degree to which it is governed by an actual event, and at the same time invites the reader's imagination to work like the child's, extending its significance.

Mr Witheford has 'wrung the neck of rhetoric'—but so has Mr Baxter. It is a matter of personal development in each case, not of literary history; and it hardly needs to be said that however apt some of Mr Witheford's strictures may have been fifteen years ago, Mr Baxter was then and remains the larger and more important poet. That is not to say we could afford to dispense with either. Mr Witheford's is a distinct talent. His new book deserves to be read.

FLEUR ADCOCK:
A COOL INTELLIGENCE

The modes of poetry in this century, no matter how they vary, all build on the personality of the poet (Eliot's talk of 'impersonality' notwithstanding). *'Le style c'est l'homme'* seems more and more meaningful. Felicity of phrase that doesn't carry along with it the breath-pauses of speech, the hesitancies and fluxes of thought and feeling, the grittiness of the actual, seems facile, academic. I once wrote 'the words a poet uses will . . . declare the lies he tells to be lies and expose his vanities' and I still feel that this was a way of saying something important and true. A poem which lays claim to a strength not possessed by the poet will seem falsely rhetorical; one which fluently lacquers over his weaknesses will seem superficial, decorative. Skill, technique, craft are the measure of verse; honesty is the measure of poetry. Perhaps this has always been so and the current modes only make us more conscious of it.

Fleur Adcock's poems suggest not only a woman's sensibility and preoccupations but a woman's voice—as distinctly as handwriting can suggest a female hand. She is (if I can speak loosely for the fraternity) better than most of us. She always writes well. She seems gifted with that slightly detached female intelligence that can marshal even the most wayward feelings and make verbal sense and shape of them. But her poetic virtues are also her poetic limitations. She lacks the will, the passion, the ebullience, buoyancy, egotism on which great or strongly original structures are flung up.

High Tide in the Garden will sustain her reputation. There are no bad poems and no strikingly new departures. Everything is well done and there are a few poems as good as Miss Adcock's best, which is very good indeed.

A review of *High Tide in the Garden*, in *Landfall* 100, December 1971.

At that best she is tender, subtle, precise, and this is always when her heart is in the poem—when she is expressing some phase or aspect of love towards place, child or lover.

> Come closer. Listen. Be brave.
> I am going to talk to you quietly
> as sometimes, in the long past (you remember?)
> we made love. Let us be intent, and still. Still.
> There are ways of approaching it. This is one:
> this gentle talk, with no pause for suspicion,
> no hesitation, because you do not know
> the thing is upon you, until it has come—
> now, and you did not even hear it.

('Afterwards')

There are no 'images', no poetic devices, only an exact dramatization of a moment of feeling in which the reader becomes the lover addressed and is rendered passive by a voice which seems bell-like, hypnotic, anaesthetizing. The poem's meaning is thus enacted, or enforced, as experience.

She is least engaging when she is merely accomplished, when she seems to write out of an idea rather than out of the conjugations of actual pain and pleasure. Even 'Gas', the long poem which concludes the book, doesn't take hold of me in the way the merits of the writing, which I very well recognize, suggest it should. It interests me as an exercise, a construction, rather than as a living poem.

Perhaps the best poems in the collection are three which express an expatriate's feeling for New Zealand. 'Stewart Island' is a poem of rejection. 'On a Son Returned to New Zealand', merging the image of the loved child with that of the landscape he inhabits, finds release for nostalgia without committing the poet to it totally:

> He was
> already in his father's house, on the
> cliff-top, where the winter storms roll across
> from Kapiti Island, and the flax bends
> before the wind. He could go no further.
>
> He is my bright sea-bird on a rocky beach.

'Ngauranga Hill Gorge' is a rich evocation of the life which it is the poem's purpose to reject, and that life is weighed against the simple and feeling conclusion 'But I think it was a barren place.' There is great intelligence, or real style (it may come to the same thing), in a simplicity which can so effectively by-pass a whole area of profitless sociological debate. The positive and the negative confront one another and I am left admiring and liking the personality that has contrived to give conviction and force to

both. By comparison, poems like 'Saturday' and 'Trees', deriving from the
poet's ease in her present environment, although beautifully composed out
of precise imagist fragments, seem a fraction too cosy, lacking that tension
which gives the New Zealand poems their intensity.

There are three other poems which don't fall into any distinct category
but which deserve special mention. 'Country Station' is a beautifully successful poem which will speak best for itself:

> First she made a little garden
> of sorrel stalks wedged among
> some yellowy-brown moss-cushions
>
> and fenced it with ice-lolly sticks
> (there were just enough); then she
> set out biscuit crumbs on a brick
>
> for the ants; now she sits on a
> deserted luggage-trolley
> to watch them come out for dinner.
>
> It's nice here—cloudy but quite warm.
> Five trains have swooshed through, and one
> stopped, but at the other platform.
>
> Later, when no one is looking
> she may climb on the roof of that
> low shed. Her mother is making
>
> another telephone-call (she
> isn't crying any more.)
> Perhaps they will stay here all day.

'Against Coupling' is the comic counter-statement to the love poems
—wry, frank, witty, not in the least cynical. 'A Surprise in the Peninsula' is
a fantasy or dream poem (or perhaps it merely seems so). I had the peninsula firmly in mind as Coromandel until I noticed the 'bitter local coffee',
which might suggest Greece, or nowhere. The protagonist arrives home
and finds the skin of a dog nailed to her wall, a coarse map of the 'peninsula' singed in the fur, 'the town' marked by a bullet hole that goes right
through the wall. Literalness and understatement (as in so much of the
book) are the qualities of the style:

> It seemed freshly killed—
> There was blood at the edges. Not
> my dog: I have never owned one,
> I rather dislike them. (Perhaps
> whoever did it knew that.) It

was a light brown dog, with smooth hair;
no head, but the tail still remained.

A balance is maintained on a fine line between terror and the absurd: hysteria is just out of the picture, giving it its sharpness and point.

With such a transparent style, a good deal of any poem's interest will depend on its subject matter, or on (to return to my opening) the personality of the poet. If there is anything lacking in this collection it is certainly not accomplishment. It is true that poets whose intelligence and sense of decorum are as highly developed as Miss Adcock's sometimes suffer at their own hands. Careful selection can look like meanness, and control like lack of feeling. But to complain of it would be to do the injustice of asking Miss Adcock to be another poet than the one she is.

DAVID MITCHELL:
HE SING FR YOU

First, who is David Mitchell? I know him as a poet whose work I've become aware of by attending poetry readings around Auckland in the past four or five years. Otherwise it would hardly be possible to know anything of him at all. A note (a fatuously modish note) on him by M. D. Edmond in *Freed* 3, 1971, tells us that Mitchell has published only five poems in magazines in the past ten years. I would guess him to be in his early thirties. Two years ago he was reading mostly from a sequence called 'Davy Mitchell's Tripbook' which contained poems drawn from his experiences travelling in France and England. More recently the poems of 'Pipe Dreams in Ponsonby' have replaced the 'Tripbook' poems. Mitchell is an ingratiating though not at all an assertive or histrionic reader. He is probably very much the man of the moment, or the man of the mode, among the young who are interested in poetry in Auckland.

The following information about Mitchell's poetry is derived from the note in *Freed* 3, by M. D. Edmond: At that time Mitchell's finished poems were contained in a thick red folder the whole of which bore the title *Davy Mitchell's Tripbook*. It was divided into five sections: 1. 1960-65 Europe, 'The Trip', 29 poems; 2. 1962-66 'Blind Rooms', 20 poems; 3. 'Pipe Dreams in Ponsonby', 14 poems; 4. 'Brothers & Heroes'; 5. 'Soixante-neuf', 15 poems.

The book under review contains 38 poems, so the 'Pipe Dreams . . .' sequence has undergone some change since last year. These are evidently not Mitchell's earliest nor his latest poems.

It seems that Mitchell is reluctant to commit his poems to print. For this

A review of *Pipe Dreams in Ponsonby*, in *Islands* 1, Spring 1972.

reason, and because they are good poems, Stephen Chan of Auckland deserves special congratulation for his first venture as a publisher. The book is well designed, it has three pleasant 'graphics' by Pat Hanly, and my only complaint about it as a book (not an insignificant one) is that the pages are not numbered.

Listening to Mitchell read I've found myself increasingly enjoying and admiring. Two qualities seemed to come through—the personality of the poet and the music of the poetry, and the two were not really distinct. They were two aspects of the same harmony. But it seemed a complicated kind of music, not a simple one. The poetry could be surprisingly lyrical, gentle, almost sweet—but 'surprisingly', because the material was so often *raw* material. It was rough. It was real. It was abrasive. That perhaps was what appealed to me so much—the flavour of the lion and the honeycomb, sweetness drawn from the guts of life, two extremes kept in harmony so you felt here was a man who had been through it, who had been through the mill, and he was still writing lyrically.

What I've wondered was how well my admiration would last if I had the poem in front of me. I can say now that it lasts very well. If anything this book has dispelled a few last precautionary doubts. After a Mitchell reading I used to remember occasional clichés and moments when the sincerity of feeling seemed to be lost in verbal posturing, and I would think if I can remember these having only heard the poem read, surely I would find many more if I had the poem in front of me. In fact there are no more, and on the printed page they seem less significant. As I read these poems over and over I find myself accepting them as wholes, and consequently accepting their parts. Here is an example of a weakness I remember noticing on hearing the poem read:

> shaming th precise blue
> evenings
>   with th proud
>   eternity
> of her flesh

It comes from 'White Room', one of the most unguardedly lyrical poems in the book, and it looks too much like a slice off the old stale cake, a piece of poeticizing. But take it in context and it seems to pass. The poem begins

> i remember her
> as a fifth season
>
> she
>
> who came unheralded
> into those lean months

> shaming th precise blue
> evenings
>   with th proud
>   eternity
> of her flesh

The 'i remember her/as a fifth season' is a stroke of—what's it to be called?—of talent at least if not of genius. You feel the poet has been given it as a reward for true feeling and it's a gift almost sufficient to sustain the lyric as a whole.

Mitchell's poems have strength of feeling and they have wry detached humour. Sometimes one predominates, sometimes the other, but the conjunction, when it is felt through a number of his poems together, is strong and pleasing. He has the courage of his emotions and knows not to undermine them too far with irony. At the same time he doesn't dress them up in worthy clothes. You feel he has felt too much, made too many mistakes, gone too close to the borders of common sense and sanity, to treat his emotions with solemn reverence. They are tides to be respected and dealt with as they come. His poems are reports on experience which as often as not has left him bruised, but he is still capable of extraordinary bursts of joy:

> a beautiful day!
> th blues then &
> th dead
> th oranges & th red
> in th same old sweet
> familiar way . . .
>
> very cold logic drains out th green head
> & th rooms of this day fill
> with friendly ghosts
> shuffling/ rolling cigarettes
> whistling, humming, caressing
> th gentle flesh of th invisible
> year. . . .   ('Reunion')

Mitchell is very much a modern poet—'modern' in the sense (a perfectly proper sense) which renders Eliot and Yeats poets of a former age. The contemporary influences are apparent without being obtrusive. The effort in the way the poems are set down is to match the line to the natural breath pauses and this works well. But Mitchell's use of 'th' for 'the' is a pointless gesture in the direction of phonetic script when nothing else is phonetically represented, and especially so when (as in 'th invisible' above, or 'th illusion' below) it misrepresents actual pronunciation.

Beneath this determinedly modern surface, however, there beats a traditional heart. Here are some lines from 'Silences':

who is there, here, with heart
who does not fear at last or least
in some fool part or wise/ th dark
    blue frieze of
    silences
        to

come?

It needs only a rearrangement of the lines to turn them into three perfect
iambic pentameters, ten syllables neither more nor less per line, and with a
distinct Shakespearean ring:

Who is there here with heart who does not fear
At last or least in some fool part or wise
The dark blue frieze of silences to come.

And how little the typography conceals the closeness of the following, in
language and spirit, to the *carpe diem* refrain of some seventeenth century
lyric:

so hold/ time! & let us stand
since we are naked &
th blood is up
stay your bitter hand!   ('At Pakiri Beach')

I think it was Pound who said of the poet 'by his language shall you
know him', and I see it was by his language that I knew David Mitchell at
those public readings. There is no way of adequately representing his book
because no short extract will properly stand for the diverse yet unified effect of the poems in bulk. Embedded in what seems to me a traditional
music there are sharply contemporary elements both of speech and of subject matter (the 'young kiwi bird' who 'kicks the living shit out of th kids')
like a pattern of hard grains in a smooth texture. And there is sometimes a
rhetoric which seems curious, unanalysable, entirely Mitchell's own and
very fine:

once again
    houses across th bay hang red
    & savage
    through a veil of thin sun . . .

once again
    dressed in vivaldi's rosethorn cloak
    you whisper
    through th dust motes of my untenanted
    body
        th illusion of blood. . . .

                                              ('Ritual')

To turn, as I have done, from this book to James Baxter's *Jerusalem Sonnets,* is to be reminded of how much language a poet can do without and how strong the effect of making do with little can be. No doubt Mitchell will pare down as he goes on and when he does there will be a balance of gain over loss. But in the meantime there is quite enough to rejoice over in this rich and curious talent which can somehow contrive to throw up and hold together within a few lines a Thomasish sonority like

>   . . . th clear bright voice of time
>   within th sheltered chapel of its tree

the extraordinary simile

>   like some young cousin to th hawk

and the beautiful irony of

>   in this hemisphere's best/ bombing weather.

'O masters', as that poem ('Harlequin at Home') goes on 'he sing fr you!'

PART III:
A POET'S VIEW

FOR THE HULK OF
THE WORLD BETWEEN

Wholehearted he can't move
From where he is, nor love

Wholehearted that place . . .

Allen Curnow

I

I suppose it is a point of general agreement that in any developed civilization which is not in the process of regressing to the primitive, the artist must maintain a living contact with the tradition in which he is writing or painting. This contact with the tradition is as important as the living contact with society, because the tradition is not only an inheritance of experiment in forms; it is a record of the life of the civilization—a record which itself lives. A knowledge of the tradition implies a perspective of values.

For the New Zealand writer our remoteness from Europe is no obstacle to the maintenance of that contact, as it is for the painter. In an article in *Landfall* 46 Mr Tomory wrote, 'There is not one single great example of European art in this country'; and 'printers' ink [cannot] be substituted for oil paint'. This is a point Mr Tomory chose not to repeat in his lecture last

This was one of the Auckland University Winter Lectures for 1960. The topic for the series was the effects of remoteness on New Zealand and I was to deal with literature. The other lecturers were E. J. Godley (flora and fauna), Jack Golson (Polynesian settlement), Keith Sinclair (European settlement), R. M. Chapman (politics), Peter Tomory (the visual arts), and E. H. McCormick (New Zealand Society). The topics and speakers had been chosen by Dr T. H. Scott before his death in a climbing accident and the lectures were published by Paul's Book Arcade and the University of Auckland under the title *Distance Looks Our Way* and dedicated to Scott's memory.

week, but it suggests to me that remoteness sets an immediate problem for the New Zealand painter—a problem which does not exist for the writer. Almost anything of significance that has ever been written is obtainable if the writer wants it. The effects of remoteness on our literature are of another kind.

Two lectures in this series—Dr Sinclair's and Mr Chapman's—have made it clear that our remoteness does not amount to anything like isolation. Our society has been shaped more by external influences than by internal pressures. But there is a sense, I think, in which the word 'isolation' can be applied to this country: as New Zealanders, we suffer a certain isolation from experience. Most often where this is recognized, it is expressed as part of our good fortune. We say that we have no slums, no class distinctions, no extremes of poverty and wealth, no big unmanageable cities, no memory of bombing or occupation by foreign troops. We are 'banned by tides from the sorrows of continents', as Keith Sinclair's 'Chronicle of Meola Creek' puts it. But in this description of our condition there is the implication that our good fortune has isolated us from a richness and variety of human experience—social and political experience. And for the writer this is not necessarily a source of satisfaction. Even Sinclair's poem says we are '*banned* . . . from sorrows'.

In Maurice Duggan's short story, 'Voyage', two tourists try to explain to a waitress in Mallorca that they come from New Zealand:

> With a little malice we showed her the school-atlas map of the world and pointed to New Zealand. It is small, Catalina cried. Is there room? She examined the map as though she had never seen such a thing before: it was a gesture of politeness. But people in Oceania would be French, she believed. She thought she had heard it said. We compared the size of Mallorca with the size of New Zealand: Catalina stared at the tiny dot in the Mediterranean. But it is central, she said. It is near. And she smoothed her fingers over Europe.

That passage, set in a context which extracts the full rich essence of the New Zealander's image of Europe, is an expression of a *kind* of isolation. Catalina, the native of a tiny Mediterranean island, feels herself part of the community of Europe. It's of no relevance to question whether or not the real Catalina would feel this. What matters is that the New Zealander, Duggan, feels himself an outsider, a privileged visitor to the world where things happen.

It should be clear that what I am calling an 'isolation from experience' is not simply a matter of geographical remoteness. A great nation, remote from other nations, would not feel its remoteness as we feel ours. It is the combination of remoteness and *insignificance* which New Zealand writers feel. And to the insignificance of New Zealand I should add the thinness and uniformity of its society, its dependence on Europe and America, and a certain sourness that underlies its achievements. Our forebears had, I imagine, two principal aims in coming here: to escape from the sordidness of English industrialism, and to advance themselves materially. These aims, expressed in terms of the present, have become the ideals of New Zealanders: to live in a country with fresh air, an open landscape and plenty of sunshine; and to own house, car, refrigerator, washing machine, bach, launch, fibre-glass fishing rod, golf-clubs, and so on. These aims are relentlessly pursued, and widely achieved; but they are often achieved at the expense of close human associations, and perhaps at the expense of a true sense of community. We tend not to think of cities as places in which our consciousness as social beings finds its fullest satisfactions. They are places in which to work and earn money, and from which escape is made to dormitory suburbs or, at holiday times, to the beaches and the open country.

This is what he had come for [Maurice Gee writes in his story 'The Widow'], to swim, and be by himself, and wander about wherever his feet took him for just two weeks before going back to wear out that office chair, and worry about other people's money, and taxes, and profit and losses. He had his own losses to worry about; four years of lost time since he had taken that job; and now he had fourteen days to use as he had always wanted to use his days; wandering along beaches, climbing cliff faces above dark cave mouths, swimming to tall little islands.

Mr Gee does not call the attitude into question; as a New Zealander he accepts it. But it is surely this attitude which drags our cities outward from the centre, and their inhabitants away from one another. (If I think of the suburb in which I live, I am tempted to add our remoteness from one another to the list of our remotenesses.)

This description of New Zealand is nothing more, I think, than an acknowledgement of one obvious fact: the political and economic 'advantages' we enjoy as New Zealanders are not guarantors of the good life, or of a healthy literature. 'A citizenship like ours', Mr Curnow writes, 'confers no spiritual privileges, no singular virtue or liberation of mind . . . The true poet is more apt to feel underprivileged in his geographical isolation.'[1]

The New Zealand writer, then, is committed, as the Irish poet W. B. Yeats was committed, to a country he is frequently prompted to describe in terms of its limitations—a society which cannot always satisfy his appetite for experience. One reads a remark like James Baxter's: 'The only language which our society speaks with understanding is the language of money and status',[2] and one is reminded of Yeats's address to Dublin in 'September 1913':

> What need you, being come to sense,
> But fumble in a greasy till

> And add the halfpence to the pence
> And prayer to shivering prayer, until
> You have dried the marrow from the bone?

But remoteness means that the New Zealander is unable to find any solution as simple as that available to Yeats. For most of his literary life Yeats ferried his Muse back and forth between London and the Lake Isle; he was able to enjoy the richness and variety of London without ever losing contact with the country of which and for which his poetry was primarily written.

So our remoteness cannot be discussed on its own; it can be discussed only as one of a number of elements that go to make up the particular situation in which the New Zealand writer works. The ways in which it exerts pressure on the writer are indirect. A tension exists somewhere in the mind of every New Zealander between 'here' and 'there'. That tension has produced this series of lectures. For the writer it may be directly acknowledged in the form of a choice between staying and leaving. Or it may remain unrecognized, displaying itself in affirmations of our absolute independence of spirit—affirmations which would be unnecessary if the independence were real. But the tension remains and influences a good deal of our writing: and where it has been recognized, come to terms with, and exploited, it has on the whole served the literature well.

II

The remoteness that concerned writers in this country in the nineteenth century was a remoteness from their home, England. The remoteness that has concerned our writers in the last thirty years or so is the remoteness of their home, New Zealand, from the centres of the civilization which initiated their society and which has continued to shape it. For the rest of this lecture I want to look for some of the effects on our literature of the condition I have described—a condition in which remoteness is a significant consideration.

Writers in New Zealand have always paid a great deal of attention to the landscape of the country. But in the past thirty years that attention has ceased to be merely in the interests of scenic exploitation. There has been an expenditure of intellectual energy on unbroken landscape—an expenditure deliberately planned and pursued in the interests of assimilation.

> Man must lie with the gaunt hills like a lover,
> Earning their intimacy in the calm sigh
> Of a century of quiet and assiduity . . .

These lines from Charles Brasch's 'The Silent Land' illustrate the conscious effort to assimilate the visible scene. The poem continues:

> So relenting, earth will tame her tamer,
> And speak with all her voices tenderly
> To seal his homecoming to the world. Ah then
> For him the Oreads will haunt the fields near the snowline,
>
> He will walk with his shadow across the bleaching plain
> No longer solitary, and hear the sea talking
> Dark in the rocks, O and the angel will visit,
> Signing life's air with indefinable mark.

It seems to me for at least two reasons inevitable that this kind of effort should have been made: first, because in normal circumstances the writer is quick to realize all that our society lacks, and at the same time to feel the strong attraction of the natural scene which has pressed itself into his mind from an early age; and second, because our history—our forebears' escape from industrial England—leads us to distrust cities and inclines us easily to the feeling that Virtue resides in inanimate landscape. The landscape, then, becomes a form of compensation for all that our society lacks; and in this sense there has been a real antipathy in New Zealand between landscape and community. A form of romanticism has been bred, in which topography becomes a substitute for human society. The man alone in the mountains, M. H. Holcroft tells us:

. . . is able to know, with a proof expounded by the senses, that the body and its environment have merely an illusory separateness. The margins grow indistinct, and the spirit has command of a larger self, mysteriously preserving its identity even in the moments of renewal and surrender.[3]

I don't think anyone aware of the emptiness of New Zealand's intellectual life at the time Mr Holcroft began writing could blame him for finding it necessary to discuss literary problems with hills rather than with human beings. In *The Deepening Stream* he speaks of 'the intellectual solitude of those who do their work twelve thousand miles from the central scene of literary activity in the British Commonwealth. It is not easy [he goes on] to preserve any freshness of outlook when there are so few—and they so widely separated—who care for things of the mind.'[4] The situation Mr Holcroft describes is the situation that drove out Katherine Mansfield and D'Arcy Cresswell in turn, and no one can have felt anything but gratitude in the thirties to have the vacuum filled by a voice. But the dangers of Mr Holcroft's romanticism need to be recognized, and have in fact been discussed in *Landfall* by D. M. Anderson and by Allen Curnow.

Holcroft himself seems to acknowledge the dangers of his own isolation when he adds that the New Zealand writer may easily 'find himself developing wayward or extravagant forms of expression'.

While M. H. Holcroft was writing the first of his essays on New Zealand, with his eye fixed firmly on the mountains, Allen Curnow's attention was directed at the society. His volume of prose and verse, *Not in Narrow Seas,* is an attack on New Zealand society—on Canterbury society in particular—in terms of the social realism that was fashionable at that time. 'Apparently there was a chance for a clean break', he writes in one of the prose passages. 'The dark places of industrial England, its poverty and diseases, were left behind. Only the best had been taken, it seemed, of the English tradition.' This settlers' falsehood is set in ironic contrast to the actual achievement:

> Reproduction, reproduction
> Of the curved, the angled, the tangible
> Street measurable block by block.

In Auckland, A. R. D. Fairburn conducted the enterprise on both fronts. His long poem, 'Dominion', alternates between assaults, less pointed than Curnow's, on New Zealand society; and libations, more mellifluous and less reasoned than Holcroft's, to the landscape:

> Fairest earth,
> fount of life, giver of bodies,
> deep well of our delight, breath of desire,
> let us come to you
> barefoot, as befits love,
> as the boy to the trembling girl,
> as the child to the mother:
> seeking before all things the honesty of substance,
> touch of soil and wind and rock,
> frost and flower and water,
> the honey of the senses, the food
> of love's imagining; and the most intimate
> touch of love, that turns to being.

The separateness of community and scene remained. Curnow's attacks in *Not in Narrow Seas* were valid, but lacking affirmative power. Holcroft's thinking was a sort of intellectual primitivism. Fairburn alternated between the attack and the primitivism. Only Denis Glover at this time welcomed frankly the roadbuilders' assault on the landscape. His delight in the work of

> Crosswire of the theodolite, pickpoint, curved shovel,
> Small tremor of a touched-off charge

was a more 'intelligible hope' for islands than Holcroft's.

Of these four, Curnow and Glover developed significantly in the forties. Curnow in particular succeeded in bringing together the two images of New Zealand—the impressive landscape and the unremarkable towns—which had hitherto existed separately in our poetry. This process of joining landscape and society, without falsification of either, can be seen at its best in his recent poem, 'A Small Room with Large Windows'.

But while Curnow was ascending rapidly to an achievement quite unequalled, I think, by any other New Zealand poet, a new generation of poets appeared who found it convenient to link him with a man as unlike himself as Holcroft, and to set them both aside (together with Brasch) under the label of the 'South Island Myth'. There has never been a specifically South Island myth. If the 'myth' is the exercise of the pathetic fallacy in viewing our landscape, that is a fault as common in the North as in the South—a fault in Holcroft's work and in Fairburn's, but absent from Curnow's. If, on the other hand, the 'myth' is as Eric Schwimmer described it in the *Poetry Yearbook* for 1951—'a myth . . . concerning a lonely island-desert,★ discovered by navigators and developed by baffled explorers'—then it seems to me not a myth at all, but a statement of geographical and historical fact. New Zealand *is* geographically 'lonely': it is remote. It *was* discovered by navigators, and it *was* developed by explorers.

Many recent confusions in the discussion of our poetry seem to me to have sprung from a failure by this later generation to distinguish clearly and evaluate justly among the writers who preceded them. James K. Baxter, in his Macmillan Brown lectures, speaks of Mr Curnow's 'myth of insularity', as though new Zealand were in fact part of a continent. And on page 300 of his *History of New Zealand* Dr Sinclair writes:

Allen Curnow wrote, in a critical essay, that 'our presence in these islands is accidental, irrelevant; that we are interlopers on an indifferent or hostile scene'.

What Mr Curnow in fact wrote went as follows:

The idea that . . . our presence in these islands is accidental, irrelevant; that we are interlopers on an indifferent or hostile scene; that idea, or misgiving, occurs so variously and so often, and in the work of New Zealand poets otherwise so different, that it suggests some common problem of the imagination.[5]

Mr Curnow was drawing attention to an idea present in the work of a number of poets; Dr Sinclair attributes to him the making of the idea.

Why should this habit of misunderstanding have developed during the

★ 'Desert' is, of course, Mr Schwimmer's own invention.

immediate postwar years? First, I think, because many of these younger writers felt—as Mr Chapman told us at the beginning of his lecture—that New Zealand was in some *special* way a good country to live in. The feeling was prompted by New Zealand's emergence from depression and war, and by the progressive legislation of the Labour Party in its first ten years of office. Young writers felt impelled to reject the image of New Zealand implicit in the work of a number of their predecessors: the image of an immature society existing in a state of limiting and felt remoteness. Any notion was rejected if it implied that New Zealand society had shortcomings which could not be surmounted in a short time by hard thinking and good government. One could acknowledge limitation, but not immovable limitation. So for example Robert Chapman's 'Fiction and the Social Pattern' is a fine sociological study which discovers in our society a 'powerful frustration, loneliness, and lack of love'.[6] But in obedience to the general optimism, it concludes, naïvely I think, by implying that this deep-seated condition would find a ready cure in welfare legislation.

The ideas about poetry that have been expressed most frequently during the past ten years spring directly from this optimism. The idea, for example, that New Zealand's remoteness might impose certain strains on the writer, has been countered by claims for the internationality of literature—its independence from the specific New Zealand scene—as if poetry could be switched at will from its traditional pasture, the immediate and the particular, and taught to graze on abstraction. This is the claim that has been made repeatedly in the *Poetry Yearbook,* and it is made, more cautiously, in Mr Chapman's *Oxford Anthology.* Poets here, Mr Chapman claims, 'feel so at ease in their environment that they can simply assume it and find themselves freed to deal directly with the concerns of poetry everywhere'. Louis Johnson, in search of this shortcut to universality, has swung the sights of poetry on to what is commonest, most general, in the suburban scene. But his praise of the city Everyman brings us no nearer to the true flavour of universal human experience than the most extreme examples of mountain mysticism.

> I praise Saint Everyman, his house and home
>   In every paint-bright gardened suburb shining
> With all the age's verities and welcome
>   Medalled upon him in contentment dining;
>   *And toast with gin and bitters*
>   *The muse of baby sitters.*   ('Here Together Met')

This national optimism of the late forties was damaging to a plain view of ourselves, and to a correct estimate of our senior poets. The most successful of these younger writers were those like Kendrick Smithyman and Maurice Duggan, who remained indifferent to the optimism; or those, like

Keith Sinclair, who could shake off most readily the defensive attitudes that accompanied it.

It seems to me that the poetic development of Allen Curnow, of Denis Glover, and of Charles Brasch, has in each case been more consistent, less subject to sudden setback and failure, than the development of almost any one of their younger contemporaries; and if we leave aside the important consideration of the ability each man is born with, it may be possible to argue that this consistency of development by three earlier poets is a sign of the assurance with which they have been able to hold to their view of New Zealand.* The remoteness and the limitations they felt and acknow-ledged in their country were not imagined. If they expressed themselves wrongly or extravagantly at times, they had only to adjust the expression. But the unwarranted optimism of the younger men could only collapse, as Dr Sinclair implies in a recent note to *Landfall* on the death of Harry Scott. (This collapse was acknowledged, I think, in Mr Chapman's lecture.) And further, while that optimism lasted, the making of special claims for their country became inevitably the making of claims for them-selves; the error could extend itself unnoticed, and become a lack of humility, a lack of proportion. It could become almost a duty to forget what Glover so easily reminds himself:

> Be a man never so proud,
> He is only thistledown planted on the wind.

Keith Sinclair, in those years which he recently described as a 'postponed, post-war adolescence', wrote

> We were brave, were mapping the coasts of mind
> Where we strove to plant, in the soil of speech,
> The truth that was born on a Rock, a Creek:
> Our random home, grown native now,
> Was the pith in life that our past assigned.
>
> Our minds were making the shape of years.
> ('The Chronicle of Meola Creek')

(I can think of less interesting examples of the same sort of thing in my own poetry.) These men may have been 'mapping the coasts of mind' and 'making the shape of years', but the claim to be doing it was less easily turned to poetry than the apparent gestures of defeat by Curnow and Glover:

> These songs will not stand—
> The wind and the sand will smother.

* From the perspective of 1980 it seems more relevant to recognize that Baxter and Smithyman proved to be more important poets than Glover or Brasch.

Not I but another
Will make songs worth the bother:

> The rimu or kauri he,
> I'm but the cabbage tree,

Sings Harry to an old guitar.

This by Glover, or R. A. K. Mason's 'The Lesser Stars', or Curnow's sonnet which concludes

> Not I, some child, born in a marvellous year,
> Will learn the trick of standing upright here

—these negatives were paradoxically more positive in their effect than the
affirmations of the younger men; more effective, because for a moment the
poet seemed to have taken on the recognizable persona of the country as a
whole—a country with no momentous present, but with a future. Allen
Curnow's poem commemorating Tasman's discovery of New Zealand
wrings the fullest possible excitement out of the discovery, and then, in the
concluding section, turns that excitement like a judgement on the present:

> But now there are no more islands to be found
> And the eye scans risky horizons of its own
> In unsettled weather, and murmurs of the drowned
>   Haunt their familiar beaches—
> Who navigates us towards what unknown
>
> But not improbable provinces? Who reaches
> A future down for us from the high shelf
> Of spiritual daring? Not those speeches
>   Pinning on the Past like a decoration
> For merit that congratulates itself,
>
> O not the self-important celebration
> Or most painstaking history, can release
> The current of a discoverer's elation
>   And silence the voices saying
> 'Here is the world's end where wonders cease.'
>
> Only by a more faithful memory, laying
> On him the half-light of a diffident glory,
> The Sailor lives, and stands beside us, paying
>   Out into our time's wave
> The stain of blood that writes an island story.
>   ('Landfall in Unknown Seas')

New Zealand is seen with a correct sense of proportion; 'here is the world's end where wonders cease'. The discoverer, because of the necessarily limited nature of our achievement in these islands, earns only 'the half-light of a diffident glory'. But again the negative becomes a kind of affirmative; it achieves dignity, and escapes all the brashness that commonly accompanies the realization of post-colonial identity.

III

The point of all this has not been to suggest that all the members of an earlier 'generation' or 'group' of writers succeeded in coming to terms with the limitations imposed by life in New Zealand, and that a more recent generation has failed. Groups tend to express themselves in terms of a common viewpoint, but it is as individuals that writers succeed or fail. The fact that Mr Curnow expressed for his generation a point of view which our New Zealand situation still confirms, did not save Fairburn from falling often between an effusive love of the land and a facile abuse of its society. On the other hand the dangerous optimism of the late forties failed to rob Kendrick Smithyman of an admirable diffidence and tact in affirming his experiences as a New Zealander. Of those experiences he says:

> Somewhere there is value to them. As the piano stumbles
> something grows into being. It will take shape in the end.

My point is simply that a limiting factor—remoteness or any other —must be acknowledged by the writer if it is relevant to his poem or story. If it is not acknowledged and come to terms with, it will force him into defensiveness or some form of romantic compensation.

Since I have spoken almost exclusively of poetry, I want to take an example of this process from our fiction: Maurice Shadbolt's 'The Woman's Story', from his recently published book, *The New Zealanders*. In this story, Mr Shadbolt's principal character, Bridget, is a girl who has been brought up in New Zealand, by an English mother, to believe that she is English. At the climax of the story, after some obscure emotional experiences, involving a rather unconvincing Maori girl, Bridget discovers her true identity. She is a New Zealander, a native of a country which the story presents in terms of thick bush, kauri, rimu, kahikatea, supple jack, cabbage trees, nikau palms, bell-birds, 'mangroved' tidal creeks, and 'bare coast-line where surf creamed the rocks'. It is this Tarzanesque setting that the girl comes to identify herself with; and life there, Mr Shadbolt implies, must not be conceived of in terms of limitations. It is not accidental that one of the minor characters who describes New Zealand as 'rather limited', is depicted as 'affected', 'not particularly pretty', a disruptive element in the Maori girl's love life, and a university graduate. The story concludes with Bridget's 'moment of revelation' in which identification with New Zealand is accompanied by rejection of England:

The dew scented the morning, and the air was cool and still. A stranger to myself, I had a longing to walk barefoot, clean-limbed, through green forest where clear waters fell: to tread softly banks of moss dappled with new sunlight: to bed in silver fern with the slender fronds tickling my cheeks: to sleep flesh to flesh with the warm earth.

I felt an immense peace, a drowsiness of spirit within a tranquillity of body; and when the moment of revelation overtook me, I felt faint, and I reached out, to the side of the window, and held myself steady.

I should never go to England.

I should never to to England; and I was glad.

And I was no longer afraid.

The strain under which the writer has worked is evident. In trying to assert an identity for New Zealand independent of the outside world, Mr Shadbolt has been driven to the very worst kinds of cliché. How many steps backwards is it from the weakest moments of Brasch's and Fairburn's poetry to this example of Mr Shadbolt's prose; from Brasch's 'man must lie with the gaunt hills like a lover' to Bridget's desire 'to sleep flesh to flesh with the warm earth'; from Fairburn's 'Fairest Earth . . . let us come to you / barefoot, as befits love' to Bridget's 'longing to walk barefoot, clean-limbed, through green forests where clear waters fell'? Brasch, with his customary tact, spoke of adaptation, however romantically conceived in that poem, in terms of 'a century of quiet and assiduity'. And Fairburn, whatever weakness or naïve enthusiasm gripped him from time to time in his poetry, was never deserted by his verbal felicity. Mr Shadbolt's 'moment of revelation' fails because it is an attempt to evade a true realization of ourselves.

A passage from Frank Sargeson's 'The Making of a New Zealander' will point the difference. A New Zealand farm labourer, the narrator of the story, talks to a Dalmatian fruit-grower:

I asked Nick about his trees and he said they were all right, but there were too many diseases.

Too much quick manure, I said.

He said yes, but what could they do? It would take a long time to make the soil deep and sweet like it was in the part of Dalmatia he came from. Out here everybody wanted money quick, so they put on the manure. It was money, money all the time. But he and his mate never had any. . . .

Well, maybe you're right, I said, but what about the grapes?

Oh, Nick said, they grow, yes. But they are not sweet. To make wine we must put in sugar. In Dalmatia it is not done. Never.

The most important elements in Mr Shadbolt's story are present in this one by Sargeson—but because Sargeson is not concerned to romanticize people or scene, they are differently and more convincingly disposed. The chemical manure serves as an image of the eager materialism of our society. The deep sweet soil of Dalmatia, and the wines that require no sugar to sweeten them, are simple facts; but they acknowledge indirectly, and without a hint of self-pity, that something has been lost in the transfer from Europe. The Dalmatian's farm in the context of the story as a whole widens in its implications and becomes New Zealand itself:

He said it over and over, and I couldn't look him in the face. It had too much of that sadness. I mightn't have put it the way Nick had, I mightn't have said I was born too soon, but Nick knew what he was talking about. Nick and I were sitting on the hillside and Nick was saying he was a New Zealander, but he knew he wasn't a New Zealander. And he knew he wasn't a Dalmatian any more.

IV

Images of arrival and departure, and emotions bred out of the tensions between our New Zealand identity and our European background—these recur so frequently in the work of our best writers that remoteness cannot be seen as other than deeply relevant to the discussion of our literature. One thinks inevitably of the lines by Charles Brasch that Dr Sinclair quoted:

> Remindingly beside the quays, the white
> Ships lie smoking; and from their haunted bay
> The godwits vanish towards another summer.
> Everywhere in light and calm the murmuring
> Shadow of departure; distance looks our way . . .

or of three much-quoted lines of R. A. K. Mason's:

> here in this far-pitched perilous hostile place
> this solitary hard-assaulted spot
> fixed at the friendless outer edge of space;

of Glover's and Cresswell's poems written on leaving New Zealand; or the verse letter by Curnow which includes the lines:

> O I could go down to harbours
> And mourn with a hundred years
> Of hunger, what slips away there . . .

Some of the finest passages of Cresswell's prose, and of E. H. McCormick's, spring from the consideration of remoteness. More recently there have been the stories of Maurice Duggan; and poems by young New Zealanders in England—Pat Wilson's 'Staying at Ballisodare', W. H.

Oliver's 'In Fields of my Father's Youth', and one or two others—attempts to draw together the opposite ends of the earth in a single operation of the imagination. But the poles remain obdurately opposite, creating in our writers, whether or not they have ever left New Zealand, a permanent dramatic tension in which much good writing has been generated.

> Seas will be seas, the same;
> Thick as our blood may flood, our opposite isles
> Chase each other round till the quiet poles
>   Crack, and the six days top
> Totter, but catch us neither sight nor hold;
> Place will be place, limbs may not fold
>   Their natural death in dreams.
> I pray, pray for me on some spring-wet pavement
> Where halts the heartprint of our salt bereavement,
>   Pray over many times,
> Forgive him the seas forgive him the spring leaf,
> All bloom ungathered perishable as grief,
>   For the hulk of the world's between . . .
>
> ('When the Hulk of the World')

Those lines by Allen Curnow convince me that remoteness is not something our writers should deny or regret, but something to be acknowledged, and exploited as an analogue for the immovable tensions which are universal in human experience.

A POET'S VIEW

When Mr Dennis McEldowney invited me to contribute to this series of lectures I hesitated, and I've gone on hesitating ever since. My brief is first to adopt, of all the roles I might and do adopt from time to time, the role of the poet; and second, to speak of Books and Writers in New Zealand as this poet sees those things. It's not an easy task because I'm not invited quite to take an objective view—the view of the historian or the scholar or even the critic—but the more personal view of the writer of poems. In other words I'm somehow required to keep myself in the picture. The two reefs between which I have to steer, or if you prefer, the two stools between which I'm invited to fall, are those of literary autobiography on the one hand and literary history on the other. No doubt by confronting the problem I've made it larger than it need be; but I want it clear from the beginning that I will be trying—no doubt trying and failing—to steer the appropriate middle course. I will in fact be trying to convert literary autobiography into literary history.

Let me begin then by placing myself historically as others in this series have done. I was born in 1932. That means I remember learning at school that the population of New Zealand was one-and-a-half million and that the British Empire was an Empire on which the sun never set. Before I'd turned seven a war began. Six years later when it stopped the headmaster of the school I was attending instructed me to ring the school bell and keep on ringing it for as long as I could. I didn't know, and I don't suppose he did either, that fifty million people had died violently during those six years. I remember enjoying ringing the bell but worrying about what Peace might be like.

This is the text of one of the 1974 series of Winter Lectures at the University of Auckland delivered under the general title of 'Books and Writers in New Zealand'. Other lectures were delivered by Keith Sinclair ('A General View'), Wystan Curnow ('A Critic's View'), Maurice Shadbolt ('A Novelist's View'), Dennis McEldowney ('A Publisher's View'), Simon Cauchi ('A Librarian's View') and Michael Noonan ('A View from the Media').

One other memory places me pretty exactly. It's the memory, a little before the bell-ringing episode, of my sister reading out of the Auckland *Star* that an atomic bomb had been dropped on a Japanese city called Hiroshima, and of myself, about twelve years old, never having heard the word 'atomic' before, correcting her and saying that it must have been an automatic bomb. There may be an apt irony in the fact that this incident stuck in my memory, not because I understood what had happened at Hiroshima and what it signified, but simply because I was embarrassed at being wrong about a word.

What was happening on the New Zealand literary scene during those years when the fifty million were dying violent deaths and I was passively enduring the interminable fathomless boredom of primary school? Could anyone have been finding words to fill that enormous gap between the unremarkable and the unspeakable? Poetry is limited to what the human imagination can assimilate. It can't deal with fifty million deaths but it can deal with one. Here's a sonnet by Allen Curnow:

> Weeping for bones in Africa, I turn
> Our youth over like a dead bird in my hand.
> This unexpected personal concern
> That what has character can simply end
>
> Is my unsoldierlike acknowledgement
> Cousin, to you, once gentle-tough, inert
> Now, after the death-flurry of that front
> Found finished too. And why need my report
>
> Cry one more hero, winking through its tears?
> I would say, you are cut off, and mourn for that;
> Because history where it destroys admires,
> But O if your blood's tongued it must recite
>
> South Island feats, those tall snow-country tales
> Among incredulous Tunisian hills.
>
> ('In Memoriam, 2/Lt. T. C. F. Ronalds')

In Christchurch during those war years Curnow was writing the poems for which he's probably still best known. In Takapuna Frank Sargeson was writing stories which in their way represent a fictional parallel to Curnow's poems. Both men were to go on to different, more baroque, less obviously public works. But at the time they must have seemed like literary cartographers, each charting country that had never been charted before— Sargeson with his musical elaborations of the cadences of the vernacular, Curnow with his witty and finely structured questioning of our history, both with a capacity to catch, as no writers before them had done, the distinct physical quality of what lay around them.

It hardly needs saying that as a schoolboy I didn't hear of either, but it was of great consequence that they should be there, and it's of great consequence thirty and more years later that they should still be here and still writing. What the subject 'Books and Writers in New Zealand' conjures up is something altogether more substantial than it would have been without them.

My initiation as a poet came a year or two after the end of the war. New Zealanders sent food parcels to Britain and my sister corresponded with the daughter of a family in Rugby to whom our food parcels had been sent. This girl sent my sister a copy of the Collected Poems of one of Rugby School's most celebrated old boys—Rupert Brooke. My sister didn't read the poems but I did, and I began at once to write Brookish imitations. The effect was immediate, compulsive, and long-lasting. My long boredom was over, and you might say I've never looked back.

There was still as far as I was concerned no local literary scene. Secondary school pupils now seem to be made at least aware of the existence of New Zealand books and writers. In the late forties we read *Macbeth* and Keats's 'Ode to a Nightingale' and Wordsworth's 'Tintern Abbey' and Milton's sonnet 'On his Blindness'—and I'm glad we read them. But there was no mention of New Zealand poems or fiction. Literature and life were separated by 12,000 miles of water. There was what Maurice Duggan calls 'a discrepancy between the real and the written'; and Duggan catches it beautifully in his story 'Along Rideout Road that Summer', where the teenage rebel, Buster O'Leary, driving a tractor over farm paddocks shouting Coleridge's 'Kubla Khan' above the noise of the engine, is suddenly aware of a girl called Fanny Hohepa with her ukulele. Does she compromise the poem's vision of the damsel with a dulcimer? Or is she a materialization of it?

Almost happy, shouting Kubla Khan, a bookish lad, from the seat of the clattering old Ferguson tractor, doing a steady five miles an hour in a cloud of seagulls, getting to the bit about the damsel with the dulcimer and looking up to see the reputedly wild Hohepa girl perched on the gate, feet hooked in the bars, ribbons fluttering from her ukulele. A perfect moment of recognition . . . in spite of the belch of carbon monoxide from the tin-can exhaust up front on the bonnet.

That 'discrepancy between the real and the written' continued for me—it didn't bother me, but it was a fact—until I was sixteen when I read my first New Zealand book, *Man Alone*. That was a powerful experience which set me writing Mulganish short stories. I discovered a few Sargeson stories in the same year, and a year later one poem by R. A. K. Mason. Those few things, a couple of stories by Katherine Mansfield, and what I could find in the *New Zealand Listener* edited by M. H. Holcroft, constituted 'Books and Writers in New Zealand' for me almost up until the time I came to this university as a student.

> Suddenly exhilaration
> Went off like a gun, the whole
> Horizon, the long chase done,
> Hove to. There was the seascape
> Crammed with coast, surprising
> As new lands will, the sailor
> Moving on the face of the waters . . .
>
> ('Landfall in Unknown Seas')

If you can see me for a moment as the literary sailor moving on the face of the waters I mean those lines of Curnow's to catch the excitement I felt arriving at this university in 1951. 'There was the seascape/Crammed with coast'. In the library of the old Arts building there was a room—not a large room—which housed English literature. English literature seemed of manageable proportions. But more important, there was in that room a small case for which the key could be obtained from the lending desk, which contained the work of New Zealand poets. (I don't know how many people who are let into the air-conditioned closely guarded room which is called the Glass Case in the new library realize that the name has been directly transferred from what was once literally a glass case.)

And finally, as if the existence of the books wasn't itself sufficient, some of the poets could be seen walking about. Allen Curnow had just given up his job on the Christchurch *Press* and come to lecture in Auckland. An absurdly youthful-looking and very emphatic Robert Chapman, who wrote verses in those days, was my Stage I tutor in History. Keith Sinclair, whose poem 'Strangers or Beasts' I used to quote to girls at parties with varying effect, was a lecturer. M. K. Joseph in the English Department was just beginning to be known as a poet. Rex Fairburn had transferred from a tutorship in English to a lectureship in the History of Fine Art, and he, like Frank Sargeson, put in occasional appearances at Somervell's Coffee Bar. R. A. K. Mason was a remoter figure. And later there were others—notably Kendrick Smithyman and Maurice Duggan.

This is not meant to be an exercise in nostalgia. My subject is Books and Writers in New Zealand, and I'm trying to communicate the particularity and vividness with which both—both the books and the writers—materialized for me in 1951. I studied the books in that glass case more intensively than anything set down in the courses I enrolled for. They were mostly finely printed, put out in small editions; and if they had one quality in common it was a kind of freshness in the writing. The voices were distinct, the subject matter stood out sharp and clear. Nobody was aiming

for a commercial, or a foreign, or an academic, market—there were no such
markets to aim for. Maybe they were writing for one another, or for the
future, or to please themselves; whatever they thought they were doing the
predominant qualities seemed to be confidence, excitement, and sharpness
of definition, as if each writer believed he had a subject ready to hand and
the means to deal with it. What I was discovering, I suppose, was the wave
of literary energy that had begun to move in New Zealand in the thirties,
had gathered momentum and achieved remarkable work in the forties, and
was to fade—that particular wave, anyway—was to fade away in the fifties.

For myself at eighteen and nineteen, publishing my first poems and having them noticed by these people, it was a good beginning. I was accepted
into a literary world as intimate, as personal, as compact and comprehensi-
ble as I imagine the London coffee-house scene might have been in the
eighteenth century. And in addition there was a periodical, *Landfall,*
edited by Charles Brasch in Dunedin, which provided a forum for new
writing from all over New Zealand. I think it's worth making the point
that without *Landfall* as a centre of activity, as a platform, and even as a
target, the literary scene couldn't have produced and sustained the body of
writers it did during the years of Brasch's editorship. Writers need a
periodical as much as actors need a stage.

For a moment now I'm going to put aside the role of the poet and speak as
a literary historian.

The significant literature of Western Europe has seldom or never been
unconnected with the great political and social movements of its time. In
this century war, depression, revolution, and short of revolution the
political surges to left and right—these have all influenced, or incited, or
provided subject matter for, or found correspondences in, literary
developments, particularly developments in poetry.

The first World War not only prodded a number of talented young men
into poetry before killing them off; it seems also to have liberated the sur-
vivors (mostly American) into literary experiments which were radical and
successful to a degree unmatched in English poetry since the Romantic
revolution of more than a century before. The thirties, the Depression, and
the Spanish War set off secondary shock waves of modernism, closely
associated with hopes for a socialist revolution. The forties brought the
war, which had its own intensities and reverberations. The post-war
decade, by contrast, brought nothing but intellectual and cultural exhaus-
tion, the Cold War, the Korean War, McCarthyism, an inevitable shocked
withdrawal, as the body count went on, from everything new and fresh and
exciting that the twentieth century had seemed to offer.

Poetry needs a head of steam. It lives off euphoria. If I had been able to adopt the role of the literary historian in 1951 I might have shaken my head over the emerging young poet and told him not to expect much of himself, even if he was talented, because talent is never enough. Soon the English literary heroes of the fifties would begin to appear—Kingsley Amis, John Wain, John Osborne—even Philip Larkin. Who could sustain for long the initial excitement that each of them produced? Weren't they just what the literary historian might have predicted—an expression of the directionlessness of the time? And in New Zealand, where 1949 saw the defeat of Labour, and 1951 the Waterfront Strike and the defeat of the unions, we had Louis Johnson.

As the fifties went on there was some recovery of the political idealism of those pre-war years, but not enough to shake the predominant conservatism. Towards the end of the decade I was in London when Harold Macmillan won an election on what must have been the most blatantly unidealistic slogan of the century: YOU'VE NEVER HAD IT SO GOOD.

I remember someone saying, when she was asked why she wouldn't try marijuana, that she didn't need it because she was 'auto-euphoric'. To survive the fifties I think a poet had to be 'auto-euphoric'. Of the seven or eight students who used to meet and read poems to one another when I was an undergraduate I was the only one who went on writing.

I've sketched two opposite impressions of the poet stepping on to the scene in 1951—as it seemed to the poet himself, and as it seems in retrospect to the literary historian. Everything is relative. To emerge in 1951 from the silent wastes of the volcanic suburbs on to an intellectual scene had to be exciting, even if the intellectuals themselves were in retreat and political and literary radicalism was exhausted. I didn't see then what I see now: that I had no great subject; that 'the age' was not 'demanding' poems of me as it had seemed, for example, to demand them of Ezra Pound; that consequently I had no obvious material to work on but myself, a self that was unformed, provincial, uncultured, and erratically educated.

These were the things I *didn't* see, and of course not seeing them was necessary to keeping going.

Allen Curnow and his contemporaries had imbibed from the wider world of the thirties the feeling that poetry should reach out towards public statement, and Curnow in particular found his themes during the forties in our history, the voyages of discovery, the sacrifice of blood on which the new nation was founded, and the gap between the colonial dream and the postcolonial fact. Stylistically he and fellow poets owed most to the Auden group in England. Like the Auden group they set themselves against the stylistic vices of their Georgian predecessors, spoke with firmer voices, replaced whimsy with wit and romantic nostalgia with a disciplined candour. A cloud of sentiment was rolled away and New Zealand appeared almost for the first time *plausibly* in our poetry.

Such an exercise wasn't to be repeated in the fifties, and in the post-war years the only poet on the New Zealand scene who had any kind of new programme, the only one who ran up a banner under which younger poets might gather, was Louis Johnson. Johnson (if I remember correctly) proposed to 'people the New Zealand scene'. His subject was the suburbs, which, he argued, being like suburbs everywhere were 'universal'. The new subject was to be, not what was (in Allen Curnow's phrase) 'peculiarly New Zealand's', but what was *typical* in New Zealand. It was to be the world, or the Western world, as it's found immediately to hand.

Expressed in this way Johnson's programme doesn't seem absurd, and I suppose wasn't absurd. It made a kind of sense, and I can see now, although I couldn't see then, why a poet as talented as James K. Baxter seemed to rally to it. But I preferred the measured affirmation, the element of deliberated nationalist assertion, in the best of Curnow's poetry, to the international suburban drabness of Johnson's. There was a ring of authority, of authenticity, I suppose of sheer talent, one looked for and didn't find in Johnson. Certainly I favoured Curnow in that protracted argument. But I knew there was no point in trying to repeat what Curnow had done; and in any case my own temperament, and the particular bent of such talent as I possessed, was bound to take me off in another direction.

> A damsel with a dulcimer
> In a vision once I saw:
> It was an Abyssinian maid,
> And on her dulcimer she played;
> Singing of Mount Abora.
> Could I revive within me
> Her symphony and song,
> To such a deep delight 'twould win me,
> That with music loud and long,
> I would build that dome in air,
> That sunny dome! those caves of ice!
> And all who heard should see them there,
> And all should cry, Beware! Beware!
> His flashing eyes, his floating hair!
> Weave a circle round him thrice,
> And close your eyes with holy dread,
> For he on honey-dew hath fed,
> And drunk the milk of Paradise.

Those are among the great lines of English lyric poetry. They're from the end of Coleridge's 'Kubla Khan' and they are the lines which Duggan's Buster O'Leary is shouting above the noise of the tractor. And it has to be admitted that if Buster were driving his tractor in Somerset where Coleridge wrote the poem, rather than in New Zealand, his sense of there being 'a discrepancy between the real and written' might be just as acute; because although the lines do create their own reality, it's a reality of a peculiarly inward and visionary kind.

'Kubla Khan' is usually discussed in terms of its symbolic structure or in terms of the sources of its imagery in Coleridge's reading, or the peculiar circumstances surrounding its composition. But if any critic really tried to come to grips with how the poem works he would have to confront the element in poetry that's never discussed in any depth or detail because it's at once too elusive and too complex: that is, the element of music.

If I say the music of poetry is the prime vehicle of feeling and the true fabric of imagination, I mean by 'music', not merely the way the words are gathered into groups to create a texture of sound, not merely how that texture moment by moment is relating to an overall sound structure, but in addition, how those sound patterns affect, and shape, and space out, and regulate, our rational apprehension, and our visualization of the images placed before us word by word, phrase by phrase, line by line. The whole business is so dense and so simultaneous, the mind staggers trying to comprehend it; and the totality of elements could only receive expression in something that might look, in fact, very like a score for full symphony orchestra.

Now why have I gone off at this tangent, or out on this limb? Only, I'm afraid, in order to make one small (or large) assertion on my own behalf. I've described myself as a young poet in the fifties who lacked both culture and a great subject—and I meant what I said. What I did have I think was an acute sense of the music of poetry—a sense of the poem as *composition* and of myself as composer. So when I wrote a long poem called 'Pictures in a Gallery Undersea' in London in 1958 I was at least half conscious of doing something that hadn't been done in New Zealand poetry before, tapping sources that hadn't been tapped, and that the special effects were musical in the way I've tried to describe. Just how I was doing it wasn't quite as clear to me then as it seems now. I knew that I wasn't—as a number of people thought when the poem appeared—writing a pastiche of T. S. Eliot. I knew that though there were some echoes of Eliot for particular effect, technically the poem owed everything to Ezra Pound's innovations in 'Hugh Selwyn Mauberley' and in the Cantos. I think I was aware that those innovations of Pound's were parallel to developments like the use of atonality in music, or to cubism in painting. And I think I could have said that the musical structure of my poem was built up partly by putting contrasting things alongside each other—bits of literary history alongside obvious fictions, a passage in long lines after one in short lines, resonant romantic statements after curt ironic ones. But I may not have had even this degree of consciousness. One of my failings perhaps has been a fear of doing things consciously. I've preferred to be acted upon in the old wind-harp tradition, rather than act. And as a result I've tended to make technical advances in my writing and then lose them through working too exclusively by instinct. In fact I should say it's only in the past few years, reading the thesis work of my colleague in the English Department, Roger Horrocks, that I've come to see more clearly how Pound's technique works and consequently what it was I'd derived from him by a sort of osmosis.

'Pictures in a Gallery Undersea' was successful. I had at first to twist Charles Brasch's arm a little to persuade him to print it in *Landfall*. But then by one of those unpredictable chances it won an award voted on by the subscribers to *Landfall* for the most popular poem printed there during fifteen years of publication. Meanwhile Allen Curnow (who saw the Pound connexion at once and didn't read it as a pastiche of Eliot) had selected the poem for his Penguin anthology of New Zealand verse. And later it went into two other anthologies.

Now this will seem a lot of fuss about one poem. But it has been my unfortunate brief as I've understood it in preparing this lecture to keep myself in the picture; and it struck me that here was a point at which I added something distinct, and the addition was technical—it was in the realm of poetry as an *art*, not poetry as a bearer of tidings. So much of the argument about poetry in New Zealand has been about subject matter—what should we write about? 'What can I take that will make my song news?' Charles Brasch asks himself despairingly. In 'Pictures in a Gallery Undersea' I demonstrated to myself what I knew anyway, that the distinctive poetic element was not *in* the subject—that in fact, as Mallarmé said, poetry is not made of ideas, or subjects, it's made of words.

> Each day He dies to do me good.
> I sign a protest, join a march.
> What Wolf began, Eagle accomplishes.
>
> Minerva had a mouse in mind.
> It was a weasel, tore her beak.
> What Owl began, Eagle accomplishes.
>
> Eagle bears the Snake to die.
> Up there it twists about his throat.
> Out of the sun they fall like brass.

> I signed a protest, joined a march.
> Today he dies to do me good.
> What Eagle began, Serpent accomplishes.
>
> (C. K. Stead, 'April Notebook')

Poetry is made with words; but during the middle and late sixties a very large *subject* forced its way into my poems. Ever since the Korean War being angry at American foreign policy and at what I saw as our own slavish involvement in it had been a more or less continuing state of mind. But in 1965, when Lyndon Johnson began the bombardment of North Vietnam and simultaneously put half a million American soldiers into South Vietnam the ineptitude and brutality of that policy was all at once exposed and magnified. The movement of protest one had looked for for years developed and grew rapidly—first in America, then in Europe. By 1968 it had broadened to become something of a minor revolution in Western society.

One personal fact that deepened my feelings about these events was that by now I had children. My family and the war seemed to grow larger together. That made the war seem more real. The deaths weren't abstract, as they had seemed to be when I was a child. They were a dark stain over everything; and correspondingly the political commitment I felt was deeper and more implacable. I learned from that how people must have felt in the thirties, and in fact during any time when a great wrong seems about to precipitate radical change. Because as well as horror there was a compensating excitement. So much was going on at the emotional level one was very largely relieved of the burden of reason; and however dangerous such a state may be it has, as well as force, its own kind of purity.

All this strong feeling got into the poems I wrote during those years, which are domestic poems, suburban New Zealand poems, clouded by world events, and they're printed in the first section of my book *Crossing the Bar*.

How important is the 'subject' in such poems? This is a question which defeats analysis, because the 'subject' is an abstraction. Perhaps we can say that what gets into the poem is not the piece of history which we call its 'subject' but the poet's feeling about that piece of history; and it's that feeling which remains durable and vivid while the events of history fade. There is a sonnet from which we learn that Milton felt strongly about certain 'slaughtered saints' whose bones lay 'scattered on the Alpine mountains'. Only a history book will tell us exactly who they were and how their bones came to be scattered. There are numerous instances of this, from Horace's ode on the defeat of Cleopatra, through Marvell's celebrations of Cromwell, to Auden's poem on the Spanish civil war. Time takes the heat out of every cause, blurs the memory of the most memorable events, and dulls even the colour of blood. But the feelings remain intelligible, because they are constantly renewed in the present; and it's the feelings, not the events and causes, which survive in the verbal music—as in the sonnet by Curnow:

> Weeping for bones in Africa, I turn
> Our youth over like a dead bird in my hand . . .

We talk of turning something over in our minds; we talk of a bird in the hand being worth two in the bush; and those casual colloquial phrases are gathered into the elegaic cadence and played upon. The pathos, the finiteness, the loss, are all there in the lines—more durable than the event which brought the poem into being.

What does the poet so far presented to you see when he looks round at the literary scene as it is in 1974? It's always difficult to be clear about what's happening *now*, and I'm going to try to arrive at an impression of it by reminding you of some of the things Keith Sinclair and Maurice Shadbolt said in their lectures and then attempting both to confirm and to qualify their views.

Keith Sinclair's lecture was for me one of those rare occasions when one is made to see and to recognize one's own society in a new and dramatic light. His image of the uncovered floors, the kerosene lanterns, the butter-box larders, all in living memory, was a reminder of how close the colonial bare boards are to us all, how they lurk in our consciousness, and how, correspondingly, our intellectual and cultural life is one which has only recently emerged from a state of colonialism. His lecture also revealed the degree to which a kind of cultural oppression, what I think the Australians call 'the cultural cringe', has lingered in New Zealand and hampered our intellectual growth.

I think Sinclair is right, that the colonial, or post-colonial lack of confidence has pretty well gone, in literature as in everything else. But while losing it we have also been losing the distinctness that gave colonial life an inherent sharpness of definition. Life in New Zealand has become more like life everywhere in the West—the same mix, but milder, the same colours, but paler, the same sounds, but quieter. Our physical environment still offers the most extraordinary possibilities—but they are possibilities to be taken or left; they don't press upon us as necessities.

Thirteen years ago Keith Sinclair and I were among the contributors to a Winter Lectures series on the effects of remoteness on New Zealand. Less could be said on that subject today. The ease of air travel and its cheapness relative to earnings means that a very high proportion of New Zealanders are able to travel abroad if they want to. Even more important are the effects of television and the growth of cities. Thirteen years ago Auckland was still just recognizably a South Seas port. Today it looks like a modest city in the Great Nowhere of Western affluence. Buildings, motorways, domestic interiors—the whole visible fabric of our lives is becoming increasingly anonymous.

And that brings me to what was chiefly celebrated in Maurice Shadbolt's lecture—the arrival of literary professionalism. Shadbolt's narrative went something like this: Twenty years ago fiction writers in New Zealand were part-time amateurs who soon gave up in despair. Today our fiction writers can live by writing. That phrase 'live by writing' begs a lot of questions. They 'live by writing' journalism, advertising copy, television plays, guide-books, even university lectures. I know of only two who have lived for any significant period of their lives by writing *fiction* and they are Barry Crump and Ngaio Marsh.

But I accept that on the whole Maurice Shadbolt is right. Literary professionalism has arrived—along with motorways, television, tall buildings and national confidence. It's also true that the necessities of professionalism can cut through a lot of preciousness and pretence. And I suppose no one should complain of a development that promotes a market for the commodity he produces. Nevertheless I see it as a mixed blessing. The professional is answerable in the first instance, not to the traditions of an art, but to public taste, to the state of the market. Sometimes public taste matches pretty exactly what is meritorious and durable. At other times, obviously, what is professionally successful is worthless, while something that goes unheralded and unread except by a few devotees proves to be of permanent value. My fear is not, of course, that worthless things will be praised, which hardly matters, but that valuable things may be lost. I wonder, for example, whether some of the smallest and finest work in that original Glass Case would ever have got into print in a time of literary professionalism.

So I offer two cheers for professionalism, as E. M. Forster offered two cheers for democracy. But I believe it needs to be accompanied by a criticism which is not destructive but which reserves its fullest celebrations for those various excellences the study of literature teaches us are always rare and never impossible.

The national confidence Keith Sinclair celebrated I celebrate too. Without it we would labour under the old crippling illusion that the excellence which is rare here is abundant somewhere else. It's rare everywhere, but I repeat—it's never and nowhere impossible. . . .

Ebullience, energy, eloquence, wit—and perhaps something beyond all these that lacks a word in English: what I think the French call *réalisation*—realizing in the sense of making real, bringing to life, so that the literary moment is lived through by the reader, experienced and retained like a piece of real life: these are the qualities to be striven for and celebrated.

Of course there's no need to see the professional and the artist as belonging to different camps. They may occupy the same skull. But it's in his consciousness as artist, not as professional, that the writer achieves these qualities; and that is a consciousness reaching back, not 12,000 miles to the European marketplace, but centuries back into the European past.

ON *QUESADA*

Being invited to write about my own book and critical reactions to it is disconcerting. I flick through it and each poem triggers a recollection and a possible set of observations. There is too much to say.

In general the most important thing is that the book is there and that it is authentic. Not that it's good or bad (others will decide that, over a period of years) but that I know it to be my own authentic production. Once you have survived as a poet to an age where you can be sure on that point, other people's reactions are of tremendous interest (and still a matter for thin-skinned response) but not crucial. The poet must not try to be other than he is to fit the requirements of his readers. (Wordsworth has some excellent stiff-backed statements on this in his Preface to the *Lyrical Ballads*.) He must make the best of what he is. And if there is some reasonable confidence, then one must be prepared to wait. Everything really new is slightly disconcerting—even to the poet who wrote it. I felt that in the title sequence of *Quesada*, whatever initial reactions there might be, I was putting something solid down on the poetic landscape.

The second poem in the book, 'Under the Sun', was the first to be written. I hadn't written any poems, except a few lines now and then, for some time—it might have been as long as three years. I had been slowly buried under work and felt anxious about it. (Don't most poets carry about with them the fear that they will never manage it again? Allen Curnow's longest dry spell appears to have lasted about fifteen years.) 'Under the Sun' was written after and about a traffic accident in the South of France. I felt pleased to have written poetry again but depressed that it had taken a near disaster to shake it out of me. That was in the European summer of 1972. In the Autumn, in London, I wrote 'Cold Moon', a poem I had to work hard at, a piece of nostalgia for the South of France; and in winter 'North-

One of a series in *Pilgrims*, Autumn 1979, in which poets were invited to discuss a recent book. My subject was *Quesada : Poems 1972-4*, published in 1975.

amptonshire Notes', an inconsequential page of satire. So at the beginning of 1973 when I returned to New Zealand I had some poems, but not in sufficient number to suggest I would have enough for a book for a very long time.

Why not force it? Frank Sargeson believes a writer should do his page every day. In my case that would work for an article; it might work for fiction if the idea was good and the impulse genuine; but for poetry acts of will have been of no use. When I was younger I used to force myself and the results were always artificial and had to be thrown away. The right kind of discipline is not a discipline exercised at the moment of composition. It is more difficult than that—the arrangement of one's life so that nothing is closed off—so that the mind is alive, free, flexible, open. Then at the moment of composition the felicities come unbidden; everything is integrated. If I feel less enthusiastic than I used to about a poet like Yeats it is because there is too much deliberation, too much conscious labour and the labour shows. More and more I feel with Keats that 'if poetry come not as naturally as the leaves to the tree it might as well not come at all'. But of course the process by which the leaf comes to the tree is no less complex for being 'natural'.

Acting as advocate for 'Under the Sun' I recommended to Alan Roddick, as lines that pleased me almost as much as any I had written, the opening four of section 3:

> Do you remember how the leaves chattered in Provence?
> They were telling us something.
> Every stone had a blood stain.
> Every rock had thrown back a human cry.

Perhaps they depend a little too much on my own almost physical recall of how the poplar leaves *do* chatter in Provence. But challenged to explain why I had recommended them, wondering why they pleased me, I noticed among other things that each line had its half concealed half-rhyme —'remember' / 'chatter', 'telling' / 'something', 'stone' / 'stain', 'rock' / 'back'. There was also the full rhyme of 'stone' and 'thrown', so that the ear could run from 'stone' to 'stain' to 'thrown'. There was the sinister balancing of the statements and at the same time the way each line was grammatically blocked off and complete. None of that had got there in the ordinary sense in which things are done 'consciously'. This aural element, the verbal music which is such an important element in poetry, is best achieved I think as an automatic eloquence. It is a matter of being in a particular frame of mind which permits the brain to move very fast—so that if one were an orator the images and alliterations would come as the sentences formed. Worked out in advance, deliberately planted, they would sound laboured, they would seem to have a design upon the hearer, they would be less subtle, and above all (as in Swinburne, for example) less integrated into all the other things (designating, stating) which the language is doing. The true felicity I think is really a speed of action with which the mind can act manifesting all its faculties at once. You cannot do that 'consciously', because there is a limit to how much you can be conscious of at one time. This is surely the basis for the traditional notion of 'inspiration', not so much a matter of being unconscious as superconscious. It is what permits a line like (in the same section) 'But filled the wide fields with their wild music' to make perfectly the sense required there (it is what the birds are doing) while itself making the music of the half-rhymes 'filled', 'field', 'wild' and 'wide'.

'Under the Sun' was for me a new beginning, and I was pleased with it. But it was not something new. Reviewing *Quesada* in *Islands* Martin Edmond disliked the title sequence and preferred 'Under the Sun' precisely because he thought 'Stead's older style still serves him best'. As Ezra Pound observed when he reviewed Yeats's *Responsibilities* in 1914, there will always be critics disappointed because a poet has declined to mark time.

In 1973 I was back at work in Auckland. In October I was invited to Melbourne to address the Fellowship of Australian Writers. I took with me a book called *Zen Flesh, Zen Bones* and was housed in the Zebra Motel, which was the occasion of '15 Letters from the Zebra Motel'. Reactions to that sequence have varied. Peter Crisp in his *New Argot* review seemed to feel it to be a piece of self-indulgence; Rob Jackaman in *Landfall* thought it lacked depth. Allen Curnow (in conversation) liked it; so did Martin Edmond in *Islands*. My own feeling about it is technical. It is (roughly) an Imagist sequence, and Imagism, though I think I do it quite well, always feels evasive. It is clean writing, but there is no space for sustained feelings; there is insufficient density, insufficient texture. There is also the problem of persona. In '15 Letters . . .' I speak in my own voice, out of my own circumstances. But the technique of Imagism and the confessional mode seem alien—the one not expansive enough for the other. Though there are things I like very much in the sequence—particularly sections 6, 10, 12, and in 14 the lines

> I watch the trees dancing
> Oak arms
> Fig torsos
> Spine of one tall pine—

this cramping of the self seems a sign of unease.

A month later the opening lines of 'Quesada' were triggered off by a conjunction of personal and literary accidents, and I continued writing the sequence through December and into January. It was the end of the academic year, and while marking examination scripts I began reading *Don Quixote*. At the same time I was dipping into Whitman. And my colleague Roger Horrocks sent me from New York a large piece of his PhD thesis which I was supervising. It was a survey of various kinds of experimentalism in modern poetry and it gave me a renewed feeling of excitement about purely technical matters. (The idea for the 'double poem'—section 11—came straight from Horrocks.) The name Quesada is a variant of Quixote. Quesada himself is not strictly a persona (there is no first person speech in the poem) but a character. He is like Quixote but not Quixote. Like Quixote he has a mistress (real or imaginary) called Dulcinea. His mood is a sort of controlled hysteria—exhilaration in despair. He suffers defeat and is glad to suffer because he values intensity more than comfort. He wills his own defeat because he knows his life requires it (long ago I had written the line 'Willing to get to where I'm sent') but the defeat is painful. The poem shares his 'madness' to the hilt, yet sees it objectively. I remember that Father Frank McKay liked the full-blooded Romantic passages so much he could not quite take the moments of irony or mockery. ('The real Stead is the Romantic Stead' he told me.) But I don't think these passages are the sort of self-destructive academic irony that used to kill every full-blooded feeling expressed in poetry in the 1950s. The Romantic feeling is unequivocally the life of the poem, and it is only shown the more sharply by juxtaposition with its opposite.

It was the longest poem I had written and I felt in many ways the best—that was reassuring for a poet just past 40. But it did not leave me feeling significantly less dependent on accidents. There was, however, one section—13 ('Our cameramen are hoisted on a boom')—which had felt different from all the rest in composition. There had been a great deal of trial and error in writing it, put and take, rearrangement and revision, a great deal of deliberation but no sense of strain, of undue effort. There was a feeling of objectivity, of shaping something, not to a fixed form, and not to something that required to be said, but as you might put and take and rearrange a number of coloured objects to form some pattern which only emerged slowly out of the process of doing it. I had had before the sense, but never so sharply, of what Mallarmé meant when he told Degas that poetry was not made with ideas, it was made with words. (New Zealand poetry at the moment is full of 'ideas' done into verse.)

I make no special claims for that section in itself. It simply happens to mark for me an advance in consciousness as a poet; and it, more than any other item in 'Quesada', leads on to things I have done more recently (not to the sonnets which I will discuss in a moment). I would like to think that in due course I will be able to say it represented for me a path out of being dependent on accidents. I would say it now but I do not like to tempt fate.

There were, however, examples of various kinds of word-play in other sections of 'Quesada', including the punning section, 9 (in which Mallarmé's statement is alluded to), which Martin Edmond found 'simply embarrassing'. I was glad to find it defended by John Davidson in a recent issue of *Climate* (no. 28) who wrote 'In my opinion, embarrassment about puns is almost on a par with Victorian embarrassment about sex. After all, even Homer puns on the name of Odysseus.' I was also pleased that Davidson was able to say with emphasis that he found the character of Quesada credible.

I had now almost enough for a small book and that made me alert and hopeful for opportunities. Most of another teaching year intervened, however. Then in late October 1974 I was with friends and family in Northland. Maurice Duggan was dying of cancer and I dreamed of saying goodbye to him. Next morning by the golf course at Ahipara beach someone turned on a transistor radio and I heard that Norman Kirk had died. I spent the hours driving back to Auckland thinking out a poem that would bring these two facts together. The images were right but it felt shapeless until I tried it in the form of the open sonnet Baxter had adopted from Lowell—and there it could be made to fit and feel tight. That set me off, and for the rest of that October and into November life kept presenting itself in 14-line packages. I must have written about twenty and kept twelve. They ought to have been kept together as a sequence in the book but were broken up into three groups, I've forgotten for what reason. In the following Autumn, after *Quesada* was published, I wrote more sonnets, eight of which seemed worth keeping; and in my new book, *Walking Westward*, I have reprinted the ones from *Quesada* and run them all together as a single sequence of twenty sonnets, with one added by way of recent postscript.

The open sonnet is really something of a compromise between traditional forms and the open form which the Modernist movement has led to in America. Fourteen unrhymed lines look about as free as poetry can get, particularly when the five-stressed line is observed as loosely as Baxter observes it. But in fact to shape experience again and again to fourteen lines is a very tight discipline. It must be brought to a conclusion there—even rhymed stanzas, which look tighter, in fact allow you to run on and on. The sonnet is the most artificial of forms, and the absence of rhyme only relaxes it superficially. As the reader runs from sonnet to sonnet in Lowell or Baxter (particularly the latter) it all has a loose free-and-easy feeling about it. But look at it from the poet's end, and compare it with the openness of a Canto by Pound or a poem by W. C. Williams, which must find its own length and its own shape, and the tightness is obvious. No sonnet is truly 'open'. So it is very hard to do well; and at the same time it avoids the harder thing—just to launch out and let the poem discover its own shape.

The sonnet suits the confessional mode (as Baxter and Lowell use it) which at the same time can be the vehicle for commentary on public events. My sequence begins with the death of Norman Kirk. It ends (in the 21st sonnet, added in *Walking Westward*) with the para-military operation to clear Maori land protesters from Bastion Point. In between come the end of the Vietnam war, the death of my mother, literary reflections —private and public intermixed. It has the kind of substance interesting to readers for whom poetry is more a vehicle than a pure art—a wider appeal than some other things I have done in recent years.

But since these sonnets I have gone back to open form; and the title poem in *Walking Westward* is itself conceived of as section 1 of a longer poem, of which the second is already written and the third projected.

The translations from Baudelaire and Apollinaire were done because those poems were connected with themes and preoccupations running through the book. (A phrase from the Baudelaire poem serves as epigraph to 'Quesada': 'Je pense . . . aux vaincus'—I think of the defeated.) I don't think my version of the Baudelaire succeeds as a poem, though it is an excellent translation. But the Apollinaire is a good lyric in its own right in my English version—and it's nice to demonstrate now and then that one can still work in rhyme and fixed form.

Part of my brief has been to refer to published critical comment and I have tried to do this in passing. But I have to acknowledge special gratitude for the encouragement I got from Peter Crisp's review in Stephen Chan's excellent and now defunct paper, *New Argot*. It was not just that Crisp permitted his enthusiasm to show, but that he was discriminating (I mean he didn't like everything), analytical—all that a critic ought to be—and he was someone I had never met. He, Bruce Beaver in *Poetry Australia,* and I think one or two of the newspaper reviewers, mentioned economy, tightness in the writing. This is for me no abstract 'rule'. It is a matter of trying to write so that a very few syllables cause a maximum agitation in the responding mind, so that the words seem active in a high degree. It counters any tendency to Swinburnian excess in the purely aural (or musical) aspects of the poem. And it is something one gets better at the longer one works at it.

DATES OF AUTHORS WHO ARE THE SUBJECT OF INDIVIDUAL ESSAYS

Part I: Fiction

Katherine Mansfield 1888-1923
Frank Sargeson 1903-
Sylvia Ashton-Warner 1908-
John Mulgan 1911-45
Ronald Hugh Morrieson 1922-72
Maurice Duggan 1922-74
David Ballantyne 1924-
Janet Frame 1924-

Part II: Poetry

A. R. D. Fairburn 1904-57
R. A. K. Mason 1905-71
Charles Brasch 1909-73
Allen Curnow 1911-
Denis Glover 1912-80
James K. Baxter 1926-72
Hubert Witheford 1921-
Fleur Adcock 1934-
David Mitchell 1940-

Part III: A Poet's View

C.K. Stead 1932-

REFERENCES

Katherine Mansfield: the Art of the 'Fiction'

1. 'Frau Fischer', *In a German Pension*, London, 1911.
2. *In a German Pension*, Penguin reprint, London, 1964, Introductory Note, p.7.
3. *Don't Never Forget*, London, 1966, p.255.
4. Mansfield biographers have never offered any explanation for Stephen Swift's disappearance, which left Mansfield and Murry in debt for their periodical *Rhythm* which Swift had undertaken to publish. The anecdote about a bigamy charge occurs among verbal reminiscences of Martin Secker, recounted by Mervyn Horder in the *T.L.S.*, 10 December 1976, p.1565.
5. 'Their flavour and vigour raise a question—could she have made a regional writer? Did she, by leaving her own country, deprive herself of a range of associations, of inborn knowledge, of vocabulary?' *34 Short Stories*, Katherine Mansfield, selected by Elizabeth Bowen, London, 1957, p.17.
6. *The Lonely Voice*, London, 1963, p.136.
7. p.140.
8. *34 Short Stories*, p.15.
9. One in *Katherine Mansfield and other Literary Portraits* (hereafter referred to as . . . *Portraits*), London, undated (1949), the other in *Katherine Mansfield and other Literary Studies* (a completely different book despite the similar title), London, 1959 (hereafter referred to as . . . *Studies*).
10. . . . *Studies*, p.86.
11. *The Letters of Katherine Mansfield to John Middleton Murry*, London, 1951, p.149 (hereafter referred to as *Letters* 1951).
12. . . . *Portraits*, p.14.
13. . . . *Portraits*, p.12.
14. *The Journal of Katherine Mansfield*, London, 1954, pp.93-4 (hereafter referred to as *Journal* 1954).
15. *Journal* 1954, p.79. Carco was later, however, to be the chief model for Raoul Duquette in 'Je ne parle pas français', though Duquette was also drawn in part from the painter Mark Gertler.
16. *Letters* 1951, p.26.
17. *Journal* 1954, p.68. 'Brave Love' survived in manuscript and was recently transcribed by Margaret Scott and published in *Landfall*, 101, Christchurch, March 1972, pp.3-29.
18. *Letters* 1951, p.33.
19. *Letters* 1951, p.14.

20. *Letters* 1951, p.40.

21. *Letters* 1951, p.42, italics mine.

22. *Letters* 1951, pp.47-8.

23. *Journal* 1954, pp.93-4.

24. *Journal* 1954, pp.94-5.

25. *Journal* 1954, pp.97-8, italics hers.

26. *Katherine Mansfield*, Antony Alpers, London, 1954, p.219. Compare this fact with the following examples of statements by Murry: 'Now let us remember that the months at the Villa Pauline were the days when she was writing *Prelude*'—introduction to *The Life of Katherine Mansfield* by R. E. Mantz and J. M. Murry, London, 1933, pp.5-6; and 'Katherine and I now entered on a period of simple happiness together, when every day was pure delight. . . . There was Katherine, there was the book I was writing: both engrossed me. . . . We sat on each side of a tiny table. . . . And on her side of the table Katherine was writing the first draft of *Prelude*'. *Between Two Worlds*, London, 1935, p.393. Both Alpers and Sylvia Berkman in their books on Mansfield (1954 and 1951) appear to have the evidence in front of them but to be confused by Murry's account which conflicts with it. Both, consequently, make statements about the writing of the first version of 'Prelude' which are partly correct, partly inaccurate or misleading.

27. *The Letters of Katherine Mansfield*, edited by John Middleton Murry, London, 1928, v.1, pp.82-3.

28. *Weir of Hermiston*, The Works of Robert Louis Stevenson, Colinton Edition, v.12, London, undated, pp.9-10.

29. *The Lonely Voice*, p.140, and p.139.

30. *Between Two Worlds*, p.463.

31. *Katherine Mansfield, A Critical Study*, London, 1951, p.154.

32. *Letters* 1951, p.160.

33. *Letters* 1951, p.166 (letter dated 14 February 1918).

34. . . . *Portraits*, p.12. And compare 'At first Katherine was very happy at the Chalet des Sapins. She was once more "in some perfectly blissful way, at peace"—the mood in which she could return to the vein of "Prelude". She wrote "At the Bay", its companion piece. . . .' *Letters* 1951, p.641. Here Murry's commentary links 'Prelude' and 'At the Bay', Bandol 1916 and Chalet des Sapins 1921, and once again invokes (in the phrase 'in some perfectly blissful way, at peace') the letter of 3 February 1918.

35. *Letters* 1951, p.268.

36. These include Ian A. Gordon, Saralyn R. Daly, Max A. Schwendiman, L. M. [Ida Baker] (in a footnote, provided by her editor, to her memoirs of Katherine Mansfield), and Antony Alpers.

37. British Museum MS.52921. In his new biography of Mansfield (1980, and the best to date) Antony Alpers (p.336) refers to my conclusion that this story was written in Switzerland, and insists that it must be the story referred to in letters as having been written in Looe. He offers no new evidence for this. It appears to me he has not read Murry's letter to Schiff but only my transcription of a part of it; and I believe his footnote must be a late addition to his book, attempting to cope briefly with an article that does not confirm his own account. In the letter from Looe (28 May 1918) in which the story is referred to which is held to be 'A Married Man's Story', K. M. says 'This new story has taken possession, and now, of course, I can't go out without my notebook and I lean against rocks and stones taking notes.' 'Taking notes' suggests observation, and outdoors Cornwall would hardly have helped her write 'A Married Man's Story'. Another point in my favour I think is that the story 'Poison', written in Menton late in 1920, has the same theme—the lover who 'poisons' (metaphorically) his/her beloved. K. M. had thought it good but Murry persuaded her not to include it in *The Garden Party*. (He later acknowledged that he had been wrong and that it was 'a little masterpiece'.) It would be

logical for her, having rejected 'Poison' from the collection, to try to use the idea again. I concede that Alpers knows much more about Mansfield than I do, and that therefore he may yet be proved right. To date, however, I have more solid evidence on my side—chiefly in the form of Murry's letter to Schiff.

38. *Letters* 1928, v.2, p.126.
39. *Journal* 1954, p.259.
40. British Museum MS letter from Murry to Schiff (see note 37 above).
41. British Museum MS letter from Murry to Schiff. See also *Letters* 1928, v.2, p.129.
42. *Letters* 1928, v.2, p.134.
43. *Letters* 1928, v.2, p.143, and *Journal* 1954, p.266. The letter to Violet Schiff on p.137 of v.2, *Letters* 1928, which also refers to *The Garden Party* as the title of the new book, is dated there as belonging to September which conflicts with the sequence I have outlined. But the MS of this letter in the British Museum is marked 'Received October 26 '21', so the dating of the published text is incorrect.
44. 'They sought to renew English poetry. . . . Several of them, including Hulme and Flint, were aware of the relevance of modern French Poetry to such an enterprise. As far back as 11 July 1908 Flint had written in *The New Age* of a similarity between Mallarmé and Japanese poetry and of the possibility of a poetry composed of suggestions rather than complete pictures; and he had declared: "To the poet who can catch and render, like these Japanese, the brief fragments of the soul's music, the future lies open." ' *The Life of Ezra Pound,* Noel Stock, London (Penguin edition), 1974, p.81. '. . . the art of attending to radioactive moments, "simply", in Pater's phrase, "for those moments' sake", had preoccupied two English generations. A central tradition of 19th-century decadence, a hyperaesthesia prizing and feeding on ecstatic instants, fragments of a psychic continuum . . . endorsed the kind of attention fragments exact if we are to make anything of them at all'. *The Pound Era,* Hugh Kenner, London, 1975 edition, p.60.
45. *The Dove's Nest and Other Stories,* Introductory note, p.xii.

John Mulgan: a Question of Identity

1. 'Our Cousin, Mr Poe', *Collected Essays,* Denver, 1959, pp.457-8.
2. *The Making of a New Zealander,* Wellington, 1958, p.28.
3. *The Making of a New Zealander,* p.125.
4. *John Mulgan* by P. W. Day in the Twayne World Authors Series, New York, 1968; and *John Mulgan* by Paul Day in the Oxford New Zealand Writers and their Work Series, Wellington, 1977. Hereafter these will be referred to as Day (Twayne) and Day (Oxford).
5. Day (Twayne), p.89.
6. Day (Oxford), p.11.
7. *Landfall,* March 1948, p.51.
8. Curnow in conversation with the author.
9. Day (Oxford), p.14, called it the Publications Committee and I followed him in *Islands,* 25. Mrs Jean Bartlett corrected the fact in her letter to *Islands,* 26.
10. *Report on Experience,* p.30.
11. R. A. K. Mason, *Collected Poems,* Christchurch 1962, Introduction p.13.
12. Day (Twayne), pp.40-41.
13. All page references are to the Longman Paul hardcover reprint (1973), the first edition being too rare for useful reference. I have to thank Garry Tee, however, for the gift of a first edition when I was at work on this article.
14. Day (Twayne), p.106.
15. 'The Provincial Dilemma: 2. The Bit in Between', *Landfall,* September 1976, pp.247-8.
16. Day (Twayne), p.100. Italics mine.

17. *Report on Experience*, p.17-18. Alan Mulgan's *Home* in a later edition was subtitled *A Colonial's Adventure*.
18. Day (Twayne), p.83 and p.90.
19. *Comment* 39, 1969, pp.10-14.
20. Day (Twayne), p.23.
21. Day (Twayne), p.138.
22. 'Mulgan's independent attitude to the two public events cost him the nomination . . . a good man was rejected because older men in office were frightened and decided to play for safety first.' *Comment* 39, 1969, p.11.

Maurice Duggan: Language is Humanity

1. 'Beginnings', *Landfall* 80, December 1966, p.335.
2. *Aspects of the Novel*, 1926 (1960 reprint), p.27.
3. 'Beginnings', p.335.
4. In Duggan's copy of *Speaking for Ourselves*, in which this story first appeared, the pages of his own work are scored over and he has written at the end 'What embarrassing crap!'.
5. He calls it three years in 'Beginnings' (p.335) but the evidence of letters shows he left New Zealand in September 1950 and was on his way home, following a tubercular haemorrhage in Spain, in December 1952.
6. Of seventeen Duggan appearances in anthologies eleven have been stories from *Immanuel's Land*.
7. 'Beginnings', p.336. Early in his career Duggan received from Sargeson a letter dated May 5th [1944] commenting on David Ballantyne's precocity and expressing the fear that he might 'go too fast and use up material before he's in a position to do his best by it'. 'So don't go too fast if you can help it', Sargeson added, 'and don't worry about not going fast enough'. And in a letter written to Sargeson in 1951 but not sent Duggan says of what is clearly the story later called 'Chapter' that it is 'quite the clearest and sharpest thing I have done' but that 'it doesn't end' and to publish it 'would be giving away a great chunk of stuff that I should one day get into a novel'.
8. 'Beginnings', p.336.
9. In a letter to Keith Sinclair dated 28.iv.60 he writes that he has put aside his Miss Bratby novel 'for two weeks' and written 'a story of about twenty typed pages *A Blues for Miss Laverty*'. In the same letter he mentions a talk to the 'Lit. Soc.'.
10. E. A. Horsman in *Landfall*, March 1962, p.80, and Lawrence Jones, *Landfall*, September 1965, p.290.
11. *Manuka*, Auckland, 1960, p.6. 'Only Connect' is the epigraph to E. M. Forster's novel, *Howards End*.
12. A letter to me dated 28.iv.66 but not sent, and found in Duggan's copy of *Manuka* when I was preparing this volume for publication. Duggan showed me the story first in typescript in 1961. I enjoyed it, I was impressed, but I did not recognize its merits to the full. That recognition has only come with repeated readings. I remember I had only one objection. It was to the reiterated address 'Gentlemen'; and I think Duggan explained that he conceived of Buster O'Leary as an older man imagining himself in the dock looking back over his misspent life to a time of relative innocence. The 'Gentlemen' were gentlemen of a jury of the older O'Leary's imagining.
13. Bill Pearson's comment on this story in 'The Maori in Literature' (in *Essays on New Zealand Literature*, ed. Wystan Curnow, Auckland, 1973, p.114) seems to me to miss its point and to misinterpret its tone. For example: 'When [Buster] first conceived Fanny Hohepa with her guitar in the image of the Abyssinian maid with her dulcimer in *Kubla Khan*, he was asking for disillusion.' But Buster did not so conceive her (nor was she

playing a guitar). He noticed a '*discrepancy*' between the lines he was chanting and the reality confronting him. Pearson also asserts that 'by leaving Fanny, Buster confirms Puti's comment: "She is too good for you" '. Lawrence Jones agrees: 'Buster . . . finally runs from the results of his actions, evading responsibility or significant human relationship.' (*Landfall* 75, Sept. 1965, p.288). There seems something inappropriately simple, even naïve, in the idea that Buster ought to have settled down with the Hohepas. Was he to teach his 'collapsible sheila' the joys of double vision? Terry Sturm (*Landfall* 97, March 1971, p.61) finds Buster guilty of a 'sentimental racist idyll' which 'is pricked by Puti Hohepa himself, who sees the situation as raising much more complex moral and human problems than Buster is ever prepared to admit'. How Sturm has penetrated the old Maori's silences to discover this 'complex' recognition is not made clear. Duggan, I should add (but only because it seems critically justified), was never comfortable with such moralizings of his stories.

14. I have found that modern students need to be told what 'stripping' means in the context of the cowshed. After milking by machine the last of the milk has to be 'stripped' by hand. The 'cups' are the cups of the machine.
15. *Don Juan*, Canto III, stanza LXXXVI.
16. 'Beginnings', p.337.
17. Should this story perhaps have been called 'The Deposing' to avoid an ambiguity?
18. 17.vii.60 to Keith Sinclair.
19. Letter to Frank Sargeson 26.viii.60.
20. Letter to Sargeson dated (possibly wrongly?) 16.vii.60.
21. Letter to Sinclair 17.viii.60.
22. Letter to Sargeson dated 17 Aug. 60.
23. Letter to Sargeson 18.x.60.
24. It seems likely, however, that the scene was derived from the Captain Cook hotel in Dunedin where Duggan lived during the early months of 1960. He describes it in a letter to Sargeson (Feb. 7 1960) as 'like nothing so much as a translation from Dante in a local vernacular'. And he adds, in a comment which signals the chief literary influence on the writing of 'Riley's Handbook', 'the place is crammed to bursting with crazy humanity; it might be called Beckett's Reach'.
25. W. B. Yeats, 'Adam's Curse', *Collected Poems*, p.88.
26. Letter to Frank Sargeson, 27 Feb. 1951. The phrase 'some Osyth reading her ancient book' was added after 'Voyage I' first appeared in *Landfall*.
27. Letter to Stephen Sinclair, April 1 1974.

David Ballantyne: Whimsical Losers

1. See previous chapter, note 7.
2. *The Paris Review* 53, Winter 1972, p.181.
3. *N.Z. Listener*, 21 July 1979, p.69.

From Wystan to Carlos

1. 'New Zealand Literature: the Case for a Working Definition', in *Essays on New Zealand Literature*, ed. Wystan Curnow, 1973, p.146.
2. cf. Louis MacNeice: 'The nineteen-thirty school of English poets, represented by Mr Auden and Mr Spender, derives largely from Owen.' 'Subject in Modern Poetry', *Essays and Studies*, v.22, Oxford, 1937, p.149.

3. 'T. S. Eliot, himself the outstanding modernist poet, through his later work helped deflect modernism and its acceptance in Britain.' Michael Schmidt, *An Introduction to 50 Modern British Poets,* London, 1979, p.8.

4. *Unpublished Letters of Matthew Arnold,* ed. Arnold Whitridge, London, 1923, pp.15-16. Arnold's complaint exactly accords with the observation by Ian Wedde which I have used as epigraph.

5. It is, I suppose, no more than idle speculation to note that the word 'obelisk', which Curnow arranges down the page in poem five of *Trees, Effigies, Moving Objects,* is similarly spaced out on the back cover of *Freed* 4, and to wonder whether Curnow may have been leafing through that issue and consciously or unconsciously taken an idea from it. *Postcript:* In *Islands* 29 Mr Curnow wrote to say the 'brief existence' of *Freed* 'passed unnoticed' by him, and that in any case the poem in question existed in draft as early as 1961, including the word 'obelisk'. I accept his correction with only the observation that my speculation arose from the fact that in the early 1960s he had shown me those drafts of poems and my recollection was that the word 'obelisk' was not then upended.

6. '. . . we should not strive too earnestly for a cosmopolitan poetics'. Manhire in *The Young New Zealand Poets,* ed. Arthur Baysting, Auckland 1973, p.122.

A. R. D. Fairburn: The Argument Against

1. Allen Tate, *T. S. Eliot, the Man and his Work,* London, 1967, p.392.
2. M. H. Holcroft, *Discovered Isles,* Christchurch, 1950, p.70-72.
3. James K. Baxter, 'The Waves', *Poetry Australia,* v.2, no.9, April 1966, p.40.

Hubert Witheford: Rhetoric and Wit

1. Hubert Witheford, 'Background to a Magazine', *Arachne* 2, February 1951, pp.21-22.

'For the Hulk of the World's Between'

1. Allen Curnow, Introduction to *The Penguin Book of New Zealand Verse,* London, 1960, p.59.
2. James K. Baxter, *The Fire and the Anvil, Notes on Modern Poetry,* Wellington, 1955, p.54.
3. M. H. Holcroft, *Discovered Isles,* p.86.
4. Ibid., p.57.
5. Allen Curnow, Introduction to *A Book of New Zealand Verse 1923-45,* Christchurch, 1945, p.52.
6. Robert Chapman, 'Fiction and the Social Pattern', *Landfall* 25, March 1953, p.52.

INDEX

Page numbers of main subjects of essays are in italic